CURRENTS OF ENCOUNTER

*Studies on the Contact between Christianity and
Other Religions, Beliefs, and Cultures*

VOLUME 5

CURRENTS OF ENCOUNTER

GENERAL EDITORS: Rein Fernhout, Jerald D. Gort, Hendrik M. Vroom, Anton Wessels

───────── **VOLUMES PUBLISHED OR AT PRESS** ─────────

1 J. D. Gort, et al., eds. *Dialogue and Syncretism: An Interdisciplinary Approach* (copublished with Eerdmans)

2 Hendrik M. Vroom *Religions and the Truth: Philosophical Reflections and Perspectives* (with Eerdmans)

3 Sutarman S. Partonadi *Sadradh's Community and its Contextual Roots: A Nineteenth-Century Javanese Expression of Christianity*

4 J. D. Gort, et al., eds. *On Sharing Religious Experience: Possibilities of Interfaith Mutuality*

5 S. Wesley Ariarajah *Hindus and Christians: A Century of Protestant Ecumenical Thought* (with Eerdmans)

6 Makoto Ozaki *Introduction to the Philosophy of Tanabe, according to the English Translation of the Seventh Chapter of the* Demonstratio *of Christianity*

───────── **VOLUMES NEARING COMPLETION** ─────────

Julio de Santa Ana *The Church and Human Rights in Latin America* (with Eerdmans)

Rein Fernhout *Word of Absolute Authority: A Phenomenological Study of the Canonicity of the Veda, the Tipiṭaka, the Bible, and the Koran*

───────── **FURTHER VOLUMES ARE IN VARIOUS** ─────────
STAGES OF PREPARATION OR PLANNING

Volumes in this series unavailable from Eerdmans are available from Editions Rodopi, Keizersgracht 302-304, 1016 EX Amsterdam, the Netherlands, or 233 Peachtree Street N.E., Suite 404, Atlanta, GA 30303-1504.

Hindus and Christians:
A Century of
Protestant Ecumenical Thought

by

S. Wesley Ariarajah

EDITIONS RODOPI, AMSTERDAM

WILLIAM B. EERDMANS PUBLISHING COMPANY
GRAND RAPIDS, MICHIGAN

This edition first published 1991 jointly by
Wm. B. Eerdmans Publishing Co.
255 Jefferson Ave. SE, Grand Rapids, MI 49503
and Editions Rodopi, B.V.
Keizersgracht 302-304, 1016 EX Amsterdam, the Netherlands,
and 233 Peachtree Street N.E., Suite 404, Atlanta, GA 30303-1504

Library of Congress Cataloging-in-Publication Data

Ariarajah, S. Wesley.
Hindus and Christians: a century of Protestant ecumenical thought /
by S. Wesley Ariarajah.
p.   cm.   — (Currents of encounter: vol. 5)
Includes bibliographical references.
ISBN 0-8028-0504-3 (pbk.)
1. Christianity and other religions — Hinduism — History — 20th century.
2. Hinduism — Relations — Christianity — History — 20th century.
3. World Council of Churches — History.   4. Ecumenical movement — History.
5. Christianity and other religions — Hinduism.   6. Hinduism — Relations —
Christianity.   I. Title.   II. Series.
BR128.H5A75   1991
261.2'45 — dc20   91-4482
                                                                CIP

Rodopi ISBN 90-5183-206-0

Acknowledgements

I wish first to express my gratitude to Prof. Michael Barnes, s. J., who gave valuable advice on both the formulation and the development of this study, in its original form as doctoral dissertation. Mr. Pierre Beffa, Director of the wcc Library and Archives, and his staff have given me much willing and practical assistance in exploiting their facilities and for this, too, I am very grateful.

My colleagues Dr. Stuart E. Brown and Mr. T. K. Thomas read through the drafts of the chapters and made numerous suggestions for corrections and improvements. I greatly appreciate both their willingness to give of their time and their sustained interest in the progress of the work.

I am deeply beholden to my wife, Shyamala, who typed the drafts, and I am especially thankful to my colleague Audrey Smith whose commitment and sustained interest in typing and preparing the final text has been a source of much encouragement to me.

To the memory of my loving father

Contents

Introduction 1

Part 1   The Quest for Understanding   15

Part 2   The Quest for Relationship   89

Part 3   The Quest for a Future   163

Bibliography 221

Introduction

CHAPTER I

Introduction

A New Awareness

> I wish to attempt to discern and delineate something at least of the
> momentous current that, if I mistake not, has begun to flow around and
> through the Christian church. It is a current which, although we are only
> beginning to be aware of it, is about to become a flood that could sweep
> us quite away unless we can through greatly increased consciousness of its
> force and direction learn to swim in its special and mighty surge.[1]

The 'current' about to become a 'flood' to which Wilfred Cantwell Smith,
the author of these words, refers could have been called 'ecumenical,' said
he, had not the word "been appropriated lately to designate rather an
internal development within the on-going church." Smith is here alluding
to the increasing pressure on the churches to become aware of and to
cope with a religiously plural world — "which, of course, is the only
world there is."[2]

Much, however, has already been said and written about the planet
earth becoming a 'global village,' 'one world,' etc., pointing to social,
political, economic, and cultural developments as well as modern travel,
communication systems, and technological advances, all of which have
brought together communities that were hitherto in comparative isolation,
so nothing needs to be added here. Nor is there a need to recount what
great tensions and pressures all these changes have wrought in human
inter-relationships, with such speed and in such a short span of time,

---

1 Wilfred Cantwell Smith, "The Christian in a Religiously Plural World," in John
Hick and Brian Hebblethwaite, eds., *Christianity and Other Religions* (Glasgow: Collins,
1980), p. 87.
2 *Ibid.*

affecting simultaneously the lives of so many people.[3] For the study we are about to undertake, it is nevertheless important to note briefly how this current which "has begun to flow around and through the Christian Church" —the awareness of religious plurality, or the pressure for a 'new' or 'wider' ecumenism, as some have called it— is in fact even now becoming a 'flood.' But is there not an exaggeration here, some would object, for religious plurality is by no means new to the churches. There has been no period in history when Christians and the churches have not had to face plurality in one form or another. One should be aware that large Christian communities have lived for centuries in pluralist situations and learned to accept and adapt to such a context. What, then is 'new' in the Christian awareness of pluralism that has accentuated the issue in our time?

First, there appears to be a qualitative and quantitative difference in the Christian awareness of other faiths. Until recently the study of other religions was the privilege of a few, born out of curiosity or scholarly interest. Most Christians had a general awareness of the beliefs of their neighbours and learned to respect, reject or ignore them. Becoming 'more religious' meant becoming more informed and involved in one's own faith. Today there is not only a wider, more popular, and more informed interest in other faiths, but also, and here is the newness, an interest in them as part of one's own spiritual search. There are increasing numbers of people who look at other faiths as possible serious alternatives to their Christian faith. And there are still others, who no longer see religious traditions as demanding necessarily alternative commitments, who want to lower the barriers between religious traditions so that all the spiritual resources of the human community would become the heritage of everyone. Let us illustrate.

"The practice of Zazen," says Ann E. Chester, who remains a convinced Christian, "became a way to develop the inner stance": spoken words really tend to limit God to the meaning of the words spoken.

> But 'centering down,' as the Quakers put it, remaining at the 'still point' within, completely open to the all-pervading energy of God, is to be in touch with myself, with who I really am; it is also to give God full freedom to help me become what I am capable of being. ... Zazen has helped me to seek that depth, to be at home there, to deepen it, to act out of it.[4]

---

3 For a vivid description of how the religious and social map of Britain, for example, has changed, see Kenneth Cracknell, *Why Dialogue? A First British Comment on WCC Guidelines* (London: British Council of Churches, 1980), pp. 2-5.

4 Ann E. Chester, "Zen and Me," *Spring Wind* IV, no. 4 (Winter 1984–85): 25-26.

Only a few decades ago such a conviction that Zazen would help someone come to a fuller realization of the Christian understanding of God would have been seen by the more organized sections of the church as an isolated, if not erratic, enthusiasm of a person disillusioned with what life had to offer in an industrialized society. Not today. For now there are organized regular exchanges of monks between Benedictine monasteries in the West and Zen monasteries in Japan to enable them to learn from each other's meditative practices and techniques.[5] Ann Chester's interest in and use of Zazen ceases to be the particular interest of an individual. It is part of a 'current,' and the example could be multiplied by the hundreds. But the current does not stop there.

Aloysius Pieris, one of Asia's leading theologians, is on Ann Chester's side. In his view, the Christian theology which has grown out of Western culture must depend for its renewal on being 'baptized' by immersion in the waters of Asian spirituality:

> A genuine Christian experience of God-in-Christ grows by maintaining a dialectical tension between two poles — between action and non-action, between word and silence, between control of nature and harmony with nature, between self-affirmation and self-negation, between engagement and withdrawal, between love and knowledge, between *Karuna* and *Prajnu,* between *agape* and *gnosis.* ... We believe ... that the most creative encounter between East and West could come from monks whose calling it is to bring about within Western theology a fruitful interaction between Christian *love* and Buddhist *wisdom.*[6]

To this we add a reminder that on 27 October 1986, leaders of the major Protestant and Orthodox branches of the church gathered in Assisi along with the leaders of all the major religious traditions of the world to engage in prayer for world peace in response to the call of Pope John Paul II.[7] The current is indeed in the process of becoming a flood, as witnessed to also by the proliferation of international interfaith organizations and the volume of literature on religions and their inter-relationships. Has the world become irreversibly inter-faith? Are the churches ready for this?

---

5 Diana L. Eck, "What Do We Mean by 'Dialogue'?", Moderator's report, *Dialogue with People of Living Faiths: Minutes of the Seventh Meeting of the Working Group* (Geneva: WCC, 1986).

6 Aloysius Pieris, "Western Christianity and Asian Buddhism: A Theological Reading of Historical Encounters," *Dialogue,* New Series VII, no. 2 (1980): 66.

7 Thomas H. Dorris, "Leaders of a Dozen Religions Gather for Prayer for Peace," *Ecumenical Press Service* (1986), item 86.10.121 (26-31 October 1986). The one hundred and more religious leaders included heads of churches from the Protestant, Orthodox, and Roman Catholic traditions, as well as Hindus, Buddhists, Muslims, Jews, Jains, Sikhs, and Shinto.

The second aspect of the new awareness has to do with changes in our understanding of mission and evangelism. When he addressed the 1980 WCC World Mission Conference in Melbourne, Philip Potter (then General Secretary of the WCC) recalled the confidence that had marked the missionary conference of Edinburgh (1910), as signified by the challenge of John R. Mott:

> If the Gospel is to be preached to all men it obviously must be done while they are living. The evangelization of the world in this generation, therefore, means the preaching of the Gospel to those who are now living. To us who are responsible for preaching the Gospel it means in our lifetime; to those to whom it is to be preached it means in their lifetime ... [8]

Potter rightly observed that the pilgrimage from Edinburgh to Melbourne, marked as it was by momentous events and upheavals, was still a story of "extraordinary boldness, courage, courtesy, faith, hope, and love."[9] What is the situation today? Writing on "History's Lessons for Tomorrow's Mission" Tracy K. Jones, Jr., says that Christian mission around the world today is in "colossal confusion":

> There is no agreement as to priorities. There are those who give first priority to church growth. Others would give priority to the poor. Still others would see the priority as one of confronting the 'principalities and powers' of racism, militarism, repression of human rights, and economic exploitation. Then there are those who focus on the needs of women and children. Finally, there are those who argue that the most important priority of all is a fresh approach on the part of the Christians to people of other faiths. ... [10]

Jones himself was undaunted by the situation for he believed that "untidiness and confusion have characterized the great periods of missionary expansion." The 'low tides,' he was certain, would be followed by the 'high' ones. There are others, however, who are much less willing to interpret the present 'confusion' in positive terms.

In his review of developments in Mission Theology from 1948 to 1975, Rodger C. Bassham said that "the question of God's activity in the world raises one of the most acute points of tension in the contemporary discussion of mission."

---

[8] Philip A. Potter, "From Edinburgh to Melbourne" in *Your Kingdom Come: Mission Perspectives,* Report on the World Conference on Mission and Evangelism, Melbourne, Australia, 12-25 May 1980 (Geneva: WCC, 1980), p. 7.

[9] *Ibid.,* p. 20.

[10] Tracy K. Jones, Jr., "History's Lessons for Tomorrow's Mission," *International Bulletin of Missionary Research* X, no. 2 (April 1986): 50.

> That God is at work in the world is widely accepted: it is far more difficult to answer how and where God is acting, and what is the relationship between his work of salvation in Jesus Christ and his presence and activity in the whole world, including other religions. ... This question (other religions), which has such broad ramifications for mission theology, remains the key issue in the current debate.[11]

Cantwell Smith's warning, however, is based on his belief that the new awareness of religious pluralism has brought the missionary enterprise to a 'profound and fundamental crisis,' the extent and seriousness of which is often not faced. This in his view is a crisis facing the whole church, and not merely "those interested in mission."[12]

Whatever one's judgment on the present health and future prospects of Christian missions, no one would deny that Christian relations with people of other faiths have reached a crisis point, in terms both of relationship and theological understanding. The new interest in oriental religions, the steady decline in missionary recruitment, the counter-missions, the rise of militant and fundamentalist expressions within all religious traditions, the desperate need to cooperate on questions of justice and peace, inter-religious marriages, the rise of a new religious consciousness which refuses to adhere to the limits of spirituality delineated by religious institutions, Ann Chester, Aloysius Pieris, and the Pope — all are contributing to the 'current' becoming the 'flood' which, in the words we have quoted in the beginning "could sweep us quite away unless we can through greatly increased consciousness of its force and direction learn to swim in its special and mighty surge."

In the contemporary scene there are many, both in the field of Mission and in Theology of Religions, who are attempting to understand the nature of the crisis, analyse it, and suggest some ways in which we might come to terms with it. It may be fairly safely asserted that religious plurality is here to stay. If the issue has received new dimensions, we also need to seek new dimensions of the Christian faith to deal with it. This study is thus an attempt to understand one aspect of this issue, and it is offered in the hope that it will make a modest contribution to what is likely to be a prolonged and profound search in the life of the church.

---

11 Rodger C. Bassham, "Mission Theology: 1948–1975," *International Bulletin of Missionary Research* IV, no. 2 (April 1980): 57.
12 *Op. cit.,* p. 88.

The Scope and Focus

We have noted that religious plurality and attempts to relate to it are not new to the church. Plurality is at the heart of the New Testament and it also engaged the attention of the early church, especially as it began to move out of the immediate area of its birth. Much could be learnt from a deep study of the way the issue was treated in these periods of the church's life. This study, however, is an attempt to understand the attitudes to other faiths within the Modern Ecumenical Movement. Its scope has been narrowed down by a number of limitations we have imposed to ensure a clear focus and purpose.

The first limiting factor has to do with the definition of the "Modern Ecumenical Movement." There is a general agreement that the World Missionary Conference held in Edinburgh 1910, marked the beginning of the Modern Ecumenical Movement.[13] But it would be much more difficult to define or limit the meaning of the word 'ecumenical.' The Greek word *oikoumene* from which it comes means 'the whole inhabited earth' — hence Cantwell Smith's disappointment that the word which could have truly stood for a movement towards a worldwide human community had already been 'appropriated' to designate an "internal development within the on-going church." But even in its narrower sense the word presents problems of definition, for it has been used to include all those movements, impulses, and creative developments that have contributed to the churches' growing together into unity, so that they, renewed in their own lives and truly serving the world, might bear witness to the message of the gospel. It is, therefore, very difficult to decide what not to include in the definition. The ecumenical movement as such cannot, by definition, be identified with any institution.

Yet the World Council of Churches has generally been accepted as one of the primary 'instruments' and 'expressions' of the ecumenical movement. The confessional and cultural diversity of its membership and the breadth of its concerns have enabled the Council to play this role. The Roman Catholic Church and a number of smaller churches within the Protestant tradition are not members of the WCC. The Roman Catholic Church, however, works in close collaboration with the WCC and is a full member of its Faith and Order Commission. There is also collaboration on a number of programmes, including Mission, and Dialogue.

In defining 'Ecumenical' thought and discussions for the purpose of this study, therefore, we would include the discussions of the three major

---

13 W. A. Visser 't Hooft, *Has the Ecumenical Movement a Future?* (Belfast: Christian Journals Ltd., 1974). Visser 't Hooft divided the modern ecumenical movement into four periods: 1910–1934, 1934–1948, 1948–1960, and 1960–"to a date which still lies in the future."

world conferences at Edinburgh, Jerusalem, and Tambaram, which were part of the missionary movement that was eventually incorporated into the WCC, and developments within the WCC itself since its formation in 1948. There is thus an apparent institutional interest, but this is necessary to keep the discussion in focus and to trace its development. We shall, however, make every attempt to draw out general implications and we shall also keep in mind developments within the Roman Catholic Church insofar as they bear on the issue at hand. In dealing with contemporary contributions we hope to go well beyond the institutional discussions and see how wider ecumenical thinking in the field of Theology of Religions could inform and influence the on-going discussions within the structures of the WCC. In summary, we hope to cover the three major missionary ecumenical conferences, the developments within the programmes of the WCC and the broader contemporary discussions that may shed light on the problem.

Our second limitation has to do with the definition of 'other faiths.' These faiths are many and varied and a general approach would have been too nebulous. We have therefore chosen to focus on Hinduism, also because of our own knowledge and existential interest in it. This again, however, would present some problems, for while relationships to Hinduism and the Hindus have been a subject of considered reflection at some meetings, Hinduism has on other occasions been subsumed in a general discussion of 'non-Christian religions' or 'other faiths.' While concentrating on the Hindu–Christian discussions, we would incorporate the general discussions where there is no specific discussion on Hinduism. This would in any case be necessary if we are to understand the overall development of ecumenical thinking on the basic issue.

In reaching our final conclusion we will again refer mainly to Hindu–Christian relations, but we hope that our observations would apply to Christian relations with other religious communities as well. In other words, we seek in this study to ask and answer the following questions: What has been the attitude to other faiths, and especially to Hinduism in the three Ecumenical Missionary Conferences and in the ecumenical discussions within the WCC? What are the issues that have emerged? What contributions does contemporary reflection bring to this stream of ecumenical thinking? And what is the significance of these contributions for Hindu–Christian relations? Hence the formulation of our overall topic.

Resources and Method

A fairly complete record of the important meetings of the World Missionary Conference, the International Missionary Council and the World Council of Churches is available in the Archives of the WCC. Also of interest are the preparatory materials, draft reports, correspondences, and

minutes of meetings, which together present a reasonable picture of the
circumstances, choices, and interests that governed the convening of
conferences, the emphases made in them and the many struggles, compromises, and painful disagreements that lay behind the final formulation of
statements. The main reports of the major meetings, however, are mostly
also in print, although one must glean them from many sources.

A number of dissertations, books, and articles have been written on
the three major missionary ecumenical conferences, especially Jerusalem
and Tambaram. But these invariably approach the meetings from the
perspective of the theology of Mission, or of the theology of Evangelism.[14]
Hendrik Kraemer is among the most studied of ecumenical thinkers, but
again, the emphasis is repeatedly on his missionary approach. His attitude
to other faiths, crucial to any study of Kraemer, is often discussed only to
serve the missiological interest of the research. Carl F. Hallencreutz's
Kraemer Towards Tambaram is perhaps the most thoroughly researched
study on Kraemer's theological development from his time as a theological
student at Leiden University in 1911 until Tambaram (1938). In studying the
development of Kraemer's missionary approach, Hallencreutz offered very
valuable information and insights on the Jerusalem and Tambaram meetings.[15]

Strangely enough, no detailed research work has been done in the
English language in the field that we hope to cover. As far as we are
aware, only two dissertations, one in French and the other in Dutch, have
covered a part of our period, and these deal more generally with the
theology of religions in the ecumenical movement. The only English
account that seeks to study the developments that concern us is Carl F.
Hallencreutz's *New Approaches to Men of Other Faiths*, which surveys the
theological trends from Tambaram (1938) to the Uppsala Assembly of the
WCC (1968).[16] The two volumes, recently reissued, on the *History of the*

---

14 These include Arthur P. Johnston's "A Study of the Theology of Evangelism in the
International Missionary Council 1921–1961," published under the title *World Evangelism
and the Word of God* (Bethany Fellowship, 1974); Gerald W. Conway's "An Exposition
and Critical Analysis of the Theology of Missions as Proposed by Dr. Hendrik Kraemer"
(Rome: Gregorian University, 1965); O. V. Jathanna's "The Decisiveness of the Christ-
Event and the Universality of Christ in a World of Religious Plurality," dissertation
(University of Basel, 1981). A List of Doctoral Dissertations showing the same
tendencies is given in "Doctoral Dissertations on Mission," *International Bulletin of
Missionary Research*, Vol. 7, no. 3 (July 1983). Also see *Doctoral Dissertations on
Ecumenical Themes: A Guide for Teachers and Students* (Geneva: WCC, 1977).

15 Carl F. Hallencreutz, *Kraemer towards Tambaram: A Study in Hendrik Kraemer's
Missionary Approach* (Uppsala: Gleerup, 1966). Hallencreutz treats Kraemer's time as
a young missionary in Indonesia, his part in the Dutch missionary discussions, his
attitude to Islam, and his role at Jerusalem and Tambaram. He also analyses the
preparatory meetings and correspondence related to Jerusalem and Tambaram.

16 Carl F. Hallencreutz, *New Approaches to Men of Other Faiths, 1938–1968: A*

Ecumenical Movement, could not be expected to examine our specific field in any detail.[17] In the course of dealing more generally with some Christian attitudes to Hinduism of the 19th and 20th centuries, Eric J. Sharpe has mentioned personalities who would also appear in our account. Sharpe's book is of interest to anyone who would be informed about the overall issues in Hindu–Christian relations. So the resources are there — in the reports of the conferences and Assemblies, in the preparatory materials written for them, in the discussions, and in the final reports. But they have not been brought together in a critical study. Kenneth Cracknell, Executive Secretary to the Committee for Relations with People of Other Faiths of the British Council of Churches, reacted to our preliminary outline for this study in these words: "Yes, this story needs to be told; we don't know it." In actual fact the story is known, but only in bits and pieces. It is our present objective to give a coherent picture of the development of ecumenical thought on this question in order to extract the issues fundamental to Hindu–Christian relations.

The foregoing considerations have largely determined the shape and style of this study. Methodologically, it is historical and theological, for it will attempt to trace a history, not for its own sake, but to discern the theological emphasis of each phase. At every crucial point we will formulate our own evaluation of theological developments. For the same reason, we would stay close to the original sources, quoting them as often as seems necessary for an authentic account of what happened or what was said, before submitting our interpretation. At each stage, we shall choose one or more persons who in our assessment played a crucial role in the discussion of the issue. In this way, the work of Commission IV for the Edinburgh meeting, Nicol Macnicol's presentation at Jerusalem, Kraemer's preparatory volume for Tambaram, the contributions of D. T. Niles and M. M. Thomas to the post-Tambaram discussions, and similar texts will be chosen for detailed discussion. The choice is of course made on our own assessment of the relative impact on ecumenical thought about Hindu–Christian relations in any given period. The choice will become extremely

---

Theological Discussion (Geneva: WCC), 95 pages. A summary of this work is to be found in his article in *Living Faiths and the Ecumenical Movement,* S. J. Samartha, ed. (Geneva: WCC, 1971), pp. 57-71. The two theses on the Theology of Religions are: (1) J. J. E. van Lin, *Protestantse Theologie der Godsdiensten van Edinburgh naar Tambaram (1910–1938),* (Assen: Van Gorcum and Comp. BV., 1974); (2) Gérard Valléé, *Mouvement Oecuménique et Religions non-Chrétiennes: un débat oecuménique sur la rencontre interreligieuse de Tambaram à Uppsala (1938–1968),* (Tournai: Desclée and Cie.; Montréal: Bellarmin, 1975).

17 Ruth Rouse and Stephen Charles Neill, ed., *A History of the Ecumenical Movement,* x, *1517–1948* (3rd edition, Geneva: WCC, 1986); Harold E. Fey, *The Ecumenical Advance: A History of the Ecumenical Movement,* Vol. 2, *1948–1968* (2nd edition, Geneva: WCC, 1986).

difficult when we come to contemporary discussions of the Theology of Religions, for there are too many in the field and one cannot hope to do justice to any of them in a brief statement. We shall choose 'types' representative of elements that could possibly contribute to the further development of ecumenical thought.

The Structure

The study has three parts. The first, which comprises chapters II, III, and IV, deals with the three major ecumenical conferences of the modern ecumenical movement. From a theological perspective, this part is not as historical as one would normally assume. At each of these conferences there were major exponents of Hindu–Christian relations, and these expounded three different, equally fascinating, interpretations of Hinduism and approaches to Hindu–Christian relations. We shall deal with these meetings in some detail for unlike many others they specifically considered Hindu–Christian relations, and greatly influenced contemporary ecumenical thought. The period from Tambaram until the emergence of 'Dialogue' as a major emphasis in ecumenical discussions forms the second part of our study, constituted by chapters V and VI. The third part will begin by surveying current discussions of the Theology of Religions and lead into our critical evaluation of recent ecumenical thinking on other religions and the implications of this for Hindu–Christian relations.

A Note on 'Language'

In preparing this study over a considerable span of time, we have experienced some difficulty with the use of words. For example, the words 'faith,' 'beliefs,' 'religions,' 'religious traditions,' 'faith communities,' etc., have been used by different persons in different senses, sometimes interchangeably. Similarly, even though 'pluralism' and 'religious plurality' are distinguishable and can be used to represent different concepts, many authors tend to use them interchangeably. Again, while one would avoid the negative connotation of the phrase 'non-Christian' and use 'people of other faiths,' or refer to such groups simply as Hindus, and Buddhists, this desire has proved elusive in our present exercise, especially because we have so often wished to provide exact quotations. Furthermore, inclusive language was not the particular strength of our period, so after some initial attempts to 'tidy up' we have decided to leave original texts as we found them. Also, we have tried to use such expressions in a manner that will convey the originally intended meanings.

The Contribution

What then is the contribution we hope to make with this study? We feel that the 'telling of the story' is itself a major contribution, for this has not yet been done. The account of the evolution of ecumenical Christian attitudes (with the WCC as the axis) about other faiths (with Hinduism as the focus) is a revealing story from which many lessons can be drawn. For this study is not simply a historical narrative; it is primarily an attempt to record the theological struggles of a community that would be faithful to its own religious commitments, and draw on these to develop its relations with its neighbours.

This is not, however, an unbiased or 'objective' study. Perhaps there is no such study. We have taken the stand that the new awareness of plurality calls for a change in Christian attitude to other faiths; our account is therefore a critical one. If we must be severe with such thinkers as Kraemer, our criticism has more to do with the particular angle from which we look at the past than with the commitment, competence, and relevance with which these scholars accomplished a difficult task. Each generation should be faithful to its own calling.

As a secondary contribution we have argued the need for a closer examination of two issues, plurality and Christology. Here we claim no originality, for others have pointed in the same direction from other perspectives. What is original here is our analysis of the problem from within the ecumenical discussions, demonstrating that the basic challenge relates much less to the theology of religions than to the explication of the Christian faith. New as well is the link we establish between this discovery and the conduct of Hindu–Christian relations. Readers may also be interested in the connections we have drawn between recent thinking in the Theology of Religions and the earlier ecumenical discussions. Some people would perhaps like to know how we ourselves would develop the two issues of plurality and Christology. But they must wait, for this task is well beyond the scope of our present assignment. As is often the case with research, there is a sense in which one sees the beginning of the project just as one approaches its end. There is little wonder that so many agree with T. S. Eliot's oft quoted insight:

> We shall not cease from exploration,
> and the end of all our exploring
> Will be to arrive where we started
> And know the place for the first time.[18]

---

18 T. S. Eliot, "Little Gidding" in *Collected Poems* (London: Faber and Faber, 1963).

Concluding Comment

As observed earlier, there is an obvious institutional interest in this study. For it not only concentrates on the discussions within the WCC, but it also ends with a call for greater collaboration among the Faith and Order, Mission, and Dialogue components of the Council's work. This is no judgment on the present situation, for such collaboration already exists, but it needs to be greatly intensified in order to come to terms with the pluralist situation. What we seek is a vital relationship with people of other faiths, sanctioned and warranted by the explication of our own faith, and set in the context of our own witness.

Conversations with the late Dr. Willem Visser 't Hooft, Dr. Philip Potter, Dr. Emilio Castro, Bishop S. Kulandran, Dr. M. M. Thomas, Dr. Stanley Samaratha, Rev. Kenneth Cracknell, and Mr. Ans J. van der Bent have helped me to have a better grasp of the issues treated here. To them all I am grateful. No one can study the ecumenical movement without being struck by the vision, courage, commitment, and love that characterizes its history despite all the controversies and disagreements which have been essential elements in its own growth and development. Our exposure to this aspect of the ecumenical movement has been the greatest reward for undertaking this study.

As for the 'current' that has become a 'flood' and is threatening to become a 'mighty surge' — we shall certainly learn to swim. With this, let us turn to our subject, beginning with an examination of how Hinduism was discussed at the first three major ecumenical events.

Part 1

The Quest for Understanding

CHAPTER II

'The New Emergency':
The Challenge of Hinduism
to the Christian Faith
Edinburgh — 1910

"Decisive Hour for Christian Missions"

This is a decisive hour for Christian missions. The call of providence to all our Lord's disciples, of whatever ecclesiastical connections, is direct and urgent to undertake without delay the task of carrying the gospel to all the non-Christian world. ... The opportunity is inspiring; the responsibility is undeniable.[1]

These words from the Foreword of the "Findings" of Commission I represent the overall mood of the World Missionary Conference which met in Edinburgh from 15 to 23 June 1910.[2] The purpose of the conference was "to consider the missionary problems in relation to the non-Christian world." The work of Commission I itself was done under the title "Carrying the Gospel to All the Non-Christian World," and constituted a survey

---

1 *World Missionary Conference 1910, Report of Commission I: Carrying the Gospel to All the Non-Christian World* (Edinburgh/London: Oliphant, Anderson, and Ferrier, 1910?), p. 363.

2 This was the largest missionary meeting to that date to bring together the official representatives from the missionary societies. Forty-six British societies were represented by over 500 delegates; sixty American societies were represented by over 500 delegates; forty-one continental societies by 170 delegates and twelve South African and Australian societies by 26 delegates. A large number of delegates were missionaries in Asia, Africa etc. Cf. *WMC 1910: The History and Records of the Conference together with Addresses Delivered at the Evening Meetings,* p. 18-19.

of the "progress of evangelization" and the areas "yet to be occupied."[3]
The proceedings had begun with the singing of the hymn, "Soldiers of
Christ, Arise!" It was chaired by John R. Mott, whose vision of the
"Evangelization of the world in this generation" had been the rallying
point of the meeting.

At first sight it would appear that this international ecumenical
meeting did not contribute much to the development of Christian understanding of other faiths within the ecumenical movement. In fact, it is
common to assume that the serious theological debate on the Christian
relationship to other faiths began within the ecumenical movement at the
meeting of the International Missionary Council at Tambaram in 1938, with
the epoch-making preparatory book, *Christian Message in a Non-Christian
World* by Hendrik Kraemer.[4] This is not the case. A careful analysis of
the records of the Edinburgh meeting shows that it made a very significant
contribution to the ecumenical discussion of the issue, and that the debate
on other faiths within this conference was no less animated than that of
1938. This discussion, however, did not take place within Commission I,
which was primarily concerned with missionary expansion and methods, but
within Commission IV, which had the mandate to examine the "Missionary
message in relation to non-Christian religions."

Learning from Local Experiences

Commision IV adopted a methodology which brought into its work the
actual experiences of those who were in direct contact with people of
other religious convictions. This enabled an informed and sympathetic
discussion of Christian–Hindu relations in its committee work. The
methodology included sending a large number of questionnaires to missionaries living in different parts of the world among the various religious
traditions with the objective of "discovering the realities of the situation."
More than two hundred sets of answers, some of considerable length, were
received.[5]

The questions requested information on a number of points about
Christian relationships with other faiths: What are the doctrines and
observances in other faiths that seem to give genuine help and consolation
to devotees in their religious life? What are the chief moral, intellectual,
and social hindrances to their responding to Christianity? What are the
points at which people of other religions are dissatisfied with their own

---

3 One of the tasks of Commission I was to "survey the unoccupied sections of the
world, with the view to the speedy and complete occupation of these areas ..." *Report
of Commission I,* p. 279.

4 *The History and Records of the Conference,* p. 79.

5 *Report of Commission IV,* p. 2.

religious communities and faith? What should be the attitude of the Christian preacher to the religion of the people among whom he works? What are the points of contact with other religions, and what are the aspects of Christianity that appeal to others? The last question had two forms. One, sent to Western missionaries working among people of other faiths, asked whether the person's work as a Christian missionary among people of other faiths had, either in form or content, altered his or her understanding of "What constitute the most important and vital elements in the Christian gospel." The other, sent to converts, asked what in Christianity had made a special appeal to them and whether the Western form in which Christianity was preached had perplexed them.[6]

The leaders of the Commission were overwhelmed by the number and the length of the responses they received, and made a genuine effort to take them into consideration in their Commission work and in the reporting. Commenting on the material received, the chairman of the Commission pleaded that they should be committed to print, for in the opinion of the members of the Commission it contained "material of the highest importance for the student of Church History, of biblical interpretation, and of Dogmatics and Apologetics."[7] We will here concentrate only on the material received in relation to Hinduism and the way the experience and views of those who had actual contact with Hinduism and the Hindus got incorporated into the Commission's report.[8]

Christian Attitude to Hinduism

One of the difficulties of Christians relating to Hinduism, in the opinion of many who responded to the inquiry, is its complex nature. It is described as 'not one religion but many' and the fact that it has no formulated creed or body of doctrine makes it possible for it to hold within its embrace a number of religious views and doctrines that are apparently inconsistent and even contradictory to each other. Further, the responses noted, since Hinduism expresses itself in different forms —the popular religion of the village, ceremonial, and ritual Hinduism, the religion of the home, the social expression of religion, and a highly speculative and mystical religion— each demanded a different response from the Christian

---

6 *Ibid.*

7 *Report of Commission IV,* p. 3. Also see p. 292.

8 Sixty-one of the responses received on Hinduism, including those of J. N. Farquhar, G. S. Eddy, A. G. Hogg, R. A. Hume, Francis Kingsbury, Bernard Lucas, Nicol Macnicol, Pandith Ramabai, T. E. Slater, and C. F. Andrews, are available in typed form in the WCC Library. *Commission on Missionary Message: Hinduism,* Cat. no. 280.215 w893c, Vol. 2-3.

perspective.[9] Added to this was the recognition that millions of people with whom Christians are in contact and from whom the major part of the Christian community was drawn in India, had "little to do with what might be called Hinduism in the classical sense."

There are many millions who are classified as Hindus, wrote J. A. Sharrock, "who lie between (Aryanism or) Brahmanism proper and animism. Their blood sacrifices, their propitiation of devils, their worship of goddesses and not gods, and their idolatry point more towards animism than Brahmanism. At best, India was very imperfectly converted by the Brahmans. The great mass of Sudras and outcastes know nothing of, and are slightly influenced, by Hinduism."[10] The report also quoted the words of T. E. Slater to confirm Sharrock's opinion that here Christians are dealing with at least two major blocks of people who had different orientations, although classed together as Hindus: "Remember one thing — that the lower castes or the outcastes from whom the bulk of our Christians in South India have been drawn are not Hindus. When you have converted thousands upon thousands of these, you may not have touched Hinduism."[11]

Almost all the replies received emphasized that Christians "should possess and not merely assume" a sympathetic attitude towards Hinduism. They also called for prolonged and patient study of Hinduism so that such sympathy may be "based on knowledge and not be the child of emotion or imagination." In the view of the Commission, "more harm has been done in India than in any other country by missionaries who have lacked the wisdom to appreciate the nobler side of the religion which they have laboured so indefatigably to supplant."[12]

An informed understanding of the faith of one's neighbours is seen as essential to all Christians but as obligatory to those who wish to witness to them. "It is a reasonable demand," one of the responses from Calcutta said, "to any man who tries to tackle so difficult a problem as that of changing other men's faith that he should know what he is talking about, not only his own religion, but also that which he desires to lead the people away from."[13] F. W. Steinthal claimed in his response that Christian knowledge of Hinduism should go well beyond familiarity with its history,

9 It is significant to note the diversity of the understandings of Hinduism already in the answers sent by those in mission fields.

10 J. A. Sharrock in *Commission on Missionary Message: Hinduism*, I, bound copy of typed manuscript (WCC Library), p. 298, *op. cit.*

11 T. E. Slater's report to London conference of missions in 1888. Quoted in *Report of Commission IV* of World Missionary Conference, Edinburgh, p. 157.

12 *The Missionary Message: Report of Commission IV*, p. 171.

13 *Ibid.*

ritual, philosophy, etc., to the point of grasping as far as one is able, the 'real life' that throbs within:

> Below the strange forms and hardly intelligible language, lies life, the spiritual life of human souls, needing God, seeking God, laying hold of God so far as they have found Him. Until we have at least reached so far that under the ceremonies and doctrines we have found the religious life of the people, and at least to some extent have begun to understand this life, we do not know what Hinduism really is, and are missing the essential connection with the peoples' religious life.[14]

A number of responses also emphasized the need not only to know Hinduism in depth but also to respect it. "I have met among Hindus and Brahmans as deep, genuine, and spiritual a religious life as is found amongst most Christians" wrote F. W. Steinthal. Expressing a similar sentiment, J. N. Farquhar claimed that undue criticism of the Hindu faith should be stopped. "Christ's own attitude to Judaism ought to be our attitude to other faiths even if the gap is far greater and the historical connection absent."[15]

The responses also dealt with a number of points of contact, particularly highlighting the Hindu search for *moksha* (release and deliverance from that which stands between God and soul), Hindu devotion or *Bhakti*, and the Hindu doctrine of *avatar* (where one looks for God's direct intervention to help in the affairs of the world and the journey of the soul). Perhaps the most important point of contact with Hinduism was its "unquestioning belief in the supernatural," wrote one of the respondents; "we need not spend time in arguing for the existence of the unseen and eternal."[16]

Many respondents wrote at length on these points of contact as something on which Christians should build, suggesting that the apparent differences should not lead to a rejection of Hinduism as foreign to the Christian gospel. The following quotation from Bernard Lucas is typical of the overall attitude taken by a number of respondents:

> In answer to your question as to points of contact between Christianity and Hinduism I should put first and foremost the spiritual view of life as opposed to the materialistic conception of the West. Though the quality of this spiritual view may be very deficient, and though it may contain much which is erroneous, yet there can be no question that in Hinduism, religion is, and has always been, the supreme concern of the Hindu mind. The belief that the things which are seen are temporal, while the things

14 *Ibid.*, p. 172.
15 *Ibid.*, p. 173. J. N. Farquhar, well known for his *The Crown of Hinduism* wrote a 43-page response to the questions discussing the various aspects of Christian–Hindu relations. For the full text, see *Commission on Missionary Message: Hinduism*, 1, *op. cit.*
16 *Report of Commission IV*, p. 186.

which are not seen are eternal, is deeply ingrained in the Hindu tempera-
ment. Then I should say that the conception of the oneness of God,
though essentially pantheistic and bound up with polytheism, is nevertheless
a great religious asset, destined to be of immense value for the future of
Christianity in India. . . .

Again, the conception of incarnation, though presenting very marked
defects and misconceptions, is nevertheless not a foreign idea. This
conception is also associated with the idea of divine action for the good of
humanity, and *Bhakti* and the *Bhaktimarga* again have marked affinities
with the Christian conceptions of loving devotion on the part of man, and
grace on the part of God. Though the idea of salvation (i. e., *moksha*) is
always associated with the conception of rebirth, yet there is also con-
nected with it an earnest longing and passionate desire for union with
God. These are a few of the outstanding features, but a sympathetic mind
will find very much in Hindu religious ideas which anticipates fuller
expression in Christianity.[17]

The responses also dealt with many other issues, such as what in Christianity was attractive or repulsive to the Hindus, at what points the Hindus
were dissatisfied with their own tradition, etc. There were a number of
reports that pointed out the social evils manifest in Hindu society. Having
examined all the evidence the Commission shared with the Council the
ambiguity that was inevitable in any Christian attitude and response to
Hinduism. On the one hand, the Commission was convinced that a
religious system must be "judged by its moral and social results." Here
they pointed to the many ills to which their correspondents witnessed
—the immense growth of mendicant asceticism, the petrification of society
in the caste system, the incidence of child-marriage, and the manifold
hardships of widowhood— all seen to arise from "a defective conception
of God."[18] On the other hand, the Commission was deeply impressed by
the correspondents' witness to the "profound and vital truths" hidden in
Hinduism. "Tragic and mysterious as has been the course of religion in
India," they say, "the impression left on the mind by the study of the
evidence is that no other non-Christian religion approaches this in the
gravity or in the depth of its endeavours after God."[19] While admitting
that the impact of Christianity has made a "deep impression on the
educated minds of India" and has caused a "great resurgence of Hindu
feeling and thought,"[20] the report also goes on to say that by the meeting
with Hinduism "the mind of the church is profoundly stirred, and is flung

---

17 *Ibid.,* pp. 186-87. Bernard Lucas sent one of the best responses. For the full text
see *Commission on the Missionary Message: Hinduism,* II, Bound manuscripts (WCC
Library), pp. 92-107.

18 *Ibid.,* p. 246.

19 *Ibid.,* pp. 246-47.

20 *Ibid.,* p. 244.

back upon the hidden depths of the Christian revelation in a way which is very impressive."[21] What is of importance to our study, however, is the way in which Commission IV theologically responded to this witness and evidence before them, and what implications they drew about Christian relationships with Hinduism.

Christian–Hindu Interaction

Studying the evidence before them the Commission recognized a strong parallel between the Christian encounter with other faiths today and the encounter of the early church with Hellenism. The apostles had had to face a world in which there was a search for God. They could not relate to it ignoring the reality of the religious life that had both its bad and good elements. In fact the apostolic teaching grew out of the twofold endeavour "to meet what was deep and true in other religions" and to guard "against the perils which arose" from the continued existence of what was not in keeping with the gospel message.[22]

This double response of being faithful to the gospel message and yet being open to what is 'deep and true' in other faiths was seen by the Commission to be the right attitude towards Hinduism. Such an encounter, the Commission believed, would have the effect of driving the Christians back to a re-examination of some of the fundamentals of their faith, enabling them to discover new dimensions that they had never seen before. This, in their view, was what happened to the apostles when they faced Hellenism. They were driven back to their Lord to search for undiscovered riches of their faith because "the opportunities and the dangers of their task taught them the insufficiency of all their past discoveries of Him. New faith is always born out of new emergencies."[23]

The significant feature in the Commission's finding is its conviction that the "historic peculiarity of the present situation is that, after long neglect, the church is once again facing this emergency." In other words, the Commission was convinced that the Christian task in India called for an encounter with Hinduism, for which the only parallel was the encounter between the gospel and Hellenism. The implication of this encounter was that Christianity itself must search for profounder truths within its own faith in order to counter the challenge of what was unacceptable, on the one hand, and on the other to accommodate and assimilate what was vital in India's search for God and spirituality. It was a new situation pregnant with new possibilities for both Hinduism and Christianity.[24]

21 *Ibid.*, p. 247.
22 *Ibid.*, p. 215.
23 *Ibid.*
24 *Ibid.*, pp. 215-16. Here the Commission sought to go beyond the two dominant

What is of even greater interest is that in its report the Commission went into detail to illustrate the ways in which Hinduism could and did challenge the Christian faith, driving its adherents deeper into their own faith to seek new resources. Since this was a rather revolutionary attitude in the prevalent climate of the whole conference, which was that of the missionary vocation of converting the world, it would be good to look further into how the Commission worked out its conviction.

The Commission took two aspects of Hindu belief to which most of the correspondents had referred, namely, that salvation consists in being redeemed from the world, and that this salvation is attained through the realization of unity with the Supreme Being. Taking these two concepts as belonging to the core of the Hindu religion, the Commission went on to examine how they related to the Christian ideas of redemption and communion with God. Christians, in the Commission's view, had become too accustomed, for example, to speak primarily of redemption from inward sin. This was rather inadequate; the New Testament speaks of "redemption from the alien sin within and from the evil of the world without," which are viewed by all the New Testament writers, without exception, as standing in the closest organic relation to each other.[25]

The Commission was convinced that the Christian engagement with Hinduism had the effect of driving Christianity back to one of its fundamental conceptions, "which views the kingdom of God as consisting not only in inward deliverance from the power of sin, but ultimate deliverance from everything that cripples and depresses the entire life of men."[26] The Commission saw a close parallel between the "utterly unsatisfying character of the whole nature of life in the world" into which the gospel has come as a radiant hope, and the "feeling of the misery and indignity of the present lot of men, and the passionate desire for escape from these limitations which have characterized the highest religious thought of India."[27]

> Here, surely, in this dissatisfaction with 'the world' we have a primitive New Testament idea. It is here that Indian religion surpasses all other non-Christian religions. "Though we were to win all you are seeking," her sages seem to say to the Animist, the Confucian, and the Moslem, "we should still be unsatisfied." Is there not something here deeply akin to St. John's saying: "All that is in the world, the lust of the flesh, the lust

ideas, namely, that of Christian faith replacing other faiths or of fulfilling them, which were the two major trends seen in most of the written responses. It appears that the Chairman of the Commission, D. S. Cairns, introduced the idea of the 'new emergency,' comparing the contemporary situation with the first contacts of the gospel with the Hellenistic world.

25 *Ibid.*, pp. 249-50.
26 *Ibid.*
27 *Ibid.*

of the eyes, and the pride of life, they are not of the Father, but of the world" and to the constantly recurring thought of St. Paul that "our citizenship is in heaven"? Shall we ever recover the daring optimism of the early days, until we have more deeply understood the pessimism out of which it sprang?[28]

The Commission indeed recognized the number of divergences between the Christian and Hindu views of the world, and some of the evils manifest in Hindu society which might have arisen from utter disregard for the life in this world. In the Commission's view, the Hindu would see the world as basically illusory, while Christians would say that it existed "in order to be transformed by communion with God." Again, the Hindu conception of redemption, although implying in theory union with the All, was in practice intensely individualistic. The report was most critical on the question of the way the Hindu worldview was allowed to be divorced from social ethics, producing a "fatal conservatism" in relation to caste, child-marriage and the place of women in society. "The divergence here," the Commission commented, "is profound."[29] The report argued, however, that Hinduism still was a challenge to the Christian faith in the matter of its attitude to the world:

> Yet when all is said, there is deep truth in the Hindu conviction of the nothingness of the world in comparison with God. If we must choose, it is better to believe that God is all and the world nothing, than to believe that the world is all and God nothing, which is a view widely prevailing today in Christian lands. No Christian holds this latter view either in theory or in practice. Yet have not both our Christian theology and practice become deeply tinged with the prevailing naturalism of the West? Have we not lost something of the profound sense of the absolute sovereignty of God over both man and the world which lies at the very heart of all our Lord's teaching, and without which, as all history shows, nothing great has ever been achieved in religion?[30]

These and other questions framed by the Commission implied that the Christian–Hindu encounter was a mutual challenge in which the Christians were challenged to give expression to some of the undiscovered aspects of their faith, and the spiritual resources of Hinduism were challenged to respond to the newness of the message brought to it in the Christian gospel. This could only happen, however, if there was a genuine encounter in which people were willing to listen and learn:

28 *Ibid.,* pp. 250-51.
29 *Ibid.,* p. 252.
30 *Ibid.,* pp. 252-53.

Have we nothing to learn of the riches of our faith from the uncompromising idealism of India? Have we not in those uncovered riches that which alone can satisfy India's need? Are there not here in this tragic history great spiritual forces running to waste which, if they could be turned into the one true channel, would fertilize the whole spiritual life of mankind?[31]

The Commission also dealt with the second aspect of Hindu teaching —union with the Supreme Being— in its relation to Christian teaching. Here again it first acknowledged divergence, especially in the Hindu concept of the Supreme Being as that in which the soul loses its identity at the point of self-realization. "The religious thinking of India," the Commission regretted, "has never been able to retrieve that fatal moment in its religious evolution when Vedic religion lost its opportunity of rising to a true theism." For it saw that the Christian understanding of God as 'personal' was at the very heart of its faith and life.[32]

The Commission, however, went on to say that despite the obvious divergence, the Hindu conception of the Supreme Being and its relationship to the soul challenged some of the inadequacies of the Christian conception, or at least pointed to some of its teaching that had to be expounded and applied in a much deeper fashion. The Commission saw in the "inextinguishable thirst that is behind India's search for union with God" the longing to participate "in the very life of the eternal, above the flux and reflux of the world of illusion." "Have we fully realized," the Commission asked, "the immeasurable value of the idea of the Holy Spirit in the light of what Hinduism says of the inner nature of the religious aspiration of man? Much labour has been expended in discussion on the place of the Spirit in the life of God. But we still wait for any thorough understanding of the place of the Spirit in the life of man."[33]

The meeting between Christianity and Hinduism, in other words, was a challenge to the still undeveloped aspects of the mystical dimension of the Christian religion. Admitting that the mystical elements in the Christian religion had been more or less recognized throughout the history of the Christian Church, the Commission felt that the challenge of the desire for unity with God, seen in Hinduism, could never be met unless Christianity seriously explored the "full riches of eternal life of which St. John speaks as the present possession of him who believes in the son."[34] This

---

31 *Ibid.*, p. 253.

32 *Ibid.*, p. 254. In dealing with Hinduism, the Commission distinguished among the animistic religion before the coming of the Aryans, the Vedic religion where there is recognition of gods, and the Vedantic religion. The Commission saw the parallel existence of these three strands as one of the problems in dealing with Hinduism in a general way.

33 *Ibid.*, p. 255.

34 *Ibid.*, pp. 255-56.

challenge to explore fully the nature of the inner life of the soul in God was seen as the most important impact of the Christian encounter with Hinduism:

> It may be that here there will be the richest result of it all, that whether through the Christianized mind of India or through the mind of the missionary stirred to its depths by contact with the Indian mind, we shall discover new and wonderful things in the ancient revelation which have been hidden in part from the just and faithful of the Western world.[35]

The Commission also called upon Christians to see what the Hindu attitude of *Bhakti,* described by the correspondents as "heartfelt trust and love towards the Supreme Being," had to say to Christianity, particularly to the understanding of devotional life in Christianity.[36] A similar examination of the challenge of the Vedantic concepts was also recommended.[37]

In summing up its findings, the Commission reiterated its conviction that the Christian attitude to Hinduism, notwithstanding the elements which the Christian must reject, should be one of understanding and sympathy. It said that the Christian should seek the noble elements in non-Christian religions and use them as steps to higher things, for Hinduism in its higher forms "plainly manifests the working of the Holy Spirit." The "merely iconoclastic attitude," the Commission said, was condemned by the majority of its correspondents as "radically unwise and unjust."[38]

But along with this generous affirmation went the emphatic witness to the 'absoluteness' of the Christian faith in the sense that Christ fulfils the desires in all religions.[39] "Superficial criticism might say," the report commented, "that these two attitudes are incompatible, that if Christianity alone is true and final, all other religions must be false, and as falsehood they must be denounced as such."[40] The Commission claimed that the experience of those who were actually in contact with Hinduism was quite the contrary: "Deeper consideration of the fact indeed leads us to the conviction that it is precisely because of the strength of their conviction in the absoluteness of Christianity that our correspondents find it possible to take this more generous view of the non-Christian religions. They know that in Christ they have what meets the whole range of human need, and therefore they value all that reveals that need, however imperfect the revelation may be."[41]

---

35 *Ibid.,* p. 256.
36 *Ibid.,* p. 257.
37 *Ibid.,* p. 258.
38 *Ibid.,* p. 267.
39 *Ibid.,* p. 268.
40 *Ibid.*
41 *Ibid.*

The above comment is of interest, for here at the ecumenical meeting in 1910 there was an affirmation of the possibility of radical openness to other faiths arising from a firm Christian commitment. The other religions were seen, at least in their noble expressions, as the arena where the spirit was at work. This concept of 'commitment and openness' was to come back into the ecumenical vocabulary in a well-developed form again only after about fifty years, for in between theological reflection on other faiths in the ecumenical movement was to be dominated by Hendrik Kraemer's concept of 'continuity–discontinuity.' To this we shall come later. It would be important now, however, to draw out some of the implications of the Edinburgh meeting, before turning to the next major event, which took place in Jerusalem.

An Initial Evaluation of the Edinburgh Meeting

A careful reading of the volume of material related to the Edinburgh meeting shows that it was a conference that managed to hold in creative tension contradictory views on the Christian relationship with other faiths, neither seeking to allow them to come into conflict nor trying to reconcile them. The intention of the meeting, most vividly expressed in the evening addresses as well as its final message,[42] was clearly missionary in nature, in the sense of overcoming the other religions and 'occupying' the areas not yet occupied. There was the unmistakable vision of the possibility of evangelizing the world in a generation. The title of Commission I, "Carrying the Gospel to all the Non-Christian World," clearly indicated the intention of the whole meeting. It should also be noted that with a very few exceptions, almost all of the participants were Western missionaries. Asia, Africa, etc., were represented by "selected missionaries in the field."[43]

And yet the work of Commission IV shows a remarkable degree of thinking that was, in many ways, ahead of its time. This was made possible only because the Commissioners based their deliberations on the experience of, and the written material supplied by, those who were in actual contact with people of other faiths. The Commission was undoubtedly also inspired both by the rising popularity of the 'Science of Comparative Religion' and the results of 'higher criticism' being applied to

---

42 Compiled in the volume on *The History and Records of the Conference together with Addresses Delivered at Evening Meetings.*

43 It was customary for the missionaries in the mission fields to represent the countries where they worked at Missionary Conferences in early years. This was corrected at the Jerusalem meeting in 1928, and there was a good representation of Asian and African delegates at missionary meetings from Tambaram, 1938 on.

the Bible in scholarly work.[44] There is also clear evidence that the chairman of the Commission, D. S. Cairns of Aberdeen, Scotland, who also drafted the report of this Commission, was a man of exceptional scholarship, combined with the rare ability to listen and learn, and an attitude of sympathy. W. H. T. Gairdner, who wrote a comprehensive account of the Edinburgh Conference, referred to the work of the Commission as one of the highlights of the conference.[45] Robert A. Hume, contributing to the plenary discussion, spoke of the General Conclusions of the Commission IV report as 'pulsating with life' in every paragraph. "To me," he said, "the characteristics of that concluding outlook are its sympathy, insight, penetrative use of history both for encouragement and warning, progressiveness, courage, suggestiveness, and consequent hopefulness." Encouraging everyone to "make and take time to ponder on this lucid and glowing statement," he said that the strength of the report was that it brought to the forefront the most important factor in Christian engagement with other faiths in mission — "not men, not money, not methods, not organization, but the living Christ and the universal, active Holy Spirit."[46]

This indeed was the strength of the work of the Commission. Faced with the reality of the religious and spiritual life in other faiths, the Commission refused to become defensive. It did not engage in apologetics, seeking to marginalize other religious experiences or even the doctrinal formulations of other faiths, as 'primitive,' 'preparatory,' 'natural,' 'human,' etc., but sought rather to deal with them theologically. First there was the attitude of listening to and learning about the other faiths, not simply to have an adequate knowledge, but with a view to grasping their 'meaning' for their believers.[47] Second, there was no attempt to judge the other faiths on the basis of the unacceptable manifestations of their religion in social life, even though such manifestations were taken seriously and criticized. We see a willingness to examine other faiths at their best and as they receive expression in the life of the true believers of those faiths. Third, the doctrinal formulations or the belief systems of other faiths were not ruled out as incompatible with the gospel message. The Vedantic attitude to the world, the concept of the Supreme Being, the *Bhakti* tradition, the Hindu concept of *moksha* etc., were all taken seriously, and a genuine attempt was made to understand them in their own terms in

---

44 There are many references to this in the Commission's report. In its concluding recommendations it encouraged the study of Comparative Religion and familiarity with Higher Criticism to all who wished to work among people of other faiths. See pages 268-74.

45 W. H. T. Gairdner, *Echoes from Edinburgh 1910* (New York/Chicago/Toronto: Fleming H. Revell Company), p. 135 f.

46 Robert A. Hume's comment on the Report, *Report of Commission IV,* Discussions, p. 321.

47 Cf. p. 267.

order to grasp the meaning behind the formulations and the spiritual
search that had produced them.

This attitude to other religious traditions had two specific implications
for Christianity. In the first instance, there was a realization of some of
the inadequacies of the way the Christian understanding of the nature of
reality, human life, ultimate goals, etc., were formulated, or at least held
in the common belief of most Christians. The Commission was convinced,
for example, that the Hindu understanding of the 'nature of the world,'
'nature of the union between Ultimate Reality and the soul,' etc., could at
least point to the more profound dimensions in which the Christian
attitude to these should have been formulated, if only to do justice to the
New Testament teaching.

The second effect was that, in the Commission's conviction, the church
should elaborate and expand its own theology to make sense of the
religious life of the people with whom it was in contact. It saw the
Christian contact with other faiths as the 'new emergency' that the
churches had to face, like the early church had faced the religious world
around it. In the Commission's view such encounters were essential and
instrumental for the vitality of the church, for they pushed the church back
to its spiritual resources in order to understand more deeply its own faith
and so "meet the emergency." A living theology, said the Commission,
could come only from a living encounter.[48]

One should, of course, realize that this theologically dialogical and
sympathetic attitude towards other faiths, and particularly to Hinduism, was
held within the conviction that the Christians were called upon to share
the message of Christ with people of other faiths. The Commission had
no doubts that Christ would 'meet' the religious longings of India and that
the Christian faith when rightly and fully understood would also 'meet the
emergency.' This explained the call to go back to the roots of the Christian faith in order to meet the challenge of the spiritual life of the
Hindus. At no time did the Commission seriously challenge the missionary
intention of the meeting or its plan to take the gospel to all the 'corners
of the earth.' The strength of the work of the Commission lies in its use
of this very concern to evangelize the world as a theological argument for
a positive attitude to, and life with, people of other faiths.

A fuller evaluation of this meeting should await our consideration of
the two major meetings at Jerusalem and Tambaram. In concluding this
initial evaluation, however, one should say that here in the meeting of the
ecumenical community at Edinburgh in 1910, there were expressed views on
the Christian attitude toward and understanding of people of other faiths
that have much to contribute to the contemporary discussion.

---

48 *Ibid.*, pp. 264-65.

It is unfortunate that so little use is made of this meeting and its findings today, mainly because, as mentioned earlier, it fell under the shadow of the meeting of the International Missionary Council at Tambaram, where the issue became deeply controversial and hence more visible. Why did this happen? The explanation has to be sought in the developments between 1910 and 1938 both in the field of the history of religions and in world history. The meeting of the IMC at Jerusalem, 1928 illustrates these developments. And to this we turn now.

CHAPTER III

In Search of Collaboration:
Hindu—Christian Enrichment
and
Collaboration Against Secularism
Jerusalem — 1928

The Jerusalem Topic

The second World Missionary Conference took place at the Mount of Olives, Jerusalem, over Easter 1928. Many important contemporary issues demanded the urgent attention of the conference. The most obvious was the rise of secularism, predominantly in the West, but also in the East. The spread of secularism was seen not only as a threat to religious life in the West; it presented new challenges to the whole missionary enterprise and to the content of the missionary message. Another issue that called for special attention was the relationship between the younger and older churches. The younger churches had begun to assert their 'self-hood,' raising new questions regarding relationships and partnership in mission. Precisely because of the secular challenge, Christian education was also seen as a priority for many churches. It is significant that in spite of these stated new priorities, when the preparatory meeting listed the priority issues for Commission work, Christian relationship to other faiths was at the top.[1]

---

1 The seven Commissions were: (i) The Christian Life and Message in Relation to Non-Christian Systems of Thought and Life; (ii) Religious Education; (iii) Relationship between Younger and Older Churches; (iv) The Christian Message in the Light of Race Conflict; (v) The Christian Message in Relation to Industrial Problems; (vi) The Christian Message in Relation to Rural Problems; (vii) International Missionary Cooperation.

The formulation of this topic, "The Christian Life and Message in Relation to Non-Christian Systems of Thought and Life," was not an easy task. During the pre-Jerusalem preparatory work and meetings there was much disagreement on what should be the focus of this topic, for it was held that the very formulation of the topic constituted a theological stance vis-à-vis the people of other faiths.[2]

Robert E. Speer, who had attended Edinburgh as vice-chairman and secretary to the Commission that worked on "The Missionary Message in Relation to Non-Christian Religions," drew attention during the Jerusalem discussions to the significance of the different ways in which the two conferences had formulated the topics. He first noted that at Edinburgh there had been a separation between the task of carrying the Christian message to the areas of the world 'yet to be occupied' and the Christian message in relation to the other religious traditions. Priority was given to the task of carrying the gospel; the matter of the Christian message in relation to other faiths was, in his words, "relegated to the fourth place." At Jerusalem these two were brought together and given the first place. Another significant change, Speer said, was the introduction of the word 'life' into the Jerusalem formulation of the topic. The intention is that we are here not dealing only with the relationship between two systems of thought, but with lives; lives in interaction. This, in Speer's view, gave a new dynamism to the way the topic would be formulated for the Jerusalem meeting.[3]

The Jerusalem topic was formulated to focus the discussions on three fundamental issues that were seen to be important for Christian relationships with those of other faiths. First, is the Christian message meant for the whole world, and if so, what is the content of this message? Second, what is the best method for the presentation of the message? Third, how does the Christian (understanding and) view of other religions, including their life and thought, call for the presentation of the message to them? It was assumed that the basic theological issues of relating to other faiths would surface if the Commission came to grips with these three questions.

In the course of the conference, however, these questions gradually receded to the background. The challenge of secularism and the need to respond to it became the major concern of its final message. To this we shall return later. For, despite the preoccupation of the whole conference with the issue of secularism, the work of Commission I, both in plenary and in 'sectional meetings,' indicated some of the major currents that were

---

2 For a discussion of the issue see Carl F. Hallencreutz, *Kraemer Towards Tambaram: A Study in Hendrick Kraemer's Missionary Approach* (Uppsala: Gleerup, 1966), pp. 168-83.

3 *Jerusalem Meeting Report* (JMR), I (London: Oxford University Press, 1928), pp. 342-43.

prevalent at Jerusalem on the question of Christian attitude to other faiths. The organizers had asked Nicol Macnicol to prepare the preliminary paper on Hinduism.[4]

Presentation of Hinduism

The preliminary papers were normally contributed by persons reputed to be well versed in their subjects and who could, in the judgement of the leaders, reflect on them in the ecumenical context with a sense of the history of the discussions. They played an important role at the conference itself and in the post-conference discussions. Macnicol himself was unfortunately not present at Jerusalem, but he wrote responses to the discussions, and these were included in the reports printed later. It is important for our purposes to follow the main line of thought that Macnicol developed on the Christian attitude to Hinduism.

Macnicol admits that it is very difficult to deal with Christian relations to Hinduism at any one time because of the amorphous and complex nature of Hinduism. At the time of this assessment it was particularly difficult "because Hinduism appears, more than at any other time in its long history, to be undergoing a process of change and reconstruction which renders the whole religious system and organisation more ambiguous than ever in its central principles and more uncertain than ever in its boundaries."[5]

Subsequent discussions will show why he made such a characterization of the situation. It was difficult for him to decide on 'which Hinduism' he would concentrate. For the Christian attitude to Hinduism often depended on the kind of Hinduism with which Christians were in contact. "Of that type of Hinduism, a religion springing mainly from the fear of demons and of the evil eye and of the ghost that haunts the night-shadows, little needs be said," he declared, recalling Stanley Jones' statement at Edinburgh 1910 that from the Christian perspective, that religion has to go.[6] In Macnicol's view what the Christians were faced with in 1928 was a different kind of Hinduism. It is a religion that, "because of its long recorded history, because of the profundity of the speculation of its ancient sages, and because of the power that these ideas still exercise over the lives of multitudes in this land, demands to be treated with complete respect and is not afraid at times to claim to be possessed of a higher truth than any

---

4 Nicol Macnicol was at that time a missionary of the United Free Church of Scotland in Poona, India, and a reputed scholar in Hinduism.

5 Nicol Macnicol, "Christianity and Hinduism" in *The Christian Life and Message in Relation to Non-Christian Systems.* Report of the Jerusalem meeting of the International Missionary Council (JMR), I (London: Oxford University Press, 1928), p. 31.

6 *Ibid.,* p. 4.

of its rivals ... it is this Hinduism that we wish to survey from without, as she stands among her rivals, proud, self-assertive, not any longer apologetic."[7]

In surveying Hinduism for the conference, Macnicol's first concern was to present the current situation where there was already a strong reaction to Christian missions. In his view, the first Hindu response to the presence of Christian witness in terms of "reformation" was now giving way to "reaction," where Hinduism, particularly under the guidance of the Hindu Maha Sabha, was in the process of attempting to re-establish the "power and prestige" of the religion of the land. The effect of this was a profound alteration in the whole spirit of articulate, active Hinduism. Its first concern was no longer to amend its life but to assert its claims, and to reclaim those who had fallen away from its fold. Macnicol points out that the resolution passed by the Maha Sabha removing the ban of untouchability and opening the temple door to the outcastes, was, for example, less out of "a sense of brotherhood than a fear lest otherwise many more of these outcastes will, as they have done in the past, abandon Hinduism for a religion which at least will not treat them with contempt."[8]

There were two major elements in this development that were of consequence to the internal life of Hinduism itself. To begin with, this emphasis on the power, numbers, prestige, and solidarity of Hindus had slowed down the process of its own reformation. It had also fanned the spirit of communalism in the land and led to the rise of 'Hindu nationalism.' It was not so much the zeal for righteousness and reform as the zeal for the greatness of the nation that animated some of the emerging leaders.[9]

Macnicol was quick to point out that this broad generalization could in some ways be misleading, for there were large sections of Hinduism and its leadership that could not be included in this description. Many exceptions would have to be made. But any Christian attitude towards, and relationship with, Hinduism would have to take full account of this 'change in mentality.' In his view Hinduism in the last few years had changed from "quiescence to aggression, from an attitude of apology to one of self-assertion." There was much suspicion of the missionary activities of Christianity and Islam. Any consideration of Christian–Hindu relation would have to take full account of the new situation.

---

7 *Ibid.*, p. 5.

8 *Ibid.*, p. 5.

9 Macnicol, quoting S. K. Dattas's report on the National Christian Council, states that between August 1923 and July 1928 seventy-four communal riots had taken place resulting in the death of 258 persons and serious injuries to 2811 others, the conflict being contained only by military and police action. *Ibid.*, pp. 8-9.

After describing what was then the current context of Hindu–Christian relations, Macnicol turned to the major part of this preparatory presentation, to the theological basis of the relationship between Hinduism and Christianity. Here he picked up the Edinburgh debate and presented his own position which would later be debated by the participants of the Jerusalem meeting. Before we turn to this we shall take note of his comments on 'the Christian approach to Hinduism' which will help us to appreciate the sensitivity of his attitude to the religious people among whom he lived and worked.[10]

It would be an error, Macnicol felt, to separate one's attitude to the faith of a people from its expression in life. Hinduism was more than the kernel of its faith. The Hindu culture and environment, were to a large measure products of Hindu religion. In considering Christian relationships to Hinduism one must also take into account this 'secular' product. Here Macnicol pointed to Bertrand Russell's concern about what Christian Missions were doing to Chinese culture and tradition. The Chineseness of the Chinese people had been developed and nurtured over centuries. There was a 'spirit' that was particularly Chinese, with its own beauty and grace that could easily be destroyed through the Christian impact on Chinese culture, for often what was described as 'Christian' carried with it another view of life. Russell feared that Asian lands might be compelled in self-defence to adopt, like Japan, the Western ways of aggression and militarism.

Macnicol held that some of Russell's criticism was unjustified, but he saw in such criticism a warning of what one must guard against. His own position was that Christian relationships to other faiths should include the conscious presentation of the gospel message. For he was convinced that the gospel "does not necessarily destroy any gracious and beautiful character of the Hindu or deprive him of anything of which he is justly proud in his cultural inheritance." The Christian attitude to the Hindu could have no part in the hope of expanding 'Christian civilization.' Nor was there any place for aggression, which was a manifestation of egoism and not of the love of Christ and humankind. "As we draw near to the souls of our brethren with our message we must put off our shoes from our feet for the ground is holy."[11]

---

10 For discussion see Nicol Macnicol, "The Christian Life and Message in Relation to Non-Christian Systems," in *JMR, op. cit.,* pp. 11-17.

11 *Ibid.,* p. 17.

Christian Understanding of Hinduism

The key to understanding Macnicol's view of Hinduism in this preparatory statement is the word 'value.' This concept was developed during the preparatory discussion before Jerusalem and became the basis of the discussion of the Christian understanding of all other religions as well.[12] In a letter J. H. Oldham wrote to Martin Schlunk on what the methodological focus of the Jerusalem meeting should be, he makes this point clear: "What we propose to ask ourselves, not in terms of theological formulations or definitions, but in terms of spiritual experience, is first, what men live upon and rely upon for support in the non-Christian systems, and secondly, what Christianity has to offer in enrichment of and in addition to the insights and help which they attain from their own religious system."[13] Oldham, like many others in the preparatory discussions, had no doubt that Christianity had something distinctive to offer to other religions. Methodologically, however, the Jerusalem discussions attempted in the first place to examine the 'spiritual values' of other faiths and then to understand how the Christian faith 'transcended them.'

This methodology was seriously challenged by some of the continental delegates, particularly those from Germany. To this we shall return later. Here we need only to note the methodological assumptions that undergirded Macnicol's presentation of Hinduism. He said that we must go beyond the examination of the ancient documents and the rich literature that expound the Hindu view of life and see how this receives expression in human life and conduct today: "We want to see it as embodied in living men and women, in their conduct and character, in their aspiration and attainment. The important thing to know is how the personalities of men and women are being moulded today by this ancient system, what are the springs in it, still flowing, of strength and comfort." Or, in other words, "What is its *value*? we ask, and by the answer that question receives, Hinduism, or any religion, stands or falls."[14]

Macnicol turned to what he called 'pantheistic Hinduism' as the one among the many streams of Hinduism which was truly representative of the overall view of life that ruled the Hindu mind and heart. He was aware that this Vendantic view was not actively held by a vast number of Hindus. But the general sense of the essential unity of the Atman with

---

12 This is most clearly seen by W. H. T. Gairdner's treatment of "Christianity and Islam" in the preparatory presentation. After discussing the word 'value' he has two sections dealing with "Values in Islam" and "Values in Christianity." In his final section he interprets Christianity as the 'spiritual home' of the converts. See *JMR*, I, pp. 235-83.

13 Letter from J. H. Oldham to M. Schlunk, 10.2.1927 (WCC Archives: IMC, 1927).

14 "Christianity and Hinduism," *JMR*, I, pp. 17-18.

the Brahman, the view of the world as *maya,* and the *karma-samsara* theory of life were taken by him to be the key concepts shaping the life and personality of Hindus. He held that, despite the fact that much of the outward life of Hinduism was surrounded by temples, rites, pilgrimages, festivals, etc., ultimately the life and thought of the Hindu seemed "to circle continually, not around the visible and familiar objects and elements of worship, but around certain ever-present and all-controlling ideas."[15] What were the positive values of these ideas and how did they relate to the Christian message?

Macnicol felt that the Vedantic doctrine presented a worldview that was both serious and profound and that it took "extraordinary intellectual courage to conceive of an ultimate unity that includes all that is." He recognized that the Vedantic view was always under challenge from theistic views within Hinduism and that there were many strands within the Vedantic school itself that made it impossible to characterize it in only one way. He felt, however, that Vedantism could represent the general, underlying attitude to life controlling Hindu India.[16]

Christian Enrichment of Hindu Values

Macnicol saw a contrast between the Hindu view of life in terms of Brahman and the Christian conception of God the Father. "Of these two supreme interpretative conceptions," he commented, "we shall not say that, as they have been held by Hindus and Christians through the ages, the one is true and the other is false. ... One conveys a conception of power immanent in all things; and the other, a conception of a power transcendant."[17] The Hindu doctrine, in his view, was a necessary reminder to the Christian that it is in God that all things exist and that there is no reality except in God.

At the same time Macnicol's difficulty was that unless one held to the conviction of divine transcendance to the point of being able to talk of God also as the 'Holy Other' there could be no moral universe. Quoting Pringle-Pathson he said that without the acknowledgement of the 'other' the doctrine of immanence "must degenerate into the acceptance and justification of the actual just as we find it."[18]

---

15 *Ibid.,* p. 21 ff. It was common in the early Christian discussions to refer to the Vedantic school of Hinduism as 'Pantheism.' Insofar as the ideas of Karma and Samsara pervade the Indian consciousness, Hinduism is often generally referred to as Pantheist.

16 Macnicol, however, was also interested in theism as well and he examined theistic ideas in his book *Indian Theism* published by the Oxford University Press in 1915.

17 *JMR,* I, p. 31.

18 *Ibid.,* p. 32.

He saw the same difficulty with the Hindu concept of *moksha* in contrast to the Christian conception of "the victory over the world." The Hindu ideal, to him, appeared to be "shadowy and abstract." It held that the opening of the eyes to the fact of world's illusion would lead the soul to evaporate into nothingness, "contained by no love, won by no ideal good." Even of the *bhakti* tradition of love and devotion to God, Macnicol believed that it lacked clarity about the quality of the object of devotion and the effects it could produce in the worshipper's soul.[19] While he affirmed the reality of devotion, love, and mysticism emanating in the Hindu bhakta, he was doubtful whether this would lead anywhere without a strongly held moral view of both the universe and the object of the bhakta's devotion.

Hindu–Christian Relations

It is not our purpose here to examine these Hindu conceptions in more detail or even to assess the way in which Macnicol dealt with some of the fundamental conceptions within Hinduism. What is important is to notice his own understanding of the relationship between Hinduism and Christianity, for it was to become the focus of discussion for the ecumenical group gathered in Jerusalem.

Here the word 'enrichment' played an important part. In Macnicol's view, Hinduism was not wrong; it was not to be rejected. In fact, in many ways he saw in the Hindu conception a very profound grasp of some of the basic realities of the universe. But it was his strong conviction that Hinduism "needs Christ." What Christianity could bring to Hinduism was an enrichment of its concepts so that Hinduism could in fact fulfil some of its own ideals. In talking about this enrichment he sometimes spoke about carrying Hinduism into Christianity and at other times of taking Christ into Hinduism.

> The fault of Hinduism is this aspect of moral impotence. It loads man with chains and leaves him helpless in deliverance. It has its lessons to teach us that can be carried over into Christian faith and can be linked with the tremendous moral energy that are stored there in the whole ethical tradition, culminating in the divine Fatherhood that is revealed in the life of Christ and the ethical passion that is revealed in the death of Christ. But they must be so carried over. Christianity has its springs of moral energy that Hinduism plainly has not.[20]

It is interesting that Macnicol insisted that the Hindu and Christian views of life were indeed reconcilable. He did not see Vedantic Hinduism to be

---

19 *Ibid.,* p. 39.
20 *Ibid.,* p. 25.

so far away that Christian faith could only replace it.[21] But he did insist that the values and conceptions that Christianity would bring to Hinduism would amount more or less to rebuilding Hinduism on a 'new foundation.'

> Thus throughout it is by the moralization of the Indian teaching, loosening of the *karma* bonds, the bringing of it from the abstract heights down to the level of the human needs, and the bringing of God near to us as the one whom Jesus could call Father — it is by these ways of reconciliation that the Vedantists and the Christians can meet and one day, we trust, rejoice together in the experience of a world overcome. But if this is to be indeed achieved — if, to change the metaphor, the house of Hinduism is to be transformed into a habitation where the spirit of man can dwell in the faith of God and in the service of man, then it must be built again upon a new foundation, namely, the foundation of Christ Jesus.[22]

Closer examination shows, however, that while he sees that Hinduism needs the values that Christianity brings in the message of Christ, it is Hinduism itself that will be vitalized if it only opens its door to Christ.

> If the Hindu system will open its gates to Him who is the truth, then release from bondage, and victory that India has so long sought can come to her, and God's reign will begin. ... If Hinduism will let Christ enter within its ancient walls, then it will be found that he is no stranger, but one who has sojourned there before and who will find within it those who will recognize His Lordship and set him upon its throne.[23]

The Debate

At the 'sectional meeting' where Christian–Hindu relations were specifically discussed, the debate concentrated on Macnicol's interpretation of Vedantic ideas as the predominant Hindu view of life. Some were of the strong opinion that popular or village Hinduism, the ritual Hinduism, the Hinduism of the home, and the *bhakti* tradition had not played the role they should in his consideration of Christian–Hindu relations. A number of persons questioned how far the so-called 'Higher Hinduism' was representative of religion of India.

Macnicol, in his written response to this criticism, defended what he had done, claiming that in dealing with other religious traditions we should consider them in terms of their dominant ideas. He also showed how easy it was for Christians to use double standards in describing their own faith and that of others:

---

21 It is important to note this here because Kraemer in his interpretation of Hinduism for the Tambaram meeting held that the monistic conception of the Ultimate in Hinduism was totally irreconcilable with the Christian faith.

22 *JMR*, I, pp. 37-38.

23 *Ibid.*, p. 41.

If I were describing Christianity to adherents of another religion, how could I best do so? Would it not be by telling them that it is a religion which rests upon a conviction that the Ultimate Reality is an infinitely loving and holy personality whom we can call Father, and who has been revealed to men supremely in the life and death of Jesus Christ? It would not convey a true account of Christianity if I gave prominence to the fact that some hold that this truth is committed to a holy society through whose priests alone and the ceremonial they administer its virtue is communicated, while others view the religion as a matter of individual commerce between the soul and God, austere, unmediated, except through the message of a book whose authority again is variously estimated. Whatever differences there may be between Christians in doctrine, in ritual, in organisation, still what makes them Christians is the faith in the character of God and His revelation of love that underlies all this discordance. So also with Hinduism.[24]

We have quoted this passage in full because Macnicol, in arguing this way, made an important contribution to the way Christians understood Hinduism for the purpose of relating to it. It was common practice at that time to highlight the socially negative aspects of Hinduism —caste rigidities, untouchability, low status of women, etc.— with a view to showing that the Christian faith had to 'overcome' Hinduism. While recognising that the social evils were there and should be removed, Macnicol insisted that Christians should deal with the basic ideas of Hinduism. "I do not believe" he said, "that it would be fair to say that the social system of Hinduism is Hinduism. It ... rests in large measure on the ideas, which I believe truly represent the religion."[25] These ideas, however, in Macnicol's view, could not themselves lead the Hindus to their own goals without the enrichment that the gospel would bring. It is at this point that he saw the missionary relationship between Christians and Hindus.

In the plenary discussions P. Chenchiah defended Macnicol's position that Christians must deal with the more developed ideas in Hinduism. "While Christianity is challenging Hinduism at its base, Hinduism is challenging Christianity at the top," he said. Insisting that the Christians would have to respond to the "finest fruits of Hindu religion and culture," Chenchiah held that the concept of the uniqueness of Christianity or even of Christ would have to be given more content:

It is not enough to assert that Christ is unique. We should be able to say wherein He is unique that the moved may see and appreciate it. Non-Christian religions have ceased to be opponents of Christianity but like secular sciences have become the competitors of Christianity. This is the

---

24 *Ibid.,* p. 46.
25 *Ibid.*

great change in the religious situation that has occurred since the Edinburgh Conference.[26]

We shall remember, however, that Hinduism was only one of the religions under discussion at Jerusalem. The discussions on other religions also played a role in the plenary discussions, but they all had implications for the Christian understanding of Hinduism.

Macnicol's position came under pressure primarily from the German delegation, who reflected the general line taken by the preparatory meeting of the continental delegates in Cairo.[27] Their statement insisted that the Christian attitude to other faiths should essentially be a missionary one where we "work for the conversion of men" seeking "their conscious break with their past life." They disagreed that the Christian relationship to other faiths should be based on a question of values. Karl Heim, representing the German position at the discussions, said that one ought to make a distinction between true and false religions. Christianity was "not simply the higher climax of the same movement which they saw in all other religions." This for him would completely take away the missionary element in the Christian faith.[28]

The opposition was to be expected, for the continental delegates had already made a written statement on the issue, criticizing three tendencies which they saw in the preparatory materials, namely, Relativism, an emphasis on the Social Gospel, and Syncretism.

> We are disquieted by the question whether the offer of salvation to non-Christians can be made by setting over against one another the spiritual values of the non-Christian and the Christian religions, the scheme followed by most of the papers presented to us.
>
> We do not believe that the central task of the Christian mission can be accomplished by a so-called 'Social Gospel' banding together all men of goodwill across the boundary lines of different religions in a common warfare against the evils of the world, indispensable and urgent though this warfare is.
>
> In view of the ominously rising tide of syncretism in the modern world ... we regard it as an urgent duty for Protestant missions of all lands to stand firm on the basis of the way of salvation set forth in the whole Bible.[29]

---

26 Report of P. Chenchiah's intervention, *Ibid.,* p. 361.

27 A European preparatory meeting for the Jerusalem conference took place in Cairo from 16-17 March 1928. The continental group was dominated by the Germans. Kraemer acted as the secretary to this meeting. His handwritten manuscript on the meeting is in the WCC Archives, box no. 261.003. The report of this meeting is summarized in *JMR,* I, p. 418f.

28 Report on Karl Heim's intervention, *JMR,* I, p. 352.

29 Robert E. Speer, "What is the Value of the Religious Value of the Non-Christian Religions?" *JMR,* I, p. 420.

Julius Richter explained the German position in greater detail at the plenary discussion. While he saw some spiritual value in other faiths he did not agree that they could become a basis for a Christian relation to other faith communities. He saw a grave danger in the attempts of Hindus to accept Christian truth and amalgamate it with their tradition, and in the tendency of some of the missionaries in India to "accentuate more the leavening influences of Christian civilisation than direct conversions." The Christan gospel, in his view, called for a faith "willing to sacrifice even the spiritual values of non-Christian religions." Instead of looking for real or imagined spiritual values in other faiths, it was the duty of Christians to "stand decidedly and even stubbornly with both feet" on the "unique way of salvation proclaimed with one voice in the whole Bible."[30] G. Simons, supporting this view, put this position in a nutshell: "The gospel was not a supplement to spiritual values in other religions, but the giving of new spiritual values to take the place of the old."[31]

A number of other views were also expressed in the plenary. One of the controversial issues was W. E. Hocking's view on countering the mounting secular influence in the world. He held that the universal spread of this secular philosophy "required a new alignment of religious forces, a recognition of alliance with whatever was of the true substance of religion everywhere." Hocking used the word religion in an all-embracing way to include the different systems and names, which in his view were not separate, for they "merged in the universal human faith in the Divine Being."[32] The views of Hocking, which were seen as extremely 'liberal,' contributed to further tension with the continental point of view and was opposed by Hendrik Kraemer. Hocking's position, however, had an important impact on the formulation of the final message of the conference.

Macnicol's view found support among the Asian voices raised during the discussions. Francis Wei and T. C. Chao basically supported what Macnicol had to say about Hinduism from their own experience with Confucianism. Wei claimed that Christianity did not have the task of destroying Confucianism. It had, rather, a distinct contribution to make to China by "giving Chinese morality a broader basis," a "new soul," and a "definite goal." Chao supported the stance taken by Wei and looked for a Christian relationship to China that would "fulfil" the best in Confucian culture.[33]

K. T. Paul went further and made a distinction between the primordial relationship of Christ to Hinduism and the missionary conception. Christ

---

30 Report on the speech by Julius Richter, *JMR*, I, pp. 353-56.
31 Report on the speech of E. Simons, *JMR*, I, p. 353.
32 Report on W. R. Hocking's contribution, *JMR*, I, p. 369f.
33 *JMR*, I, pp. 358-59.

alone, he said, could fulfil the best in Hinduism without dominating or destroying it. Therefore there was no place even to speak of superiority and inferiority of values. "The living Christ was sufficient if He was left alone with India, interpreted of course, through human life and relationships. For Christ's relationship to Hinduism shall be seen to be both inside and outside of organized Christianity."[34]

William Temple served as the chairman of the Committee that had to draft the message of the conference, reflecting something of the ecumenial consensus among the diversity of positions held. He was strengthened in this task by the mediating role played by the position taken by British delegates between the American, Continental, and Asian positions.[35] The British position rejected the evolutionary argument about the Christian relationship to Hinduism on the ground that Christianity actually brought something different in the very act of witnessing to the Incarnation, Atonement, etc. For the British, the decisive factor in a Christian relation to other faiths was the 'Revelation in Christ,' and not the 'values' of Christianity. But this did not mean that the Christian message had no immediate relationship to Hinduism. O. C. Quick presented the general British position thus:

> A man found a new thing in Christianity only because he also recognized it as something for which he had already been seeking. The Christian gospel must always be presented in relation to non-Christian thought. Christ had used the Jewish conception of the kingdom of God in the proclamation of his message. St. Paul had used some of the language of the Hellenic religions in his teaching to the Gentiles. The early fathers had brought the wealth of Plato, the schoolmen had brought Aristotle and in its ages of creative thought Christianity had built on the non-Christian things that it had found.[36]

Thus Quick took the position that while the Christian had something unique to offer to people of other faiths: "May we still to be learners of him among the peoples to whom they went with the message."[37]

The Jerusalem Message

The final statement by the Council, entitled "The Christian Message" was an attempt to bring together the concerns expressed by the various voices within the ecumenical movement at that moment in history. Insofar as it

---

34 K. T. Paul was the General Secretary of the YMCA in India, Burma, and Ceylon. His contribution is reported in *JMR*, I, p. 362 f.

35 British delegates had a preparatory meeting in London from 4-6 January 1928. The mimeographed Minutes of this meeting is available in the WCC Archives.

36 Report on the speech by Canon O. C. Quick, *JMR*, I, p. 357.

37 *Ibid.*

was a message addressed to all the churches with the unanimous approval of the participants, it is a significant document in ecumenical history. At the heart of the Jerusalem Message lies the Christological affirmation of Jesus Christ as the revelation of God in whom "the perfect and infinite love and righteousness of God is made known" to human beings. "Our message is Jesus Christ," the statement read; "He is the revelation of what God is and of what man through him may become."[38] There was also the unmistakable missionary call for churches in all nations to cooperate in the task of "more speedily laying the claim of Christ upon all unoccupied areas of the world and of human life."[39]

The Message, however, made a number of significant references to people of other faiths, and to the Christian attitude to the faith of others; in these it had obviously been influenced by the presentations and discussions at the conference, not least by Macnicol's paper on Hinduism. Repudiating "any attempt on the part of trade or of governments openly or covertly, to use the missionary cause for ulterior purposes," the Message also spoke against any imperialistic attitude of Christians to other faiths:

> ... on our part we would repudiate any symptom of a religious imperialism that would desire to impose beliefs and practices on others in order to manage their souls in their supposed interest. We obey God who respects our wills and we desire to respect those of others.[40]

One significant aspect of the Message was the use of the word 'sharing' for the act of Christian witness to those of other faiths. This had a dialogical connotation, but such usage was later to be severely criticized by Kraemer at Tambaram. The Jerusalem Message not only used it, but wrapped it up in a theological reflection about God and God's way of relating to the world:

> Since He is love, His very nature is to share. Christ is the expression in time of the eternal self-giving of the Father. Coming into fellowship with Christ we find in ourselves an over-mastering impulse to share him with others. ... He has become life to us. We would share that life.[41]

The Message went further to assert that such an internal compulsion to share the message of Christ with a neighbour of another faith has to be exercised in humility, penitence, and love:

---

38 Statement by the Council, *JMR*, I, p. 480.
39 *Ibid.,* p. 494.
40 *Ibid.,* p. 484.
41 *Ibid.,* p. 485.

> In humility, because it is not our own message which we bring, but God's, and if in our delivery of it self-assertion finds any place we shall spoil the message and hinder its acceptance; in penitence, because our fathers and we ourselves have been so blind to many of the implications of our faith; in love, because our message is the gospel of the love of God, and only by love in our own hearts for those to whom we speak can we make known its power or its true nature.[42]

The Message also affirmed the solidarity of the Christian and the non-Christian in their common need for redemption. The Christian message is shared with others "not because they are the worst of the world and they alone are in need but because they are part of the world and share with us the same human need — the need of redemption ..."[43] Here the Message is critical of the Christians because they have not "sufficiently sought out the good and noble elements in the non-Christian beliefs" as the basis of their solidarity and of the sharing of their convictions.[44]

In its theological evaluation of the non-Christian religions, the Message draws its inspiration partly from natural theology, but also from the concept of the cosmic Christ, claiming that the "rays of light" that shone in Jesus Christ are to be found "where He is unknown or even is rejected."[45] Not only did the Message affirm the "noble qualities" in non-Christian "persons and systems" as the proof that the Father has "not left Himself without witness," it went on to illustrate such noble qualities in the other faiths, without attempting to evaluate their spiritual value either to the adherents of other faiths or to Christians:

> We recognise as part of the one Truth that sense of the majesty of God and the consequent reverence in worship, which are conspicuous in Islam; the deep sympathy for the world's sorrow and unselfish search for the way of escape, which are at the heart of Buddhism; the desire for contact with Ultimate Reality conceived as spiritual, which is prominent in Hinduism; the belief in a moral order of the universe and consequent insistence on moral conduct, which are inculcated by Confucianism; the disinterested pursuit of truth and of human welfare which is often found in those who stand for secular civilization but do not accept Christ as their Lord and Saviour.[46]

This affirmation of the noble qualities of the other faiths as part of 'the one Truth' is a theological position that would have presented difficulties to a number of persons who were at Jerusalem. It did not, however, become too controversial at that time. The backlash came later and the

42 *Ibid.,* pp. 486-87.
43 *Ibid.*
44 *Ibid.*
45 *Ibid.,* p. 490.
46 *Ibid.,* p. 491.

total impact of the reaction was felt at Tambaram. But this affirmation was to be expected because the Jerusalem meeting was primarily interested in examining the 'spiritual values' in other faiths and their relation to the message of the gospel.

Once such an affirmation is made, however, the Jerusalem Message was able only to *invite* the followers of other religions to *consider* the significance of Christ for the world and for their own lives. "We call upon the followers of the non-Christian religions to join us," the Message said, "in the study of Jesus Christ as He stands before us in the scriptures, His place in the life of the world, and His power to satisfy the human heart ..."[47] In order to make this appeal more effective the Message disclaimed Christianity as a Western religion, and asserted that it can rightly belong to "the peoples of Africa and Asia as much as to the European and American." It also denied that Christ is "the continuation of any tradition," and claimed that He is the "desire of all nations."[48]

The most controversial aspect of the Jerusalem Message in later discussion was its call to other religions to solidarity in the struggle against secularism. Here the Message is influenced by the stand taken by Hocking in the plenary sessions and by its own conviction that insofar as the other religions had spiritual values, they are allies in the struggle to keep materialism and secularism at bay. It called upon the non-Christian religions to "hold fast to faith in the unseen and eternal in face of the growing materialism of the world; to cooperate with us against all the evils of secularism."[49]

In its concluding paragraphs the Jerusalem Message accommodated another trend within the conference by speaking of the gospel as the power directed to human hearts and not to systems of belief. It said that the gospel "speaks to each man, not as Moslem or as Buddhist, or as an adherent of any system, but just as man," and that the study of other religions should help mainly in approaching others wisely.[50] Also reaffirmed was the conviction of "the fulness and sufficiency of the gospel" and the need to lay "the claims of Christ on the whole of human life."[51]

The Jerusalem Message, however, made many affirmations about the Christian relationship to other faiths and to persons of other faiths that went well beyond what had been possible at Edinburgh. These were to come under severe criticism afterwards. Before we turn to the next conference of the IMC, where Kraemer's influence was paramount in assessing other faiths, we should seek to do a comparative evaluation of

47 *Ibid.,* p. 491.
48 *Ibid.,* p. 491.
49 *Ibid.,* pp. 491-92.
50 *Ibid.,* p. 492.
51 *Ibid.*

the influence of the two major ecumenical events, Edinburgh and Jerusalem, on the attitude and relationship of Christians to those of other faiths.

An Evaluation: Edinburgh and Jerusalem

Though only eighteen years separated the meeting at Jerusalem from the one in Edinburgh, 1910, there had been remarkable changes both in the life of the church and in the world. A. M. Chirgwin, writing an interpretation of the Jerusalem meeting in the International Review of Missions points out:

> In 1910 there had been no world war, no revolution in China, no non-cooperation movement in India, no demand of the coloured races for equal treatment by the white races, no indigenous church firmly rooted in the life of the Eastern peoples ... no commercial aviation, and no International Missionary Council.[52]

It is indeed true that the historical situation of the life of the church substantially affects the issues it selects to deal with, and the way it deals with them. A reading of the full proceedings of the Jerusalem meeting shows that almost all the historical changes referred to here shaped the work of the Jerusalem meeting.[53] We shall, however, concentrate on those issues directly related to our concern. These include the rise of secular ideologies, the rise of resistant Hinduism, and the challenge made by the younger churches to incorporate their experience into the life and thinking of the church universal.[54] All these affected the way the Jerusalem meeting formulated its attitude to people of other faiths.

At Edinburgh it was the 'Christian' West that was looking to the 'non-Christian' East, and therefore, the two topics formulated for discussion were, "Carrying the gospel to all the Non-Christian World" (Commission I) and "Missionary Message in Relation to Non-Christian Religions" (Commission IV). Despite the remarkable work and report of Commission IV the final message from Edinburgh was basically missionary in nature. In Jerusalem the situation had changed. Even though there was still an imbalance in actual participation, here the churches both of the West and of the East were together facing their common problems, and there had

---

52 "The Jerusalem Meeting and the Man in the Pew," *IRM* 1928.

53 Even though the World Missionary Conference at Edinburgh, 1910, played an important role in the formal organization of the International Missionary Council, the IMC was officially formed only in 1921 and hence the Jerusalem World Mission Conference was the first major meeting organized by the IMC.

54 For example, Commission III dealt with "The Relationship between Younger and Older Churches," Commission IV with "The Christian Mission in the Light of Race Conflicts" and Commission VII with "International Missionary Cooperation."

been a shift in the way the issue itself was formulated in relation to other faiths: "The Christian life and message in relation to non-Christian systems of thought and life."

Of more importance was the decision to deal with the subject by, in the first instance, looking for 'values' in the non-Christian religions. While this provided an inbuilt advantage for those who wanted to have a 'positive' approach to other faiths, the Jerusalem meeting became deeply controversial theologically, much more so in fact than the unanimous acceptance of the final Message suggests.

Basically there were four theological currents that the conference found difficult to reconcile. Macnicol represented the first position that looked at the positive spiritual values in other religions, including the examination of their value as belief systems, and spoke of the Christian message as that which 'enriches' the values in other faiths. There was the insistence that the Christian message was absolutely necessary for the true realization of the goals of these religious traditions, but this attitude represented a tacit acceptance of other faiths as legitimate aspirations which were under the guidance of the Spirit in their 'nobler manifestations.' Even though Macnicol himself, by and large, avoided the word 'fulfilment' and used the word 'enrichment,' the Asian participants interpreted Macnicol in that way, and freely used the word 'fulfilment' as the basis for relationship between Christianity and other religious traditions.

The second current was the position held by Hocking, which represented a whole liberal tradition that was developing, particularly in the United States. This tendency sought an overall concept of 'Religion,' cutting across religious frontiers against the rise of secularism in the world. Hocking, even though he was not one of the main speakers, made several interventions at the plenary debates and put a strong case for this position. The alarming rise of secular ideologies, with which many at the meeting were deeply concerned, provided a backdrop for a more receptive mood to Hocking's view.

The third current, held by many of the continental delegates, was in dissent with both the views described above. Kraemer, who had been secretary to the preparatory meeting of the continental delegates in Cairo, gave voice to this position. But he was overshadowed by some of the German speakers who put the issues strongly in the debates, and also presented a written dissent position. This view rejected both the ideas of enrichment and universal religion and insisted that Christianity was new and different, demanding 'conversion' from those who had hitherto lived by other faiths.

The fourth current, primarily held by British delegates, sought some mediation and affirmed the positive values in other faiths, but it also insisted that the Christian message demanded a new obedience.

How was a compromise made? Carl Hallencreutz attributes credit to the drafting skill of Archbishop William Temple, who chaired the Message Committee, and the method that he adopted in putting the Message together. He quotes the letter Temple wrote to his wife on how he resolved the issue: "We got the various sections so to state their own views that they were compatible with one another: and then it was only a matter of putting the bits together in the right order."[55]

Even though Temple succeeded in getting unanimous approval, the Jerusalem Message remains, and could only be, a bundle of theological contradictions. On the one hand, it affirms the spiritual values of other faiths 'as part of the one truth' and calls upon the people of other faiths "to hold fast to faith in the unseen and eternal, in the face of growing materialism in the world," an obvious attempt to recognize the position held by the Asians and Hocking. In this respect the Message calls upon the people of other faiths "to cooperate with us, to study with us," "to share with us," etc. On the other hand it speaks in some places in a way that radically dissociates the human person from the religious life, saying that the "gospel speaks to each man, not as a Moslem, or as Buddhist, or as an adherent of any system, but just as man," adding that the Christian message is full and sufficient for all human life.

The theological compromise at Jerusalem on the attitude to other faiths may well have been a mistake. But it is unfortunate that the approach made at the Edinburgh meeting had no echo or infuence at Jerusalem. Edinburgh's penetrating insight portraying the encounter with other faiths as a challenge to the Christian faith itself was completely lost at Jerusalem. In contrast to the debates in relation to secular ideologies, the discussions at Jerusalem in relation to other faiths degenerated into a sterile argumentation on whether or not there were positive values in other faiths, and whether or not Christ fulfilled them. The element of a living encounter, the 'emergency' that drives the Christians back to the fundamentals of their faith, the spirituality of others that challenges the unexamined assumptions and claims of Christian life —all of which were so prominent at Edinburgh— as well as Macnicol's deep concern that Christians were now faced with a resurgent Hinduism which challenged the assumptions of Christian mission — did not sufficiently inform the Jerusalem Message.

It was only to be expected that when the participants had come down from the Mount of Olives, and the goodwill of Eastertide that permeated the Jerusalem meeting had past, the issues of Jerusalem would become full-blown controversies. The stage was being set for the need for a clear, concise, and considered Christian position in relation to people of other

55 Carl F. Hallencreutz, *Kraemer Towards Tambaram*, p. 195.

faiths, for the Jerusalem and post-Jerusalem debates were to show an increasing and, some would say, chaotic diversity within the church on this issue. The Jerusalem meeting not only necessitated Tambaram 1938, but almost pre-determined its outcome.

CHAPTER IV

Continuity or Discontinuity
Tambaram — 1938

Invitation to Hendrik Kraemer

The meeting of the International Missionary Council at Tambaram, near Madras, 12-29 December 1938 marked a major milestone in the ecumenical discussions about Christian relationships to people of other religious traditions. The preparations for the meeting had already begun in 1934.[1] A study of the preparatory process for Tambaram and the ecumenical dialogue that took place as a result of the 1928 Jerusalem meeting shows that a variety of problems and issues influenced the agenda and the outcome of the Tambaram meeting. To begin with, the divisive debate on secularism which had begun at Jerusalem continued and intensified afterwards. To some, secularism became the major missionary issue. J. H. Oldham, for example, held that interpreting the gospel to the 'secular man' was the 'new Christian adventure' to which the churches were called in a new way.[2] There was also controversy over Hocking's view of religion and his call for all the spiritual forces to join hands in confronting the 'menace of secularism.'[3] A number of continental theologians expressed serious

---

[1] The *ad interim* committee formed at the Jerusalem meeting met in Salisbury, England in 1934 and proposed this meeting. Hangchow in China was chosen as the site at the meeting held at Northfield, Massachusetts in 1935. But the Sino-Japanese conflict caused the abandonment of this idea. Hence Tambaram was chosen — John R. Mott, William Paton, and A. L. Warnshuis "Introduction," *The World Mission of the Church, Tambaram 1938* (London/New York: International Missionary Council, n. d., 1939?), p. 6. Also see John R. Mott, "At Edinburgh, Jerusalem, and Madras," *IRM* 27 (1938): 311.

[2] *Ibid.,* p. 312.

[3] *The World Mission of the Church,* pp. 20-24.

doubts about both Hocking's concept of religion and the need to rally together the religious traditions of the world.[4]

The preparatory discussions were also dominated by a sense of crisis in the world. Political uncertainty in Europe was exacerbated by a world-wide economic depression. There were upheavals in the Far East. Concern was expressed about the rise of nationalism, communism, and scientific scepticism. At the theological level, there were also deep concerns about the growing religio-theological relativism. There was a widespread feeling in the post-Jerusalem discussions that the apostolic obligation of the church had not been taken seriously at the Jerusalem meeting. Some felt that this conference had not given sufficient emphasis to the givenness of the message, the need for conversion and regeneration, and the urgent task of confronting secularism.[5]

The *ad interim* committee that met at the Old Jordan's Hostel in Buckinghamshire, England, in 1936 therefore recognized the need to build into the Tambaram preparations a clear statement on the Christian faith and on an evangelistic approach to non-Christian religions. After some consultation the leaders decided that this responsibility should be given to Hendrik Kraemer of Java,[6] and his volume on *The Christian Message in a Non-Christian World* marked the start of a new epoch. It dominated the discussions about other faiths, both at the Tambaram meeting and after. Kraemer, originally from Holland, and then a missionary to Indonesia, combined in himself a theologian, a scholar of religions, a convinced missionary, and an ardent ecumenist. He was familiar with the debate on other faiths at Edinburgh; he had himself chaired the 'Section' meeting on Islam at Jerusalem and actively participated in the debates that followed that meeting. Although it had originally been intended as just one of several inputs to the Tambaram meeting, Kraemer's volume became, as it were, its centre-piece.

Kraemer's missionary thought and the importance of the Tambaram meeting to the discussions on mission have already been studied at some length, and a number of dissertations exist on this subject. It is neverthe-less important for our examination of the development of ecumenical thought about other faiths to state briefly the theological position which Kraemer presented at this meeting. Drawing on the thought of Karl Barth

---

4 Cf. Eric J. Sharpe, *Faith Meets Faith: Some Christian Attitudes to Hinduism in the Nineteenth and Twentieth Centuries*, Chapter I (London: SCM Press, 1977).

5 Cf. W. Paton, "A Suggestion on Preparation and Programme for Proposed World Meeting" (WCC Archives: IMC, 1938). Also see W. W. Cash, "Missionary Policy: A New Orientation," *East and West Review* (1935): 14 ff.

6 Carl F. Hallencreutz's study on Kraemer's missionary approach in *Kraemer Towards Tambaram* (Uppsala: Gleerup, 1966), gives a detailed description of the various influ-ences that shaped Kraemer's missionary approach, especially the early influences in his life.

and Emil Brunner, Kraemer would have a decisive influence on the ecumenical thinking about other religions for many subsequent decades. After a brief statement on Kraemer's theological presuppositions, we shall here concentrate on his own interpretation of Hinduism and its relationship to the Christian faith. As well, we shall focus on his preparatory volume, even though in subsequent volumes he would alter slightly the positions he had taken at Tambaram.[7]

Kraemer's Understanding of the Christian Faith

Kraemer's understanding of the Christian attitude to other faiths was rooted firmly in his interpretation of the nature of Christian faith. Part of the 'confusion' at Jerusalem, he argued in his book, had been due to the lack of clarity about the basis of the Christian faith. Admitting the importance of translating the faith to the modern world, he insisted that "it is still more urgent and important for the Church to know its original faith."[8] And for this he looked to the Bible: "The only legitimate source from which to take our knowledge of the Christian faith in its real substance is the Bible."[9]

Kraemer held that the Bible's most important characteristic was to be 'intensely religious,' by which he meant that the Bible was radically theocentric in every respect. God, His Holy Will, His acts, His love, His judgements, was the beginning and end of all: "In calling the Bible a radically theocentric book we simply mean to say that the Bible takes in a radically serious fashion the fact that God is God, that he is absolute sovereign and the only rightful Lord, with all the consequences that are implied herein for the world, human life, and the position of man. In this point consists the originality and uniqueness of the Bible."[10]

The Bible, in Kraemer's view, offered no religious or moral philosophy, not even a theistic or Christocentric one, as some might assume. It could resist all endeavours to reduce it to a body of truths and ideals about the personality of God, the infinite value of man, or the source of ethical inspiration. These, Kraemer admitted, could be derived from the Bible but the Bible did not intend to present a theology or, more specifically, any 'worldview.' Hence it had no theory about revelation, even though revelation was the presupposition on which the prophetic and

---

7 Special mention may be made of *Religion and the Christian Faith* (1956), *The Communication of the Christian Faith* (1957), *World Cultures and World Religions: The Coming Dialogue* (1960), all by Lutterworth Press, London. Of special interest is *Why Christianity of All Religions?* (1962).

8 *The Christian Message in a Non-Christian World*, p. 61.

9 *Ibid.*

10 *Ibid.*, p. 63.

apostolic witness of the church was built.[11] What, then, was the nature of the Bible? For Kraemer, the Christian faith as expounded in the Bible was primarily God's encounter with man. God confronted the sinful man in his total being and challenged him to take decisions. This placing by the Bible of its entire emphasis on the sovereign God encountering the sinful human person for decision, Kraemer called 'biblical realism.'[12]

The phrase 'biblical realism' was much debated both at Tambaram and after, because a number of participants at the meeting could not understand, or would not agree with, the sharp distinction Kraemer made between the teachings of the Bible and its character as an account of God's encounter with man. Even those who agreed with Kraemer's emphasis doubted whether the phrase 'biblical realism' was the best way of stating it. The concept, however, was fundamental to Kraemer for he was to use this as the main thesis to distinguish the Christian faith from all other religions like Hinduism. In the post-Tambaram volume *The Authority of the Faith,* Kraemer would seek to explain more clearly what he meant by the phrase 'biblical realism':[13]

The Christian revelation as the record of God's self-disclosing revelation in Jesus Christ, is absolutely *sui generis.* It is the story of God's sovereign redeeming acts having become decisively and finally manifest in Jesus Christ, the son of the living God, in whom God became flesh and revealed His grace and truth. I coined for this conception the term 'biblical realism' in order to express the idea that the Bible, the human and in many ways historically conditioned document of God's acts and revelation, consistently testifies to divine acts and plans in regard to the salvation of mankind and the world, and not to religious experiences or ideas. Religious experiences or ideas are of course not absent from the Bible, and they are by no means unimportant, but in no sense whatever are they *central.* What is central and fundamental in the Bible is the registerings describing and witnessing to God's creative and redemptive dealing with man and the world.[14]

Kraemer's explanation as to why he chose the vague and misunderstood phrase 'biblical realism' also gives us an insight into the way by which he

11 *Ibid.,* p. 65. Also, *Why Christianity of All Religions,* pp. 78-79.

12 *Ibid.,* p. 66 ff.

13 Since Kraemer's book *The Christian Message in a Non-Christian World* was much debated at Tambaram, the organizers prepared a volume after the Tambaram meeting with contributions from the major participants in the debate including T. C. Chao of China, D. G. Moses from India, Karl L. Reichelt from Hong Kong, A. G. Hogg from Madras, Karl Hartenstein from Switzerland, Walter Marshall from the USA and H. H. Farmer from England. Kraemer defended his thesis at Tambaram in an article entitled "Continuity or Discontinuity."

14 "Continuity or Discontinuity," *The Authority of Faith: International Missionary Council Meeting* at Tambaram, Madras, December 12-29, 1938 (London: Oxford University Press, 1939), pp. 1-2.

wanted to contrast the biblical faith with the Asian religious traditions. He argued that there was no better term available to bring out this contrast:

> ... I shall be grateful if anyone will offer a better term, provided it conveys more clearly and more adequately the idea that the Bible and its contents can only be understood when it is taken as the record of God's thoughts and acts in regard to mankind, and not as a tale about the pilgrimage of the human soul towards God, however moving a tale of that pilgrimage might be told by one who surveys the religious history of mankind.[15]

Kraemer developed this notion of 'biblical realism' to show the unique character of the Christian faith as he understood it. But we should also examine briefly Kraemer's understanding of revelation for this was the second concept that he used to distinguish the Christian faith from other religious traditions.

He conceded that all religions had an idea of revelation but, he argued, they have usually misinterpreted the word. It was, said he, often used to mean the attainment of knowledge that man cannot attain by the power of his mind. Thus revelation in many religions was a special way to knowledge, such as a communication of divine truths about different things or an extraordinary form of epistemology. When revelation was understood in the intellectualistic way, even phenomena which should properly be called enlightenment, a sudden intuitive insight, a luminous idea or knowledge about the trans-human realm were loosely called revelation.[16] What then was the difference between 'revelation' as conceived in these situations and as set forth in the Bible? Kraemer defined the Christian understanding of revelation in these words:

> Revelation in its proper sense is what is by its very nature inaccessible and *remains so, even when it is revealed.* The necessary correlate to the concept of revelation is therefore faith. It lies in the very nature of revelation that the only organ for apprehending it is faith; and for the same reason faith, in the strictly religious sense, can only be appropriately defined as at the same time a divine gift and a human act.[17]

Once Kraemer had defined religious life essentially as God's confronting man with a demand for decision, and revelation as that which could be appropriated only by a response to that specific encounter in an act of faith, he drew the conclusion that such an understanding of revelation and faith was to be found nowhere except in the Christian apprehension of reality:

---

15 *Ibid.,* p. 2.
16 *The Christian Message in a Non-Christian World,* pp. 69-73.
17 *Ibid.,* p. 69.

Nowhere has revelation been taken in such a radical and absolute manner as in the sphere of biblical realism. . . . Nowhere has the inherent correlation between revelation as the act of God and faith as the corresponding organ of human apprehension and as the gift of God been grasped so fully. Nowhere is the genuine meaning of revelation maintained so consistently. . . . [18]

Interpreting the Christian faith using these conceptions of revelation and faith, Kraemer said that God had truly and fully revealed himself in Jesus Christ, and yet he had also hidden and disguised himself in the man Jesus. The incarnation as an act of revelation would thus always remain hidden from natural eyes, and the message that God was in Christ would always be an offence to others. Only the eyes of faith could recognize this revelation which, even though a revelation, remained hidden until the eyes of faith could appropriate it.[19]

Before we leave Kraemer's understanding of the specificity of Christian faith we should note the implications he drew for ethics from this understanding of reality, because this is another area where he drew a sharp contrast between Christianity and Hinduism. Here again he claimed that God and God's encounter were at the centre of Christian ethics, setting the Christian ethic apart from all others. In Kraemer's view, the other forms of ethics were centred on man's asking what was the highest good in life so that man might seek and attain it.[20] But the Christian ethic was not an ethic of eudaemonism, nor of individualism, nor of collectivism. This did not mean, argued Kraemer, that human happiness or misery or human values were not a deep concern for the Christian. But the aim of the Christian was to fulfil God's will, from which various values were derived as fruits or results. Thus the happiness of man, fundamentally speaking, was never the direct object of the Christian ethic, of which the prime motive and ultimate end was to do the will of God. The fact that it was the will of the living God that one was called to fulfil provided Christian ethics with ever-changing, ever-living flexibility.[21]

We have here attempted to give a brief sketch of Kraemer's theological frame of reference because of its importance to his understanding of Hinduism. Kraemer believed that the problem with the Jerusalem meeting had not been misguided missiology but bad theology. He therefore felt that his first task in enabling the Tambaram discussions was to set out the 'original faith' based on the scriptures. Once he had done that he could

---

18 *Ibid.*, p. 70.

19 *Ibid.*, pp. 72-73.

20 *Ibid.*, p. 86.

21 See *Ibid.*, p. 85ff for full discussion on Christian ethics. Here again Kraemer's primary intention was to contrast, as we shall see shortly, with ethics as understood in the Asian religions.

turn to his interpretation of other religious traditions, drawing on his experience in the mission field. We will limit our examination to his interpretation of Hinduism.

Kraemer's Framework to Understanding Hinduism

Kraemer's interpretation of Hinduism, on which he also built his view on a Christian relationship to it, was based on the sharp distinction he made between two types of religions. The first, he called prophetic religions of revelation in which he included Christianity, Judaism and, 'to a certain degree,' Islam.[22] All other religions he classified under the second category of "naturalistic religions of trans-empirical realization" having "a primitive apprehension of reality." By the phrase 'trans-empirical realization,' Kraemer meant such efforts as concentration, asceticism, meditation, and religious observances, which were all seen as practices directed at realizing or grasping the identity of the real self with divine reality.[23]

He admitted, as we have mentioned, that the second category of religions also had a conception of revelation inasmuch as a number of these relied on some sort of sacred scripture as revealed knowledge. He held, however, that revelation was not central to these religions and in any case that the sense in which the word was used primarily to point to some mediated knowledge was quite different from the understanding of revelation in the Judeo-Christian tradition. In Kraemer's view the naturalistic religions loosely used the word revelation to refer to some supreme moments of religious experience.[24]

It is important also to note the sense in which Kraemer used the phrase 'primitive apprehensions' of reality. Aware that the word 'primitive' would be misunderstood, he explained that this word was not used in the sense of the initial stage of cultural life or the primeval condition of man.[25] In fact, to avoid any misunderstanding Kraemer used the term 'tribal' religions to indicate those religions which in his assessment had not undergone much change in the course of history. By 'primitive apprehension' Kraemer meant a view of reality which affirmed the absolute interdependence of all spheres of life —economic, social, and religious— and which, consequently made no conscious differentiation or specialization

---

22 Kraemer acknowledges that there is the concept of revelation in Islam. But he sees revelation as a body of knowledge imparted to the Prophet quite opposite to the revelation understood as God's ongoing encounter with man. "Externalization and fossilization of revelation in Islam" he said, "seems to us to be one of the great marks of its superficiality." *Christian Message*, pp. 217-18.

23 *Ibid.*, p. 142

24 *Ibid.*, p. 143. See also discussion in *Religion and the Christian Faith*, p. 351f.

25 *Ibid.*, p. 149.

between different aspects of reality. This understanding of the inter-relatedness of all spheres of life was maintained by the rigid and unassailable authority of tradition.[26]

Kraemer understood Hinduism to be a 'primitive apprehension of reality' which held all realms of life to be interdependent and inter-related. Further, he claimed, Hinduism, like the religions of China, never broke with tradition in seeing the totality of existence as a single reality. Here lay the fundamental difference between the civilization derived from Hinduism and Western civilization.

> ... Western civilization in its history has repeatedly taken the all-decisive step of breaking *on principle with the authority of tradition.* The civilizations of India and China, which are of an amazing width and wealth of expression, never have. Perhaps nowhere in the history of the world has the human spirit soared so high and enjoyed its omnipotence with such superb self-confidence and serene placidity as it has sometimes in the civilizations of India and China,[27] yet the authority of tradition has remained throughout their history one of their immovable foundations.[28]

From this description of naturalistic religions Kraemer drew his important thesis that the only adequate way to acquire true light about the other religious traditions and to determine the Christian attitude to them was the 'totalitarian' approach, namely, "to take a religion as one whole body of religious life and expression, of which all the component parts are inseparably inter-related to each other and animated by the same apprehension of the totality of existence peculiar to it."[29]

Kraemer developed this as a fundamental thesis in order to show the inadequacy of the way in which Edinburgh and Jerusalem had, in his view, dealt with 'values' in non-Christian religions. To this we shall return later. In order to demonstrate some of the fundamental issues Christians would have to face in relating to this religious tradition, Kraemer went on to describe how this primitive apprehension of reality worked itself out in Hinduism.[30]

---

26 *Ibid.,* p. 148.

27 Kraemer adds a footnote to explain that he is here thinking about what is told of the great masters of Vedanta and Yoga, of the Taoist Wu-wei and of the great masters of Zen-Buddhism.

28 *The Christian Message,* p. 148.

29 *Ibid.,* p. 149.

30 Kraemer did this with all the major religious traditions to argue his case that 'biblical realism' marks out the Christian faith from all other religious traditions. We shall concern ourselves with only Hinduism at this point.

Kraemer's General Principles in Interpreting Hinduism

In interpreting Hinduism, Kraemer saw the importance of five considerations basic to all religions with a primitive apprehension of reality. First,
Kraemer held that in the primitive apprehension of reality all myths, rites,
rules, and regulations aspired, and indeed were founded, to justify the
existing order of social and religious life. Within this apprehension the
preservation and perpetuation of harmony, stability, and welfare constituted
the primary concern. The place, role, and duties of the individual in the
social structure, therefore, were predetermined so that the execution of
duty by all contributed to the maintenance of order.[31]

The main characteristic of this apprehension of reality was that the
macrocosmos (the world of nature) and the microcosmos (man) were
correlated entities that 'co-existed' in an uninterrupted process of living
inter-relatedness and inter-correspondence. That is to say that the world
of nature, or the cosmos in all its operations, and the world of human
social relations, were inter-related and inter-dependent.[32]

Third, the primitive apprehension divided reality into dualistic principles such as masculine and feminine, light and darkness, cold and hot,
good and evil. Yet these were not seen as contrasting absolutes. These
were not irreconcilable for they each had its due and legitimate place
within the totality of existence, contributing to the overall harmony.[33]

The fourth characteristic, which was the logical corollary of the first
three, was that the primitive apprehension of reality was essentialy monistic
whereas all things, religiously speaking, were relativistic. "In the atmosphere of inter-related and counter-balancing entities, no religious or ethical
absolute is possible."[34]

All these led Kraemer to his fifth and most significant conclusion
about the primitive apprehension of reality, namely, that it was *naturalistic
and vitalistic*. By naturalistic he meant that this apprehension of reality
had the fundamental assumption that man and nature were one. Man in
his whole being and possibilities was a part of nature and one part of a
whole, equivalent to other parts. Man thus became a part of the life of
nature, in continuity with it.

This led to the vitalistic aspect, meaning that the 'quest for life'
became the basic principle of existence. The perpetuation and strengthening of individual and corporate life became the major preoccupation. The
object and practice of religion itself had the sole purpose of attaining life,
thus manifesting the "magnificent and noble quest for eternal and un-

31 *The Christian Message*, p. 150.
32 *Ibid.*, p. 152.
33 *Ibid.*, p. 153.
34 *Ibid.*, p. 154.

perishable life" seen in these religious traditions and embodied especially in the many forms of 'higher' mysticism. Sometimes ethics became the instrument of this quest, assuming the character of 'titanic moralism,' of which there were also many grand examples in these religions.[35] Kraemer was quick to point out, however, that this naturalistic, vitalistic understanding of religion had also given way to the "crassest materialism and sensualism."[36]

Kraemer's characterization of the religions with a primitive apprehension of reality, of which he saw Hinduism as a classic example, was indicative of the measure by which he would evaluate Hinduism. For Kraemer saw the primitive apprehension of reality to be "entirely outside and opposed to the world of biblical realism, with its radical insistence on God as God, the loving Lord and creator of man and the world, and in which sin and holiness are taken radically as what they are, namely, the disobedient human will and its resistance against the pure and perfect divine will."[37]

Hinduism Considered

Building on his assessment that Hinduism was naturalistic, Kraemer contended that the bewildering variety of cults, sects, institutions, and tendencies in Hinduism, and the seeming absence of all consistency, manifest even in its foundations, was only to be expected. He held that this was characteristic of the naturalistic religions:

> Just as nature is not interested in truth, but in manifestation, in realization, in shades, so Hinduism is not really interested in religious truth but in the endless possibilities of religious realization and expression. Who would dare to deny that Hinduism stands unmatched in wealth and variety of this expression?[38]

This variety was possible, in Kraemer's view, because Hinduism in its naturalistic, monistic apprehension of reality had no transcendent criterion by which to order its life. It was therefore significant, he continued, that the only two criteria for being a Hindu in this amorphous religious universality were drawn, one from the biological and the other from the social realms, namely, "the biological fact of being born as a Hindu and the social fact of belonging to a caste."[39]

Kraemer identified here what, in his view, was the root cause of the evils of caste and other social systems within Hinduism as admitted by

35 *Ibid.*
36 *Ibid.*
37 *Ibid.,* p. 157.
38 *Ibid.,* p. 160.
39 *Ibid.,* p. 161.

those who presented Hinduism at Edinburgh and Jerusalem. Kraemer contended that those social evils were not aspects of Hinduism to be looked upon as matters for reform or transformation. He was convinced that social evils like caste arose from the apprehension of reality basic to the total religious system. The caste system, for example, could never be removed until the whole Hindu worldview was changed. For the duties assigned to a person by birth in a particular caste had the function of maintaining the cosmic order of which the person was but a small part: "Therefore," concluded Kraemer, "despite the stirring quest for truth one constantly meets within the annals of Indian religious history, the rules that one is Hindu by birth and the most characteristic and indispensable attribute of a Hindu is to live according to the *dharma* of his caste, have never become dissolved, even a little, and never can be, unless Hinduism becomes thoroughly emancipated from its ingrained naturalistic monism."[40]

Kraemer also implied criticism of those who had held that the Christian faith could learn much from the Hindu conception of the Ultimate Reality. He saw a close link between the proliferation of gods in Hinduism and the fertility of nature. Almost anything could be "made" into an object of worship for gods were "the projections of our human will, desires, and thoughts."[41] Hindus, Kraemer said, would have no difficulty in admitting this because the overall power that guided this kind of apprehension of reality was not 'gods' but the law that governed and held all things in harmony:

> ... the most important thing to note is that the many gods, exalted ones and repellent ones, belong within the sphere of the cosmic and natural process. They represent always some aspect of cosmic and natural totality. That is why gods never are fundamentally different from man. They are mortal just as man is; they are subject to the law of *karma*; the only difference is that they enjoy, as a result of good *karma*, a finer and longer state of bliss than in human category is possible. This is not an absurd conception of gods; in the sphere of naturalistic monism it is wholly logical. The power above all powers is never a god, but *karma*, the tyrannical Lord and creator of all existence. ... [42]

Knowing, however, that those who, at both Edinburgh and Jerusalem, had spoken about Hindu conceptions of God, referred to the Vedantic conception of God, Kraemer went further to claim that all conceptions of ultimate reality within Hinduism arose from its naturalistic monism. "All ideas or conceptions of God, whether theistic or pantheistic," Kraemer said, "remain in Hinduism steeped in an atmosphere of immanence, because the cosmic natural process does not permit an idea of real

40 *Ibid.,* p. 162.
41 *Ibid.*
42 *Ibid.,* p. 163.

transcendence."[43] In his view Hindu naturalistic monism treated God-ideas as ideas, that is to say, as ways in which the human mind conceived the divine.

The contrast which Kraemer sought to make here is obvious. The fundamental difference that he discerned between Hindu conceptions of God, however profound, and Christian belief about God was that the Bible spoke of God as he who stood above all created order, and as one who was not a 'conception' of the human mind but addressed the human will demanding its response. This transcendence of God as "the Lord and the God of man" was never possible, claimed Kraemer, within the naturalistic apprehension of reality. "In the religious philosophy of Vedanta," he concluded, "all conceptions of the Divine, however moving they may be, belong to the sphere of *maya*."[44]

On the question of liberation or salvation, ethics, and the tradition of loving devotion (*bhakti*) which were among the subjects influencing the debate on Hinduism at Edinburgh and Jerusalem, Kraemer was convinced that a deeper analysis would show that these also conformed to the naturalistic apprehension of reality fundamental to Hinduism. Here naturalism showed itself in the *anthropocentric* nature of the way in which these are understood.[45]

Moksha, or the search for deliverance, was interpreted by Kraemer as a 'quest for life' which is part of the vitalistic tendency of the primitive apprehension of reality. Kraemer was, of course, aware that *moksha* is commonly interpreted not as the search for life but as the release from the transiency of existence (*samsara*). He felt, however, that the haunting sense of the transiency of life and the world, magnified and intensified by the system of rebirth and *karma* leading to endless processes of birth had over-accentuated transiency to the point of making the opposite desire in man:

> This deep-seated complaint of the transiency of existence is the inverted form of an intense desire for life, imperishable life. This is the reason why the soteriological systems of Hinduism are such passionate, resolute combats for deliverance (*moksha*), and why the ways of deliverance (*marga*) are so many and so arduous. Nowhere in the world have so many people so intensely believed in the possibility of self-deliverance and so unwaveringly and courageously striven and toiled for it as in India.[46]

And yet Kraemer held that, in the absence of any truly transcendental Reality, man in search of *moksha* did not ultimately find God but the supreme assertion of reality and mystery of his own being. "At the end

43 *Ibid.*
44 *Ibid.*
45 *Ibid.,* p. 165.
46 *Ibid.,* p. 166.

the only thing that appears to exist really in this whole mirage of existence is human consciousness moving in sovereign solitude over the void abyss of void existence."[47] In this search for *moksha* there was no place for ethics as the fulfilment of the will of God but only as the means to achieve the goal of *moksha*.

Kraemer saw what he considered to be the anthropocentric apprehension of existence as the opposite of the theocentric apprehension of existence given in the prophetic religion of biblical realism. For in the apprehension of biblical realism "not the womb of nature but the hand of God is the cause of all things."[48]

Kraemer was nevertheless aware, that such a general treatment of the subject of theism and of the devotional religion within Hinduism would not suffice to answer the obvious enthusiasm many Christians had over the number of similarities between Christianity and the *bhakti* religions of India. He therefore dealt at some length with the great *bhakti* religion of Ramanuja, if only to show where the differences lay between the Hindu concept of loving devotion and the same idea in Christian faith. He recognized the *bhakti* religions as passionate and necessary protests against the absolute monism of Shankara. He also saw in these religions obvious expressions of the experience of sin and grace, of conversion and loving devotion towards God. "Ramanuja breaks in a radical way," admitted Kraemer, "with the classic Hindu ideas about God, the soul, and the world. The world is real, not *maya*: the soul and human consciousness consequently are so also. The eternal, personal God, Ishvara, is the sole and personal God and Saviour, not merely a god-representation necessary for man in a certain stage in his quest for the *summum bonum*. ... The fascinating thing in Ramanuja is that his deep religious aspiration to vindicate Ishvara as the sole and Eternal Saviour urges him to distinguish clearly between God, man, and the world. ..."

Thus Kraemer saw in Ramanuja's theology some remarkable moving away from the traditional Hindu attitudes, and in the *bhakti* religions, the sense of the "wretchedness of sin, the deep longing for the divine grace, the intense feeling of trust and faith in Ishvara's all-conquering love, the experience of being divinely elected and of being called to a life of sanctification and praise of Ishvara, the deep experience of deliverance through faith and absolute surrender to God." All these things were expressed, Kraemer said, in striking ways in prose and poetry.[49]

Despite all these theological and psychological similarities, Kraemer still insisted that "the spiritual climate and the really dominant urge in this deeply sincere and fervid religion of deliverance are radically different

47 *Ibid.*, pp. 166-67.
48 *Ibid.*, p. 169.
49 *Ibid.*, p. 170.

from the prophetic religion of biblical realism."[50] He came to this conclusion because he was convinced that deeper analysis of Ramanuja's theology would show that Ramanuja also moved in the monistic Indian atmosphere for "God does not become creator in the absolute sense of the word." Kraemer also saw in the *bhakti* religions the anthropocentric drive which considered faith as a *means to salvation.* Similarly, he argued, that sin in *bhakti* religions was more an impediment for the realization of the fellowship of the soul with Ishvara than a wilful act of rebellion against God. Therefore ethics in the *bhakti* religion was also essentially eudaemonistic.[51]

Concluding his discussion on *bhakti,* Kraemer said that it rebelled against, but was not really emancipated from, the naturalistic monism of Hinduism, for it still expressed the anthropocentric tendency inherent in monism. God was proclaimed not as the God of holy love, but as a God of compassion (*karuna*); God disregarded sin and man claimed to be entitled to fellowship with God. In the world of biblical realism, however, the roles were changed. "God is anthropocentrically interested from the soteriological point of view. Man, on the contrary, in the apprehension of faith, becomes theocentrically interested, recognizing that the saving element in the supreme divine love is rather the fact that the Holy Will of God ..." is fulfilled. "Therefore the deepest word in the soteriology of biblical realism is reconciliation, wrought by God Himself; the deepest word of *bhakti* soteriology is divine favour (*prasada*)."[52]

Kraemer's Attitude to Non-Christian Religions

We have dealt with Kraemer's interpretation of Hinduism in some detail in order to compare it with the approaches taken to Hinduism at the two earlier major ecumenical meetings. This comparison will show the fundamental theological issues that emerged after the Tambaram meeting and set the agenda for subsequent discussions of the Christian approach and attitude to Hinduism. We should, however, stay with Kraemer a little longer to examine his own approach and attitude to non-Christian religions and the discussions it provoked at Tambaram.

Kraemer insisted that we should take the other religious traditions seriously, because the world remained the domain of God who had created it. "The Christian attitude to the world should correspond to the divine 'yes' and 'no' of the Holy God of reconciliation, who holds the world under his absolute judgement and at the same time claims it for His

---

50 *Ibid.*
51 *Ibid.,* p. 172.
52 *Ibid.,* p. 173.

love."[53] Kraemer therefore rejected all aggressive attitudes towards other faiths and called on Christians to have an informed understanding of the religious traditions of their neighbours. He also advocated the presentation of the gospel message in terms and modes of expression that would make it intelligible and relevant to their lives.[54] But at the theological level Kraemer saw the question of the attitude to other faiths as "one of the greatest and gravest which the Christian churches all over the world and the missionary cause have to face at the present time." For he saw in that question a deeper theological issue: "What did you think of man, his nature, his possibilities, his achievements?"[55]

Since Kraemer saw the non-Christian religions as inclusive systems enveloping culture and civilization and a definite structure of society and state, he would not be drawn into a discussion of the 'value' of any aspect of these religious traditions. He was, of course, impressed with the moving devotion of the *bhakti* tradition within Hinduism, but to deal only with that aspect would not in his view do justice either to Hinduism or to Christian faith. The theological question had therefore to be framed in the wider context of general and natural theology: Were nature, reason, and history sources of revelation in the Christian sense of the word? If so, what was the relation of Christian revelation and its implications to the body of human self-unfolding manifest in philosophy, religion, culture, art, and the other domains of life?[56]

Here Kraemer employed the concept of biblical realism that he had set out as the foundation of his preparatory volume. The revelation of Christ, in his view, directly contradicted all human religious life and wisdom, "because it is the 'wisdom of God' which is 'sheer folly' to the Greeks." It was not the perfection of human reason and religion. Kraemer joined with Karl Barth in making a sharp distinction between revelation and religion, and supported the view that all religions including empirical Christianity were under the judgement of God's revelation in Christ. The gospel, therefore, was the crisis of all religions, which were human achievements curtailed by man's sinful rebellion against God's holy will. The gospel was not in continuity but in discontinuity with man's religious life, for it called him from disbelief to an act of faith in what God had done in Christ.[57]

53 *Ibid.,* p. 104.
54 *Ibid.*
55 Cf. *Christian Message,* p. 102f.
56 See *Christian Message in a Non-Christian World,* p. 101 ff. for a full discussion on Natural Theology; note especially pages 114f. where he deals specifically with the subject.
57 *Ibid.,* p. 123f.

But Kraemer did not go all the way with Barth in his assessment of the religious life of man. Rather, he endorsed Emil Brunner's 'protest' in favour of a critical and right kind of natural theology and contended that "no man can claim the right or power to limit God's working in revelation." He was therefore able to say that God "shines revealingly" though "in a broken, troubled way in reason, in nature, and in history" and that God "wrestles with man" in man's "religious consciousness."[58] But this 'general revelation' could only be effectively discovered in the light of the 'special revelation' in Christ. The function of natural theology was not to seek or set out the preparatory stages of unbroken or continuous religious development or revelations that led to a summit in the revelatory act of God in Christ, "but to lay bare the condition not only of the non-Christian world but all human attempts to apprehend the totality of existence, exhibiting elements both from God and hostile to God, that lie side by side within them."[59]

In this way Kraemer defined 'natural revelation.' Its relationship to special revelation enabled him to take on the critical issue of 'points of contact' between the Christian faith and other religions which had been so important at Edinburgh and Jerusalem. One of the important questions in the Edinburgh survey of the missionary situation had asked those in the field to list the points of contact that enabled relationships between the Christian message and non-Christian religious traditions.[60] Kraemer, as we have mentioned rejected the idea that one could analyze other religions to identify the parts that might provide points of contact:

> The insistent demand for concrete points of contact is quite natural. It springs from the normal desire to see one's way and from the apostolic desire to reach man with the Message. However, in this matter of concrete points of contact, it is easy to entertain fallacious hopes and reasonings. Somehow the conviction is alive that it is possible and feasible to produce for every religion a sort of catalogue of points of contact. This apparently is a misguided pursuit. Such a catalogue based on similarities between Christianity and non-Christian religions, for example, on such subjects as the idea of God and man, the conception of soul or of redemption, the expectation of an eternal life or the precedence of the community over the individual, etc., is an impossible thing.[61]

58 *Ibid.,* pp. 120-21.

59 Here Kraemer's main concern is to challenge Farquhar's conception that the Christian faith is the natural fulfilment of the Hindu quest. Kraemer is keen to show that it is not only the demonic elements in other faiths that are to be rejected. Kraemer held that the groping of man after God is itself distorted by his alienation from God.

60 See discussion in Chapter II. Kraemer felt that the attempt made at Edinburgh to find points of contact in other religions had already assumed that God was revealingly present in other religions. He rejected this suggestion.

61 *The Christian Message,* p. 134.

We have quoted this section in full to show that Kraemer faithfully listed almost all those subjects on which the respondents to Edinburgh had seen possibilities of contact.

Kraemer's objections were twofold. The first had to do with his 'totalitarian' approach to religions. In his view, every religion was a desperate effort of mankind somehow to get an apprehension of the totality of existence, and therefore "every religion was an indivisible unity of existential apprehension." Every part of religion —a dogma, a rite, a myth, an institution— was so vitally related to the whole that it could not be understood in its real significance, and particularly in its meaning to those participating in it, outside the total apprehension of reality.

His second objection was based on his understanding of revelation, for he believed that in the light of revelation in Christ these similarities became dissimilarities.

> For the revealing function of this light is that, when exposed to it, all religious life, the lofty and the degraded, appears to be under the divine judgement, because it is *misdirected*. This is the dialectical 'no' of the revelation in Christ to all religious life, and therefore also to every point of contact in the sense of it being one that, if it were properly developed, would end in the sphere of the revelation in Christ.[62]

The dialectical 'yes' would affirm that this revealing light would at the same time uncover the groping and persistent aspiration of man to become the child of God in the misdirected expressions of religious life.

Kraemer therefore turned to the incarnation for the model of the point of contact. The only point of contact between the gospel and the adherents of other faiths was the missionary himself — in himself and in his disposition and attitude to those with whom he lived. Here Kraemer stressed the importance of genuine and continuous interest in people as they are. "As long as a man feels that he is the object of human interest only for reasons of intellectual curiosity or for purposes of conversion, and not because of himself as he is in total empirical reality," said Kraemer, "there cannot arise that humane natural contact which is the indispensable condition of all real religious meeting of man with man." "In these conditions," he added, "the door to such a man and to the world he lives in remains locked, and the love of Christ remains for him remote and abstract."[63]

62 *Ibid.*, p. 136.
63 *Ibid.*, pp. 140-41.

The Tambaram Debate

(a) Introduction

Kraemer's concept of biblical realism, his interpretation of Hinduism and his views on the Christian attitude to other faiths were subjected to much debate before, during, and after the Tambaram Conference. William Paton, in his introduction to the first post-Tambaram volume, said that Kraemer had been asked only to produce a preparatory book to enable discussion on the "Christian approach to non-Christian religions,"[64] but that "he did that and much more," for what he had produced was a searching critique of the entire missionary approach to non-Christian religions and the world in which they were set, based upon certain clear cut theological positions. The value of the book, in Paton's view, was not only the fresh clarity and certainty which it brought to some about "what they already believed," but also the "inescapable challenge" to others, to whom his positions were unacceptable, to say where they stood if they did not stand where he did.[65]

Since Kraemer's book was published in advance of the conference, debate had already begun before the Tambaram meeting. One of the important responses came from India where a group of Christians, including P. Chenchiah and V. Chakkarai published the volume *Rethinking Christianity in India,* challenging some of the positions Kraemer had taken in his book.[66] The Minutes of the actual debate at Tambaram, unfortunately, do not exist. However, the organizers of the conference invited some of the persons who had led the debate to set out their positions in writing and these, along with Kraemer's own response to the debate, were published under the title, *The Authority of the Faith.* This contribution is indispensable to our understanding of the Tambaram controversy and the subsequent discussions on the Christian attitude to other faiths.[67]

---

64 In early missionary discussions a distinction was made between the 'Christian approach' and the 'Christian attitude' to non-Christian religions. The word 'attitude' was used to denote the theological stance vis-à-vis other faiths; 'approach' was used to indicate the methods, personal attitudes, and practices used in the task of presenting the gospel in missionary work.

65 W. Paton, ed., *The Authority of the Faith* (London: Oxford University Press, 1939), p. ix. This is the first of seven volumes produced following the Tambaram conference setting out the discussions, decisions, and statements of the conference.

66 D. M. Devasahayam and A. N. Sudarisanam, eds., *Rethinking Christianity in India* (Madras: CLS, 1939).

67 Contributors were: T. C. Chao of Yenching, China ("Revelation"), D. G. Moses of Nagpur, India ("The Problem of Truth in Religion"), K. L. Reichelt of Tao Fong Shan, China ("Johannine Approach"), A. G. Hogg of Madras, India ("The Christian Attitude to Non-Christian Faith"), K. Kartenstein of Basel, Switzerland ("The Biblical View of Religion"), W. M. Horton of Oberlin, USA ("Between Hocking and Kraemer") and

(b) Kraemer's Conclusions

Generally speaking Kraemer's concept of biblical realism, his interpretation of Hinduism and his view on the Christian attitude to other faiths had the following implications, particularly as they related to Hinduism:

1. Hinduism and Christianity are based on two entirely different apprehensions of reality, one prophetic and the other natural-istic-monistic, making it impossible for them to be compared or to see them in any kind of continuity.

2. All religions, including empirical Christianity, are but manifes-tations, on the one hand, of the human groping for the divine, and on the other, of debased human rebellion against the holy will of God. Christianity, however, insofar as it is based on the revelation of God's will and purpose in Christ, is the bearer of this revelation. Hinduism, devoid of a truly transcendental understanding of God, is basically naturalistic, vitalistic, monistic, and eudaemonistic.

3. Since the gospel is the crisis of all religions it cannot be seen as the fulfilment of Hinduism or Hindu values. The relation-ship of the gospel to Hinduism is one essentially of 'discon-tinuity.'

4. It is important to understand Hinduism and to make the gospel relevant in the sense of addressing it to actual human need. But there are no points of contact between the gospel and Hinduism except the missionary himself, who as one who stands alongside and with the Hindu, points in all humility to the 'wonderful things God has done' in Christ.

These are generalizations of the positions taken by Kraemer, which he qualified in many ways in the course of his presentation. In his later writings he further modified and further qualified many of the positions he had taken at Tambaram.[68] But there is no doubt, judging from the responses at Tambaram, that these were the positions that were *heard* by those who listened to him. In our summary of the debate we will concen-trate mainly on the arguments of two persons, H. H. Farmer and A. G. Hogg, who challenged Kraemer at Tambaram particularly from the point of view of Hinduism.

H. H. Farmer of Cambridge, England ("The Authority of the Faith"). The titles are indicative of the major subjects that were debated at the meeting.

68 Carl F. Hallencreutz summarises these in his *New Approaches to Men of Other Faiths,* Research Pamphlet no. 18 (Geneva: WCC, 1970), pp. 40-62. For a full discussion see O. V. Jathanna, *The Decisiveness of the Christ-Event and the Universality of Christianity in a World of Religious Pluarality* (Berne/Frankfurt–M./Las Vegas: Peter Lang, 1981), p. 102 ff.

(c) Positive Aspects

Responding to Kraemer, Walter Horton pointed out some of the positive aspects of Kraemer's positions. He recognized that there was nothing in Kraemer to discourage a friendly, appreciative attitude to persons of other faiths. There was even eagerness to confer and cooperate with them in every possible way. He also saw that there was nothing in Kraemer's view that, when fully understood, would "encourage an attitude of arrogant imperialism or intolerant dogmatism."

> What Kramer offers to non-Christian lands is no ready-made system of thought, no imposing —and invading— body of full fashioned cultural patterns, but simply a piece of news of transcendent importance for all the world: the news that, as we do verily believe, God has shown mankind His nature and His will in a series of mighty acts culminating in Jesus Christ. . . . By this divine revelation all man-made religions i. e., *all existing religious movements, including 'empirical Christianity'* as Kraemer so often reminds us — are to be judged and are being judged.[69]

This useful summary by Horton did reflect the feelings of many of the Tambaram participants. Kraemer, in the way he had presented the uniqueness and decisiveness of the Christian faith as he saw it, managed, by using Barthian categories, on the one hand to justify the mission of the Church, and on the other, to reject some of the arrogant and imperialistic attitudes and tendencies in relation to other religions, particularly to Asian religions, which everyone wanted to see condemned. But whether Kraemer's own position, when pushed to its logical conclusions, constituted 'an intolerant dogmatism' was a matter on which a variety of opinions could be expected. Horton himself said that his hesitations began when Kraemer interpreted the great Eastern religions "as various forms of self-deification, resulting from man's inveterate propensity to carry his drive for self-realization up to the transcendental level . . ." Even allowing for the fact that much of human religious history was ego-inflated self-seeking, Horton did not accept such a blanket judgement of other religious traditions:

> If presumption and self-aggrandisement appear (also) in Christianity, do not humility, awe, self-abasement in the presence of the Holy One appear in non-Christian religions, and are they not signs of a genuine though incomplete self revelation of the divine Word, operative from of old in every land?[70]

Was Kraemer using different standards in the way he presented Hinduism and Christianity?

---

69 "Between Hocking and Kraemer," *The Authority of the Faith*, p. 156.

70 *Ibid.*, p. 158. This understanding of the self-revelation of the Divine Word is expanded and argued more closely by Karl Reichelt's response to Kraemer in his contribution to the volume, "The Johannine Approach."

(d) Interpretative Principles

H. H. Farmer took this point and developed a fuller criticism of Kraemer's methodology and interpretation of the religious life of mankind. Interpretation of any religion, in Farmer's contention, depended first on the data used, and secondly, on the principles of interpretation adopted. Recognizing that Christians could use only Christian revelation as their interpretative principle, Farmer asked three pertinent questions: (a) Did Kraemer cover the ostensible data? (b) Were the interpretative principles used satisfactorily? (c) Were they the only ones open to Christians?[71]

Farmer agreed with Kraemer's main arguments that religions were 'total apprehensions of reality' and that religious life involved much self-assertion, etc. But he had serious difficulties with Kraemer's general rejection of the religious life of man as human striving. For even though Kraemer spoke about "God wrestling with man," Farmer said, "the main impression left, I repeat, is that the central driving force of all man's religious life is self-affirmation and self-insurance." Did this cover all the facts? Farmer doubted that it did:

> Religions are 'monistic.' Yes, they are, but equally much they insist on dichotomising the world into sacred and non-sacred. ... Religions are 'naturalistic.' Yes, they are, but what tremendous absolutes appear in their midst — even the crudest religion has its tabus. Religions are 'eudemonistic,' life affirming. Yes, they are, but how frequently does there spring up within them an imperious demand to surrender even life itself. ... [72]

Farmer held that the elements of an awareness of God as 'sacred' or as 'absolute demand' prevalent in religions made it difficult, when all data were taken into account, to conceive them mainly in terms of self-affirmation and enrichment. "Some of the things that Kraemer says about religions," Farmer concluded, "begin to look like sweeping generalizations in urgent need of qualification."[73]

Farmer's major difficulty had to do with Kraemer's interpretative principles. He felt this issue to be so important that one could, quite apart from the question of other faiths, have a full discussion only on the question of the way Kraemer interpreted the Christian faith in order to ascertain its relationship to other religious traditions. Farmer said that as far as he could assess them, the theological principles on which Kraemer interpreted Christian faith seemed to assert that "the primal, basic relationship in which God stands to man is one of absolute sovereign Will"; and accordingly the primal, basic relationship in which man stood to God

---

71 *The Authority of the Faith*, pp. 169-70.
72 *Ibid.*, p. 172.
73 *Ibid.*

was one of "complete and unqualified submission and obedience."[74] Was this an adequate principle for interpreting the Christian faith, particularly when one sought its relationship to other religious traditions?

Farmer lamented that this kind of conception left out, for example, the interpretation of the faith in terms of the fatherly love of God. Admitting that Kraemer would have no difficulty affirming the fatherly love of God, Farmer still contended that in Kraemer's theology the idea of love was "almost wholly submerged in the idea of sovereignty" and the situation became worse when to the original doctrine of the sovereignty of God was added the derivative doctrine of sin "as rank disobedience and rebellion." He recognized the difficulties involved in theologically relating the sovereignty of God and His fatherly love. But would Kraemer have come to a different conclusion about other faiths had he used the principle of fatherly love?

> Sovereign Will standing over against the will of man is not —I do not know how to put it— is not such a holding, binding, cleaving, seeking, yearning relationship as the Love of a Father which cannot and will not let man go; and I believe that as the mind is filled with the one thought or the other, so one's attitude is unconsciously determined in the matter under discussion. ... [75]

The curiously grudging and negative description of God's relation to men in their religious life, even when this was at its highest and best, that one could see in Kraemer's description, Farmer believed, came from the principle of the Divine Sovereign Will on which Kraemer operated. It deprived the situation of the God who stood in a continuous relationship with men in their daily lives as they strove to discover the purpose of their lives. This last point leads us to another area of concern and controversy at Tambaram: revelation.

(e) On The Concept of Revelation

Revelation became an important issue because of Kraemer's clear and uncompromising insistence on interpreting it in a particular way. He denied that there was any revelation at all in Hinduism because there was no truly transcendent God who could reveal His Will to man. Therefore, he insisted, that when Hinduism used the word revelation it was misusing it to represent trans-empirical knowledge or experience. Kraemer had of course compromised a little to allow for God's self-revelation manifesting itself in 'broken' ways as God struggled with man to manifest His will within the religious consciousness of mankind. But the impression he gave

---

74 *Ibid.,* p. 173.
75 *Ibid.,* p. 174.

was that revelation referred exclusively to "God's unique and 'once-for-all' disclosure and giving of Himself to man in Jesus Christ."[76] Kraemer had further strengthened this by insisting that revelation was an 'act' of grace directed by God towards a "forlorn man and a forlorn world" and that it remained hidden until one had the eyes of faith to comprehend and appropriate it.[77]

This position had already been severely criticized before the conference by the Rethinking Group in India. Chenchiah, reviewing Kraemer's book, said that Kraemer's problem was over dependence on Barth's crusade against relativism and that his absolutist understanding of the revelation "made nonsense" both of incarnation, which Chenchiah saw as abiding presence with mankind (Immanuel), and the doctrine of the Holy Spirit, understood by Chenchiah as God's continuous work in man towards a new creation:

> What we require today is not an absolute in heaven but a 'power greater than we are' on earth. Here absolutists do not interpret Christ aright and in consequence view the problem of life in a wrong perspective. We should not throw God beyond the regional attraction of the human heart, beyond the gravitational force of man's soul. We need as a remedy for our ills —not an absolute but a God with us— 'Emmanuel.'[78]

Similar hesitations were shown at the conference itself by T. C. Chao, who from the perspective of Chinese religions saw as very limiting Kraemer's extreme reluctance to deal with revelation in a more general way. He had problems with Kraemer's overly cautious attitude to reason, nature, and history. Admitting that God took the initiative, Chao argued that man had to exercise his power of reason and understanding in the process of grasping the truth of revelation:

> The point is that *man must understand.* If revelation in its proper sense is what is by its very nature inaccessible *and remains so, even when it is revealed,* then for those who desire to have faith intelligently, there is no hope in this world or in any other world.[79]

Chao, however, had greater difficulty with Kraemer's unwillingness to see God's relationship to nature and history as part of revelation. Nature in Chao's view revealed God's power and intelligence while humanity, especially in the lives of sages and prophets, revealed his love and righteousness. He argued further that God's revealing of himself in ongoing history was necessitated by the Christian understanding of sin and history:

---

76 This is Farmer's description of Kraemer's position.

77 Cf. *Christian Message,* p. 118 ff.

78 *Rethinking Christianity in India,* Appendix. See pp. 10-19 for Chenchiah's elaboration of this point.

79 T. C. Chao, "Revelation," *The Authority of the Faith,* pp. 33-34.

Man has sinned because he is a part of history, and because he is *made* to live within that process. Consequently no gospel is a real gospel to him, which does not have in it the key to the dynamic for the salvation of society within the historical process.[80]

Chao's chief complaint was that by having such a limited conception of revelation Kraemer had not only relegated the rest of human achievements to mere human gropings, but also reduced "the Lord of heaven and earth, the Father of mankind and the ruler within human history" into "a spirit of narrow particularism":

> Man has to be saved in the historical process if he is to be saved at all, for once taken out of the network of relations he becomes nil, a nonentity, a non-existent zero. ... There has been no time, in other words, when God has not been breaking into our human world; nor is there a place where men have been that He has not entered and ruled. He has not left Himself without witness, however dim this witness may appear to man ... Who can say that these sages have not been truly inspired by the spirit of our God, the God and Father of our Lord Jesus Christ?[81]

Farmer supported the possibility of using the word revelation both in the sense of God's continuous activity in the world and also to denote the special revelation in Christ without diminishing its importance. Kraemer's special use of the word not only made it difficult to speak of God's dealing with the world except as revelation, but also made those who used this word to denote God's direct activity in other faiths "to feel that they have done something theologically dreadful, almost betraying the gospel itself, when all that has happened is that there has been a discrepancy in the use of a term."

It was A. G. Hogg, however, who posed the most searching challenge to Kraemer's insistence that revelation was an 'act' of God demanding human obedience and that it could not be reduced to ideas and concepts. Hogg saw in this argument Kraemer's basic difficulty with Hinduism. Admitting that it was an elusive argument to handle, Hogg still challenged Kraemer as to whether the sharp distinctions he made between the 'act,' the 'content' and the 'ideas and concepts' was a valid.

> ... But it is impossible to set down the content except by *expressing* the content. And (unless, indeed, we return to the old 'intellectualist' view that 'revelation' means a Divine communication of truths and ideas) we must admit that it is equally impossible to *express* the content of a revelation except as we ourselves *clothe it in ideas and concepts* which fuse together the content of the revelation and the interpretation of it by the

---

80 *Ibid.,* p. 42.
81 *Ibid.,* p. 47.

apprehending soul. To dream of expressing without at least beginning to interpret is as vain as to seize 'matter' without 'form.'[82]

Therefore, Hogg argued, even within the religion of biblical realism there was a meeting between the historical 'intervention' of God to reveal Himself and the intrusion of a fallible human element seeking to apprehend and witness to it and in so doing somewhat distorting it.

Hogg then reversed the argument to ask how, if behind the distorted apprehension of the Christian faith there was a God who revealed himself, there could be no revelatory presence behind the distorted presentation of Hinduism. Kraemer had referred to the rash and erroneous identification of empirical Christianity with the revelation in Christ.[83] Hogg suggested that it would be equally rash and erroneous to identify other religions with their empirical forms, unless of course one wished to argue that empirical Christianity should be exempted from "the relative sphere of history." Indeed, this was what Hogg saw Kraemer doing when he was finally driven to conclude that Christianity, insofar as it derived from revelation in Christ, was not only supreme among religions but also solitary among them for, in Kraemer's words, "the Christian revelation places itself over against the many efforts to apprehend the totality of existence."[84]
This was entirely unacceptable to Hogg:

> For my own part I am persuaded that it is radically wrong for the missionary to approach men of other faiths under a conviction —no matter how sincerely humble that conviction may be— that he and his fellow believers are witnesses to a Divine revelation, while other religions are exclusively the product of human 'religious consciousness.'[85]

Hogg's own position was that whether God revealed Himself to Christian faith or to non-Christian, he did not of course reveal ready-made truths about Himself and "the thought and language in which a man expresses to himself or others this apprehension of that supernatural self-disclosure has to be in human thought, human language — always defective, sometimes gravely distorting."[86]

The uniqueness of the Christian faith, Hogg argued, was not, as Kraemer would contend, that it was based on a revelatory *occurrence*. Without the revealing initiative of God there would be *no* religions. Christianity was unique because of the unique *content* of the revelation of which it was an apprehension and product. "And that content must win

---

82 *The Authority of the Faith*, p. 176.
83 *Christian Message*, p. 145.
84 *Ibid.*, p. 113.
85 *The Authority of the Faith*, p. 106.
86 *Ibid.*, p. 108 ff.

conviction by its own direct appeal, by its illuminating and renovating power."[87]

(f) On Fulfilment

We have seen that one of the major issues that Kraemer was implicitly treating in his book was the question whether gospel was the fulfilment of Hinduism or for that matter of any religious tradition. Kraemer felt that at Jerusalem much of the theological relativism and especially the interest in the 'spiritual value' in other religions had stemmed from the misguided notion that the gospel fulfilled the other faiths. He had therefore taken a firm stand on the discontinuity of the gospel vis-à-vis all religious traditions, including empirical Christianity. Following Barth he interpreted the gospel as the 'crisis' of all religions. But did the gospel fulfil the deep aspirations of man's religious consciousness? To protect his notion of discontinuity, Kraemer claimed that the gospel fulfilled these aspirations only in an 'entirely unexpected' way. For those who wished to see their new obedience to Christ in continuity with their spiritual tradition, Kraemer's position presented unsurmountable obstacles. Naturally, it was Chenchiah who took Kraemer on in his pre-Tambaram response to Kraemer's book. Chenchiah also had difficulties with Farquhar's concept of the Christian faith as the crown or fulfilment of Hinduism. His reasons, however, were very different from Kraemer's:

> While we do not agree with the summary dismissal of the fulfilment theory which it has received at the hands of the author (Kraemer), Christianity as the crown of Hinduism does appear unsatisfactory. One main ground for rejecting this idea is that non-Christian religions not only register longings and aspirations but also satisfactions. The facile presumption that in Hinduism we have a search for salvation without satisfaction and that Christianity satisfies the longing is untrue to fact.[88]

Chenchiah further stated that the longing-satisfaction model did not work because, for example, "the supreme longing of the 'Hindu' to escape from *samsara*, Christ does not satisfy, and the Lord's gift of rebirth does not appeal to the Hindu."[89]

Chenchiah, however, saw Christ as the spirit that would transform Hinduism, and Hinduism as the spiritual home for the gospel. Agreeing with Kraemer that Hinduism was "a highly integrated socio-ethical structure forming an indivisible whole," Chenchiah argued that precisely because of this Christ should belong to the whole of Hinduism rather than

---

87 *Ibid.,* p. 125.
88 *Rethinking Christianity in India,* Appendix, p. 40 f.
89 *Ibid.*

any part of it. A great religion like Hinduism could only be changed when its mind and soul were changed or when its life impulses were altered.[90]

Chenchiah saw in Kraemer's discontinuity an interaction with Hinduism where individuals could be challenged only to accept a set of theological propositions and become members of the Church. This came from a wrong conception of Hinduism where, said Chenchiah, it was seen as "a huge tabernacle peopled with millions of Hindus." His own vision of Hinduism was of "a cosmic personality capable of undergoing profound changes in the depth of its being." And Chenchiah believed that the Christian gospel could produce this change. "Christianity will produce the same effect on Hinduism as the moon on the sea. It would create tidal waves of spirituality or reform within Hinduism."[91] Although he was responding to Kraemer's preparatory volume, Chenchiah ventured his own vision of the renewal of the whole of Hinduism by Christ entering its bosom and bringing about a new creation.

It was Farmer who challenged Kraemer's ideas of fulfilment-non-fulfilment in terms of his own conception of continuity–discontinuity. He detected that Kraemer had used the word fulfilment in three different ways. First, the non-Christian faiths might be said to find their fulfilment in Christianity in the sense that their highest insights were such that they "only require some development, correction, and supplementation in order to end in the essence of Christianity." There had been some hints in the Edinburgh meeting of this view of fulfilment, where it had been thought that if only Christ would penetrate the heart of Hinduism it would be redeemed. With the concept of biblical realism, where man was seen to be in active rebellion against the will of God, it was of course not possible for Kraemer to entertain this view of fulfilment.

Farmer said that the second sense in which the word fulfilment might be used was to mean that the religious longings and aspirations of men which found expression in the non-Christian religions found their satisfaction in Christ. We have already seen Chenchiah's protest that the non-Christian religions were not only manifestations of aspirations but also of fulfilment. Even though Kraemer was inclined to accept this understanding of fulfilment, he was quick to qualify it for he was keen also to show that Christ repudiated and negated such aspirations and longings. "The cross and its real meaning," in Kraemer's view, "is antagonistic to *all* human aspirations and ends." Kraemer therefore developed the concept that in Christ human aspirations were fulfilled in an "entirely unexpected way."[92]

---

90 *Rethinking Christianity in India,* Appendix, p. 47.
91 *Ibid.*
92 *Christian Message,* p. 123 ff.

Farmer concluded that the only real sense in which Kraemer could use the word fulfilment was to denote "the fulfilment of God's promises and his preparatory doings," which were of course to be seen in discontinuity with the religious life of mankind. The large question for Kraemer here was whether such an understanding of fulfilment corresponded to the experience of someone who, like Chenchiah, found faith in Christ and still looked upon his own tradition as his 'spiritual mother.'

(g) Faith and Faiths

Hogg had difficulty with Kraemer's interpretation and analysis of Hinduism primarily as a religious system. He admitted that Christians had to define their attitude to the complex of spiritual, ethical, intellectual, and social elements that constituted what was generally called religion. But did these exhaust Hinduism? Hogg claimed that Christians should also discover the right attitude to, what he called 'non-Christian *faith.*' Referring to Kraemer's concept of life 'hid with Christ in God,' Hogg asked whether there could not be within the non-Christian religions, especially in those for whom religion was a living personal possession, "a life which although without Christ, is yet somehow a life 'Hid in God'."[93]

Hogg's concern was based on his own experience of meeting Hindus whose deep spiritual life, devotion, commitment to the Divine and consequent involvement in social issues were matters not merely for admiration but for religious reverence. He felt that Kraemer had not paid attention to this deep personal response of faith seen in other religious traditions which corresponded in many ways to a similar attitude to God on the part of Christians:

> Is there any such thing as religious faith which in quality or texture is definitely not Christian, but in the approach to which one ought to put the shoes off the feet, recognising that one is on the holy ground of a two-sided commerce between God and man? In non-Christian faith may we meet with something that is not merely a seeking but in real measure a finding by contact with which a Christian may be helped to make fresh discoveries in his own finding of God *in Christ*?[94]

"For my part," concluded Hogg, "I am convinced that the answer to these questions must be in the affirmative." Hogg's impression was that Kraemer was also inclined to be affirmative, but with "the hesitancy that must always go with assent to what is perplexing and paradoxical."

Hogg's distinction between non-Christian 'faith' as a personal response of faith in God as against 'faiths' as systems of belief played a significant

---

93 *Ibid.,* p. 102.
94 *Ibid.,* p. 103.

role in the post-Tambaram discussions. This same distinction was also picked up in a modified form in contemporary discussions. To this we should return later.

(h)   Conclusion

Most of the criticism against Kraemer at Tambaram seemed to be directed at the sharp distinction he made between revelation and religion. This distinction, coupled with his concept of 'biblical realism,' invariably raised the Christian faith above all other faiths. Kraemer did of course try to make a distinction between gospel and empirical Christianity and did qualify his position on revelation and religion, preferring Brunner to Barth on matters of natural theology. Most of his opponents, however, felt that his positions on 'revelation,' 'fulfilment,' etc., were too narrow to recognize and affirm genuine religious life in people of other faiths.

As a result of the debate, Kraemer was able to see some areas where further qualification and clarification were needed, and he provided this in his later writings. In his response to the debate itself, however, he reiterated his overall positions on the issue. "Fundamentally speaking," he replied, "we have in regard to this problem only to choose between two positions: To start, consciously or unconsciously, from a general idea about the essence of religion and take that as our standard of reference, or derive our idea of what religion really is or ought to be from the revelation in Christ, and consistently stick to this as the sole standard of reference."[95] Kraemer has decided to go the second way. To his mind, the choice of the second of these alternatives "was inescapable."

Tambaram Report

The part of the Tambaram report dealing with Christian relations to people of other faiths is to be found under the "Findings" in Section I ("The Faith by which the Church Lives") and Section V ("The Witness of the Church in Relation to the Non-Christian Religions, New Paganisms, and the Cultural Heritage of the Nations"). One should remember that the Tambaram meeting was concerned not only with the question of witness in the context of resurgent religions, but also with the Challenge of Nationalism, Communism, and Scientific Scepticism, which were described as 'New Paganisms.' The chief intention of the meeting, therefore, was to reaffirm the Christian faith, to state its content, and to recover the missionary mandate of the Church. "The outward confusion of man's life,"

---

95 "Continuity or Discontinuity," *The Authority of the Faith,* p. 23.

said the report, "reflects, and is reflected in, the confusion in men's hearts and minds. . . . Mankind's greatest need is for a true and living faith."[96]

At the centre of the Section I report there was a restatement of the traditional faith of the Church, reaffirming also the Church's ministry in the world:

> For those who are without Christ, the Church yearns with the love of its Master and Lord. It goes forth to them with the evangel of His grace. It practices His ministry of compassion and healing. It bears witness against every iniquity and injustice in their common life. It bears their sorrows and heartaches on its prayers.[97]

Only when we come to the theological passages about relationships to other faiths can we see the stamp of Kraemer in the Tambaram Findings. The important parts are quoted here in full to indicate how Kraemer's unmistakable influence on Tambaram changed the direction of the discussions about other faiths from the course set in Edinburgh and Jerusalem.

First, the report affirmed that the revelation of God in Christ surpassed all other religions:

> There are many non-Christian religions that claim the allegiance of large multitudes. We see and readily recognize that in them are to be found values of deep religious experiences and great moral achievements. Yet we are bold enough to call men *out from them* to the feet of Christ. We do so because we believe that in him *alone* is the *full* salvation which man *needs*. Mankind has *seen nothing to be compared* with the redeeming love of God in the life and death and resurrection of Christ.[98]

Second, in making a theological assessment of God's relationship with people of other faiths the conference again followed Kraemer's position:

> We do not think that God has left Himself without witness in the world at any time. . . . Men have been seeking Him all through the ages. Often this *seeking and longing have been misdirected.* But we see *glimpses of God's light* in the world religions, showing that *His yearning after his erring children* has not been without response. Yet we believe that all religious insight and experience have *to be fully tested before God in Christ*; and we see that this is true as well within as outside the Church.[99]

Finally, it affirmed discontinuity:

---

96 "Findings," *The Authority of the Faith,* pp. 186-87.

97 *Ibid.,* p. 190.

98 *Ibid.,* p. 200. (Italics are mine to show the specific emphases which have been picked up from Kraemer's presentation.)

99 *Ibid.,* pp. 200-1.

Christ is revolutionary; He brings conversion and regeneration when we meet him, *from whatever point we may have started.* Paul said: "What things were gain to me, those I counted loss for Christ."[100]

The findings of Section V affirmed almost word for word these positions from Section I. The text admitted, however, to some of the deep divisions that had appeared in the plenary debate: "As to whether the non-Christian religions as total systems of thought and life may be regarded as in some sense or to some degree manifesting God's revelation," the report said, "Christians are not agreed." Recommending that this matter be studied further, it went on to repeat the stand taken in Section I that "all religious insight and experience have to be fully tested before God in Christ."[101]

The Tambaram report called for positive relations with people of other faiths and to "a sincere and deep interest" in the religious life of those among whom Christians lived. It recommended a "fuller and more adequate understanding of other religious faiths" and the "appropriation of all that traditional cultures may contribute to the enrichment of the life of the church local and universal." It challenged the churches to cooperate with members of other religious traditions "in all good social and community movements."[102] All these, however, were to be at the service of the church's missionary obligation "to a lost world":

> Whatever new emphasis may mark our presentation of Christianity in face of the changes in the non-Christian faiths the heart of the gospel remains eternally unchanged, and the obligation of the church to carry its witness to all mankind stands central to its obedience to the will of its Lord. Indeed the continual development of fresh adaptation of method itself springs directly from the perpetual compulsion to go out and preach the gospel unto all the world.[103]

An Evalutation of the Three Major Missionary Ecumenical Meetings

Those concerned with following the history of missions and the theology of evangelism have studied the three major ecumenical missionary events of Edinburgh, Jerusalem, and Tambaram in much detail in order to examine the various cultural factors, historical necessities, and changing perceptions on the focus of the Christian message that shaped the directions taken by these major conferences.[104] It is beyond the scope of our

---

100 *Ibid.*

101 *Ibid.,* p. 211.

102 For a full statement see Findings in Section I and Section V in *The Authority of the Faith,* pp. 201-2 and pp. 211-15.

103 *Ibid.,* p. 216.

104 The Commission on Mission and Evangelism of the WCC prepared in July 1978 an

present discussions to examine these any further except to recognize briefly the general trends. In our own evaluation we need to concentrate on the options that were considered regarding Christian attitudes to other faiths, in particular Hinduism.

(a)   Tambaram and Missions

From the missiological perspective, the Edinburgh meeting was the high-point of nineteenth-century missionary expansion. So great was the confidence on taking the gospel into all the 'unoccupied areas' of the world, and so certain was the hope that Christ's command to preach the gospel to all the nations would be fulfilled in that generation that the Archbishop of Canterbury ended the conference with these well-known words: "But it may well be that, if that came true, there be some standing here tonight who shall not taste death till they see the kingdom of God come with power."[105]

In this zeal to evangelize the world, consideration of other faiths was geared primarily to examining how best they could be overcome. In fact the survey undertaken in the mission fields had the primary aim of enabling the development of an adequate missionary approach to further the cause of evangelization cf those lands. That the replies received and the work of Commission IV on them resulted in a wealth of theological reflection on the Christian relation to other faiths was, in our view, an unexpected development. It is little wonder that the final report of the Edinburgh conference in no way reflected the profound theological work done in Commission IV described by Robert A. Hume as a "lucid and glowing statement ... pulsating with life in every paragraph."[106]

By 1928, however, when the IMC met in Jerusalem, the unbridled confidence of overcoming the world had subsided. The challenge of secularism in the West and the rise of nationalism coupled with the resurgence of the religions of the East proved to be formidable obstacles to the task of converting the non-Christian world. Suddenly the whole world, and not merely the non-Christian lands, had become the mission field. Again, the study of comparative religion, which was still a specialized field of study in 1910, had become more popular, posing searching

issue of the *International Review of Missions* (LXVII, no. 267) which set out the major conferences side by side showing how historical circumstances had influenced the major conferences. Emilio Castro described the issue as an attempt "to enable us to grasp the significance of the expressions of Christian obedience within the specific historical contexts," p. 249.

105 Quoted by W. H. T. Gairdner, *Echoes from Edinburgh* (New York: Fleming H. Ravell Co., 1910), p. 43.

106 *World Mission Conference, 1910: Report of Commission IV*, p. 321.

questions on the presuppositions and goals of mission, and so further eroding missionary confidence. Gerald Anderson says that while Edinburgh dealt with the 'how' of the missions, Jerusalem concentrated on the 'why.'[107] But in fact the Jerusalem meeting appears to have been much more diverse than it is portrayed in mission history. The mission churches, suddenly faced with the serious challenge of secularism in their own base, wavered, as it were, on the question of winning the world. The liberals led by Hocking, took full advantage of this hesitation and pushed many of their ideas into the Jerusalem Message.[108]

It was only later that those primarily interested in converting the world to Christ recognized the many theological compromises that had been made in the search for concensus at Jerusalem. The direction had shifted away from the Church towards the kingdom. There had been an implicit recognition of other faiths as part of the One Truth. And despite the many places where the Message emphasized the need to share the gospel, what stood out was the call to the people of other faiths to "hold fast to (their) faith in the unseen and the eternal" and "to cooperate with us against the evils of secularism."

Did the Jerusalem Message betray the missionary mandate? Archbishop William Temple, who chaired the meeting, did not think so. His understanding was that the mission was affirmed but within the context of a positive approach to people of other faiths. Writing to *The Student World* on the Message of Jerusalem he said that there was in the Message "... the sympathetic approach to non-Christian religions, with the sincere effort to appreciate the noble elements in them and the recognition of these as part of the one Truth." Commenting further, he held that there was "no effort to reach a valuation of those religions, that would be an impertinence; but there is an effort to sympathize and appreciate, and so to establish friendly contact."[109]

Many others were less impressed. They saw in the Jerusalem Message a betrayal of the apostolic obligation of the Church and too many theological compromises on the Christian attitude to other faiths. Kraemer interpreted Jerusalem as a crisis of faith and a loss of nerve on the

---

107 Jerald D. Gort, evaluating the Jerusalem *Message* in 1978, writes, "In contrast to the acclaim it received in Jerusalem, the Message drew a good deal of criticism later on: it allowed itself to be too easily informed by certain trends of the day; there was a certain note of syncretism in it; it may have concealed serious differences and crowded out important emphases through clever wording and composition." *International Review of Mission* LXVII, no. 267 (July 1978): 278.

108 It should be noted, however, that the continental delegates prepared a statement that was at variance with the Message. This was also published as part of the Findings.

109 "The Message of Jerusalem, 1928," *The Student World* XXI, no. 4 (October 28, 1928): 363.

evangelistic obligation of the Church.[110] Jerusalem threatened the assumption that the Christian faith had to replace all other religions, an assumption which with its many qualifications, modifications, and riders was still the hope, motivation, and goal of missions as understood at that time.

It is certain from the correspondence relating to the preparation of Tambaram that this meeting was intended to put mission theology back on its rails.[111] What was needed was a clear statement on the Christian faith, a convincing reason why this faith had to supplant other religious traditions, and a missionary approach that was adequate for the changing world. This is what Kraemer was asked to produce, and he did so admirably well. "Kraemer was in a strong position (to do this)," says W. A. Visser 't Hooft, "for no one could accuse him of failing to study, with real attention, the life of other religions and civilizations. This had started in Cairo, where he lived among the Islamic theologians wearing a fez, and under the name Sheikh Kraemer. And he had continued in the same way in Central Java, in Bali, among the Bataks in Sumatra and in India."[112]

This indeed was the case, for Kraemer had an adequate knowledge and understanding of other religious traditions. Kraemer could not be accused of misrepresenting the other faiths, nor of advocating an unsympathetic attitude towards them. He could only be challenged if one would challenge the presuppositions on which he based his whole argument. By insisting on interpreting the biblical message in entirely transcendental categories, by giving a narrow interpretation to the word 'revelation' and by assessing the other religions precisely from those standpoints, Kraemer succeeded in convincing the majority of the participants that the gosepl was in discontinuity with world religions. At Tambaram the church-centred mission theology that sought to replace the world religions regained its place in mission history.

Commenting on the impact of Kraemer's book and the Tambaram conference on the churches, Bishop S. Kulandran recounts the story of Kraemer visiting him and complaining that the Church seemed "withdrawn into a shell" and not leaning over towards the non-Christians. "Dr. Kraemer's complaint and observation were quite correct" wrote Bishop Kulandran. "I was sorry to have to tell him that what had produced that attitude had been his own book. Dr. Kraemer might have been surprised,

---

110 Discussing the issue Kraemer concluded, "all the evidence ... drives irresistably to the conclusion that the Christian Church is not at the end of the missionary enterprise in the non-Christian world, but just at the beginning," *Christian Message in a Non-Christian World,* p. 40.

111 Cf. Carl F. Hallencreutz, *Kraemer Towards Tambaram,* p. 253f.

112 W. A. Visser 't Hooft, *Has the Ecumenical Movement a Future* (Belfast: Christian Journals Ltd., 1974), pp. 58-59.

but it must be confessed that the book 'Christian Message in a Non-Christian World' did have the effect of making the church to a large extent break off conversation with the non-Christian religionists."[113]

Commenting on Kraemer's stress on the uniqueness of the gospel, Kulandran interpreted the Tambaram meeting (which he referred to as the Madras meeting) as an attempt to check the two significant developments in Christian thinking on other faiths represented by Hocking, and J. N. Farquhar's book *The Crown of Hinduism*. Kulandran felt that *Rethinking Missions* was largely the embodiment of the logical conclusion to which these ideas led and that "the Christian Church was posed with sardonic frankness the question whether it had anything to preach." Then he added this characteristically vivid comment on Kraemer's role in countering the ideas represented by Hocking's book:

> What Kraemer did was to seize hold of the main idea of the book with both hands and throttle it to death. Its ghost still occasionally haunts the theological field here and there. But as a full-blooded and serious figure to be reckoned with it certainly died with the appearance of Kraemer's book and the Madras conference of 1938. It is this punitive aspect of Kraemer's book that made the deepest impression on people. It was not that there was no constructive aspect, but once the chief item in the show was over, whether people stayed through the rest of the programme or not they paid little attention to it.[114]

We should now leave this discussion of the way the three conferences struggled to find a basis for the mission of the Church and turn to a consideration of their contribution to the contemporary search for models for a Christian attitude to other faiths, and to Hinduism in particular.

(b) Tambaram and Religions

Our deep disappointment with the Tambaram meeting lies not in its re-enthronement, this time with what appeared to have been a firm theological basis, of a church-centred theology of missions that sought the displacement of other faiths, but in its ignoring or totally rejecting some of the tentative ways in which people had been struggling to come to theological grips with Hindu-Christian relations at Edinburgh, at Jerusalem, and also in Tambaram; Hocking was by no means the only casualty of 1938.

It is interesting to note that while Kraemer had all his opponents lined up in his mind as he wrote his book, shooting them down one by

---

113 S. Kulandran, "The Renaissance of Non-Christian Religions and a Definition of Approach to Non-Christians," mimeographed paper presented to The Study on the Word of God and Men of Other Faiths (WCC Archives), Box 26.32.10, p. 25.
114 *Ibid.*, p. 26.

one, he rarely took them up for consideration in terms of what they had actually put forward. Nor could he. For Kraemer seems to have applied the 'totalitarian approach' to the writing of his book as well. So much so, that his interpretation of the Bible, his theology of religions, his missiology, and his understanding of the missionary approach were all "closely interconnected and linked into an integrated whole." The mutual interdependence of his arguments meant that it was difficult to be critical of Kraemer only in one aspect of his argument; one was either with him or against him!

This seems to be the reason why the discomfort of Hogg, Farmer, Chao, Chenchiah, and many others with Kraemer's position could not be represented in the Tambaram Message. In other words, to use Kraemer's own paradigm on Hindu–Christian relations, he was in a real sense in 'total discontinuity' with the discussions that had gone on about Hindu–Christian relations at Edinburgh and Jerusalem. This was the tragic reverse side of the success of the Tambaram meeting. For both at Edinburgh and at Jerusalem, particularly in the area of Christian–Hindu relations, there had been an intense soul-searching accompanied by the realization that when one treats the faith of another person one treads on 'holy ground.' Within this willingness to explore, which stands in contrast to the theological over-confidence of Tambaram, there are some lines of thought that could make a meaningful contribution to the contemporary debate.

The strength of the Edinburgh and Jerusalem discussions is that in both, those who presented Hinduism were willing to recognize the diversity of Hinduism and the fact that while there was much that had to be rejected (the merely social manifestations of religion), there was at the heart of Hinduism a searching and finding that must be a challenge to any Christian who wanted to relate to it. This observation is not based on assumptions but is reported by those who had actual dealings with Hindus and whose own faith had been challenged by the realization of what appeared to them to be a two-way inter-communion between God and man.

Edinburgh and Jerusalem said: "Let us deal with this reality." Kraemer refused to accept its existence. It is interesting to see how he analyses the intensely devotional religion of Ramanuja, which he admitted had many parallels to Christian devotion, and still insisted on interpreting it in terms of his naturalistic–monistic–vitalistic model of Hinduism. Hogg attempted here to give him a handle by distinguishing between faith as a personal response to God and faiths as religious systems in discontinuity with the gospel. Kraemer had no use for this either, but today this distinction has become the major interpretive principle for Wilfred Cantwell Smith, who sees the need to separate 'faith' and the 'cumulative tradition' in our understanding of the religious life of humanity.

Another important insight that was lost at Tambaram was Nicol Macnicol's concept of 'enrichment.' He argued that the Christian faith would enrich and deepen the Hindu faith by the 'moralization of its teaching' and the 'loosening of the *karma* bonds,' so that Hinduism itself would be "transformed into a habitation where the spirit of man can dwell in the faith of God and in the service of man." Chenchiah shared this belief that the encounter with Hinduism should transform Hinduism itself 'from within.' Macnicol saw a similar transformation of Christianity by the deepening of the Christian conceptions of God, man, and the world, and his concerns reflected some of the contemporary discussions on the purpose and goals of dialogue between faiths to which we shall return later.

In our view, the deepest disappointment at Tambaram was its failure to pick up the lines of thought presented by the Edinburgh meeting's Commission IV. Here the encounter of Hinduism with Christianity was compared to the contact between the Judaism-based Christian Church and the Hellenistic world. The Edinburgh discussions not only saw the Christian faith as a challenge to Hinduism, but also considered Hinduism as a formidable challenge to the Christian faith. "By the meeting with Hinduism," the report said, "the mind of the Church is deeply stirred." The participants saw this meeting as "pregnant with new possibilities" for here was the 'new emergency' that should drive the Church to search for deeper and more profound dimensions of the gospel. "New faith," the Commission believed, "is born out of new emergencies." The Hindu–Christian meeting was such a 'new emergency,' calling the Church to a radical reappraisal of its own theology.

Such a view was, of course, too much for Kraemer to handle for he had the mandate to put missions, which were almost derailed at Jerusalem, back on their tracks. In our concluding chapter we will return to this line of thought followed by Commission IV in 1910. For our own thoughts are in this direction of seeing the Christian–Hindu relationship as 'the new emergency' that should drive us back to a deeper reappraisal of our own faith and theology.

Part 2

The Quest for Relationship

CHAPTER V

In Search of Community

Seven months after the Tambaram Conference, the churches were faced with the reality of the Second World War. The International Missionary Council (IMC) was among those institutions that were severely affected by the war years. Commenting on the effect of the war on the IMC, Carl Hallencreutz observes that "Missionary theologians and missionary agencies had to face other questions than theoretical considerations of the Christian attitude to men of other faiths." Assistance to "the churches under the cross" and to "orphaned missions," he adds, was such a priority that the whole question of the approach to people of other faiths became "in a sense secondary." Its was not until the latter part of the 1950's that the Christian attitude to men of other religions again got high priority.[1] Before we turn to this period a brief consideration of the post-Tambaram developments is in place.

The Post-Tambaram Developments

Even though Kraemer had made a significant impact on the Tambaram meeting and its outcome, the Tambaram debate itself was inconclusive. Even those who had welcomed Kraemer's clear and forcefully argued rationale for mission had lingering questions on some of the strong positions he had taken vis-à-vis other faiths. The other divisive issue was Tambaram's emphasis on the Church.

Among those relating to the Hindus, E. Stanley Jones, to take one example, felt that the excessive emphasis on the Church in the Tambaram

---

1 Carl F. Hallencreutz, *New Approaches to Men of Other Faiths*, WCC, Geneva, 1970, p. 40.

Message seemed to limit the work of God to the Church.[2] Already in 1910 Jones had responded to the questionnaire of the Edinburgh meeting suggesting the Kingdom of God as the broad concept for understanding the relationship with Hinduism. Some of the other Indian theologians like Chenchiah and Chakkarai took Jones' side and felt that the Tambaram Message left little room for a creative understanding and appropriation of the religious and spiritual elements manifest in Hinduism.[3] Others, like P. D. Devanandan, welcomed the emphasis on the Church, but did not fully agree with Kraemer's interpretation of Hindu–Christian relations. To this we shall return later.

Whitby and Willingen

After several years of preoccupation with war, the IMC began to incorporate Tambaram's evangelistic emphasis at its next meeting, held at Whitby, Canada in 1947. There was no attempt at a fresh discussion of the Christian attitude to people of other faiths, for Whitby assumed that despite the dislocation resulting from the war, and perhaps also because of it, the assumptions and policies on missions worked out at Tambaram were still valid. What Whitby sought, therefore, was "fresh insight on the broad strategy of the missionary task" in a world ravaged by war.[4]

The war had also heightened a sense of history and of its revolutionary motion towards the future. Hence Whitby did not attempt to make too many distinctions within the human community. What was important was a relevant message that addressed the needs not only of individuals and nations but of the whole human race. Feliciano V. Carino has this to say in a recent assessment of Whitby's comparative silence on the question of relations with other faiths:

> At Madras ... much attention was given to the distinctiveness of the Christian message embodied in the Bible in relation to the non-Christian world into which it is to be brought. While Whitby did not disavow the importance of affirming the differentia between the Word of God and words of man, its attention seems to have been less fixed upon the question of the 'continuity' and 'discontinuity' of the gospel than upon the question of its relevance. As one Whitby participant succinctly put it, the critical issue for the Church's mission is not so much the search for *Points of Contact* —a term drawn from the Madras debates— between the

2 E. Stanley Jones, *The Guardian* (Feb. 23, 1939): 101f.

3 Cf. V. Chakkarai, "The Kingdom of God vs. The Church at Tambaram Conference," *The Guardian* (April 6, 1939): 197-98.

4 C. W. Ranson, ed., *Renewal and Advance* (London: Edinburgh House Press, 1948), p. 6f.

gospel and the non-Christian world, but the search for the gospel's relevance in terms of the stark realities of history.[5]

Whitby and the next meeting of the IMC at Willingen, Germany, in 1952 are important for our discussion of the Christian attitude to people of other faiths, for in our opinion they represent one of the major theological streams within the ecumenical movement that would run parallel to the new discussions of the Christian relationship to people of other faiths that were to reopen in the late 50's. It is difficult to decide whether the more conservative evangelical attitude to people of other faiths that was represented at Whitby and also at Willingen, drawing on some of the missionary implications of the Tambaram report, or the more open attitude to other faiths that would result from the discussions in the late 50's, was the true heir of the Tambaram meeting. Kraemer himself qualified the positions he had taken at Tambaram, thus enabling a fresh discussion of the Christian attitude to other faiths. But Willingen, following Whitby's example, paid too little attention to this question, as it was keen to spell out what it considered to be "the missionary obligation of the Church":

> It is open to us to do again what our brethren three centuries before us set their hearts and hands to do. We must take up the cutting edge of our confidence and our commitment and, with urgency and intensity, seek to bring the world to acknowledge and serve the kingship under which we stand. The conflict is on between Him whom God in His almighty purpose has raised up and made both Lord and Christ and the rival loyalties and commitments which govern the hearts and minds of men of our time. The missionary task of the Church is to make its obedience to the Lordship of Christ plain and persuasive wherever this Lordship is still unknown and still unacknowledged.[6]

Referring to the "total missionary task," Willingen affirmed that the Church was called to carry out his work "to the ends of the earth, to all the nations, and to the completion of time." "No place is too far or too near for the exercise of mission" said the report. "The command 'go forth' requires the Church to exercise its mission both in the actual area where the Church is already established and in an area where it is not yet established." And on the basis of this obligation it drew out the following implication for the Church's attitude to people of other faiths:

---

5 Feliciano V. Carino, "Partnership in Obedience," *International Review of Mission* LXVII, no. 267 (July 1978): 322.

6 Norman Goodall, ed., *Missions Under the Cross: Addresses Delivered at the Enlarged Meeting of the Committee of the IMC* at Willingen, Germany, 1952, with Statements Issued by the Meeting (London: Edinburgh House Press, 1953), pp. 238-39. The five themes discussed at Willingen were expressive of its mood: The Missionary Obligation of the Church; The Indigenous Church; The Role of the Missionary Society in the Present Situation; Vocation and Training; Reviewing the Pattern of Missionary Activity.

This means that the Church must direct its mission to those places and societies where men are living by a faith that denies or rebels against the faith of Christ, whatever form that faith may take.[7]

This church-centred view of missions, however, came under sharp attack at Willingen itself. J. C. Hoekendijk, for example, challenged this thinking as primarily interested in transplanting the Church. In his view the Church was only an instrument of God's redemptive action in the world, and therefore "a church-centric missionary thinking is bound to go astray because it revolves around an illegitimate centre."[8]

In fact the whole attempt to formulate a theological basis for mission under the concept of the "missionary obligation of the Church" became too controversial and the meeting was unable to adopt a resolution. The Willingen meeting was nevertheless a very important milestone in the ecumenical discussions, for it introduced a number of key concepts, such as *Missio Dei* (first coined by Karl Hartenstein), the trinitarian basis for mission and the affirmation of the relationship between mission and unity. These are outside the immediate scope of our present discussion.[9]

It is important to note that the attitude of countering the liberal ideas on relationships with people of other faiths emphasized at Tambaram was reaffirmed at Willingen and became one of the main streams within the Protestant churches both inside and outside the World Council of Churches. In fact one of the deep suspicions at Whitby, held only a year before the formation of the WCC, was that the evangelical emphasis would be lost within the World Council when large and established churches joined its membership.[10] Discussions also took place at Willingen on the IMC's becoming part of the WCC and these may have induced those with more conservative evangelical leanings within the IMC to affirm more clearly the evangelistic dimension of the Church's relationship to people of other faiths.

These tendencies were clear in the report which the meeting adopted on "The Indigenous Church — The Universal Church in its Local Setting." While emphasizing the Church's need to incorporate "into the service of Christ whatever cultural values it may have been given by God's grace" the report recommended that the local church be not rooted "but *related* to the soil." There was, of course, the emphasis that one should

---

7 *Ibid.,* p. 242.

8 J. C. Hoekendijk, "The Church in Missionary Thinking," *International Review of Mission* XLI, no. 163 (1952): 332.

9 In 1963 Lesslie Newbigin, who had played a crucial role in drawing up the Willingen statement on "The Missionary Calling of the Church," spelt out the trinitarian basis for mission. See CWME study pamphlet no. 12, *The Relevance of Trinitarian Doctrine for Today's Mission* (London: Edinburgh House Press, 1963).

10 Cf. Arthur P. Johnston, *A Study of the Theology of Evangelism in the International Missionary Council, 1921–1961* (Geneva: WCC Library, 1969) –mimeographed thesis.

strive to outgrow the 'foreignness' of the Church 'with all possible speed.' At the same time the report advised the younger Church to take "a positive and yet a critical attitude to the national cultures" recognizing, as the report warned, "the intimate dependence of these cultures on religions and philosophical concepts which differ fundamentally from the basic tenets of the Christian faith."[11] The overall note was one of caution against possible syncretism and the loss of the sense of mission:

> At a time when religious relativism and syncretism are rampant, it must be made abundantly clear that Christ's Lordship is a unique Lordship. There are, therefore, situations in which churches have the duty to sever themselves completely from those elements in cultures which are directly antagonistic to the Christian faith.

And yet, the authors were aware that such an isolation of the church from the culture could not be a permanent solution:

> The churches have to return to the task of seeking to fill cultural forms with Christian substance; to transform, under the power and guidance of the Holy Spirit, the ideas, practices, and traditions of the people, so that the Christian message may become an integral part of the life and experience of the people.[12]

Willingen appears to have represented the typical attitude to people of other faiths and cultures prevalent in the Protestant churches in general. It was not overly critical of other faiths, but it sought to replace them. It did not reject the other cultures but it was excessively cautious about relating to them. Even though it admitted at the theoretical level that aspects of these cultures could be transformed and filled with Christian meaning, the fear of syncretism and compromise resulted in the isolation and alienation of the Church from the local culture and religious life. The primary motivation for a Christian relationship with other faiths in these situations can only be understood in terms of the 'missionary obligation of the Church.' It is of interest to note here that despite the fears nurtured by some within the IMC, the WCC in its formative years inherited an attitude to other faiths very much in keeping with that of Whitby and Willingen.

The report of Section II of the Amsterdam Assembly on "The Church's Witness to God's Design," received unanimously by the Assembly, made the following bold proclamation:

> Three things are perfectly plain:
> All we need to know concerning God's purpose is already revealed in Christ.

---

11 Norman Goodall, *Missions Under the Cross, op. cit.,* p. 196.
12 *Ibid.,* pp. 196-97.

It is God's will that the gospel should be proclaimed to all men everywhere.

God is pleased to use human obedience in the fulfilment of His purpose.[13]

Building on this premise, the Amsterdam report sought to describe the Christian relationship to others primarily in terms of witness: "To the Church, then," the report continued, "is given the privilege of so making Christ known to men that each is confronted with the necessity of a personal decision, yes or no." It went even further to categorize the world into those who believed and those who did not:

> Those who obey are delivered from the power of the world in which sin reigns, and already, in the fellowship of the children of God, have the experience of eternal life. Those who reject the love of God remain under His judgement and are in danger of sharing in the impending doom of the world that is passing away.[14]

It is significant that Amsterdam, like Whitby and Willingen, had no special Section on other faiths; nor did it make any attempt to define the Christian attitude to any given religious tradition. In fact, the whole tradition of dealing with each of the major religious traditions of humankind, so prominent at the earlier meetings of the IMC, ceased with the Tambaram meeting. Kraemer's concept of 'discontinuity' and his tendency to classify all religious life as 'human attempts' had the effect of levelling all religious traditions into one common cluster of reality to which the gospel had to relate. The question after Tambaram was not how Christianity related to Hinduism, Islam, Buddhism, etc. It was, rather put in terms of the gospel on the one side and non-Christian religious traditions on the other. This was a very unfortunate development. The very rich discussions led by D. S. Cairns (at Edinburgh), Nicol Macnicol (Jerusalem), and Kraemer (Tambaram) on Hinduism, for example, was not to appear again with the same specificity in later ecumenical considerations. A shift had taken place from an examination of actual doctrines and beliefs and how they were experienced and practised in other faiths to a general consideration of 'religions.' This tendency would be corrected only much later when 'dialogue' became a reality within the WCC.

A New Beginning

The turbulence caused by the Second World War was only one of the factors affecting missionary thinking in the 40's. Much more important from the perspective of Christian relations with other faiths were the

---

13 W. A. Visser 't Hooft, ed., *The First Assembly of the WCC* held at Amsterdam, August 22–September 4, 1948 (New York: Harper and Brothers, 1949), p. 64.
14 *Ibid.*

developments in the East. The independence of India in 1947, the Communist revolution in China in 1949, the war in Korea, the resurgence of religions, the rise of nationalism, etc., demanded a thorough re-evaluation of the problems and prospects of missions, certainly in the way they related to people of other faiths.[15] In contrast to Whitby's confidence that the difficult days of mission at last lay behind with the end of the Second World War, M. A. C. Warren had warned in Willingen "that the most testing days of the Christian mission in our generation lie just ahead."[16]

Kraemer was among those who agreed with such a judgement. As an active missionary and ecumenical theologian Kraemer was aware that the religious resurgence of Africa and Asia and the increasing impact of Eastern religions would pose fundamental challenges to the Christian assumptions about other religious traditions. In his later writings Kraemer attempted to correct some of the postions he had taken at Tambaram in order to prepare for what he called the "coming dialogue."[17] Commenting on this development, M. M. Thomas said that "in the post-war world, Kraemer himself had turned post-Kraemerian," and that the search "to discover a new positive approach to the relation between the gospel of Christ and man's spiritual quest in religion and secularism" appeared to be the only way forward. "There are signs today," he added, "that in the area of the theology of mission, a post-Kraemer approach is emerging with Kraemer's own blessing."[18]

Something of this change of mood in relation to other faiths was evident at the WCC's Second Assembly in 1954 at Evanston. The emphasis on evangelism and the need to preach the gospel to all the nations was very much there, but unlike the Amsterdam statement, the Evanston declaration was clothed in studied humility:

> ... Where the gospel has found true lodgement in men's hearts, they have been inspired with compassionate desire to share it with their fellows. The love of Christ constrains them through their understanding of His death for all men. It impels them, in loving gratitude to Him to whom alone they owe their salvation, to share with others the unspeakable benefits they have themselves received, so that all may enter into the joy of the Lord.[19]

---

15 Cf. Rodger C. Bassham, "Seeking a Deeper Theological Basis for Mission," *International Review of Mission* LXVII, no. 267 (July 1978): 329.

16 Norman Goodall, ed., *The Christian Mission and the Cross, op. cit.,* p. 40.

17 In his later books like *World Cultures and World Religions, Religion and Christian Faith,* etc. Kraemer concentrated on man's religious consciousness and on the need to have more effective communication between Christians and non-Christians. He did not, however, give up his stand on 'discontinuity' and he refused to accept Hogg's distinction between faith and faiths.

18 M. M. Thomas, *The Christian Response to the Asian Revolution* (London: SCM Press, 1966), pp. 94-95.

19 W. A. Visser 't Hooft, ed., *The Evanston Report: The Second Assembly of the WCC,*

It is significant that the word 'share' reappeared at Evanston in relation to evangelism. The Jerusalem Message had preferred this word to other words like 'proclaim,' 'announce' etc., as being more relational, but it had been rejected at Tambaram because of the emphasis on 'announcing' the gospel with the call to man 'to make a decision.' But it is even more significant that the Evanston report, unlike the one from Amsterdam, took special note of the developments in the world of other faiths:

> ... the renascence of non-Christian religions and the spread of new ideologies necessitates a new approach in our evangelizing task. In many countries especially in Asia and parts of Africa, these religious revivals are reinforced by nationalism and often present themselves as effective bases for social reform. It is not so much the truth of these systems of thought and feeling which makes the appeal, but rather the present determination to interpret and change oppressive conditions of life. Therefore they confront us not only as reformulated creeds but also as foundations for universal hope.[20]

Evanston was thus able to incorporate into its report the emphasis made by leaders from Asia, such as Paul Devanandan, D. T. Niles, and M. M. Thomas, who believed that the resurgence of other faiths involved not only a revival of religions, but also attempts at nation-building and a search for community life, which the newly independent nations badly needed in the post-colonial period. Christians dared not ignore their own part in this search.

The report, however, contrasted these hopes "based on man's persistent desire to be master of his own destiny" to the "gospel hope" built on "God's promise," and so sought to maintain the necessity of evangelism in the new context. And yet, the mood was different:

> The Christian will proclaim the gospel of God's judgement upon all human quests and questionings. But in his approach to men of other faiths he will humbly acknowledge that God has "not left himself without witness." Wherever he finds light he will not try to quench it but bear witness to Jesus Christ, the true light — "the light which lighteth every man."[21]

Evanston gave the impression of being hesitantly accommodative of the realities faced by the younger churches in Asia. With no firmly stated theological basis to deal with the resurgent religions, it fell back on the escape route taken in both the Jerusalem and Tambaram Messages, namely, to describe the non-Christian as 'a man' and not as someone possessing and living by a faith. "The ambassador of Christ," the report

---

1954 (New York: Harper and Brothers Publishers, 1955), p. 99. (The report of Section II on "Evangelism: The Mission of the Church to those Outside Her Life.")
20 *Ibid.*, p. 100.
21 *Ibid.*, p. 106.

stated, "is primarily concerned not with the faith that man possesses, though he should understand it with sympathetic insight, but with him as he really is, a sinner like himself and one for whom Christ died."[22]

Evanston's immediate response to the crisis emerging from the challenge of resurgent religions in Asia was to call for the injection of more humility into Christian relations with neighbours of other faiths. It stressed "identification and alongsideness," "the demonstration of the transforming power" of the gospel. "The seeds of the kingdom," it maintained, "are not words and arguments, but the children of the kingdom themselves, scattered and sown in the field of the world" and these children, it concluded, should "walk the way of the cross, in complete self-sacrifice and faithfulness unto death."[23]

Evanston's answer, however, could only be partial, for the time was ripe for a more extensive consideration within the ecumenical movement of Christian relations with people of other faiths and this would in fact go beyond Tambaram. It was not surprising therefore that only a year after Evanston the WCC Central Committee decided to launch a specific study on the "Word of God and the Living Faiths of Men" to pick up the question where Tambaram had left it. We shall now turn to this study.

The Issues for the New Debate

Which major theological issues about Christian relationships with other faiths were left unresolved at Tambaram? How could they be followed up in the new situation? These were major concerns of those who met at Davos, Switzerland in 1955 to prepare the ground for the study to be jointly launched by the WCC Department of Studies and the IMC. The meeting was envisaged as "merely a first informal reopening of the 'Tambaram debate'," but there was also a sense of 'history being made' for the participants were conscious of breaking "a virtual silence of twenty years on the great issues involved."[24] The Davos meeting defined the basic question unresolved at Tambaram in these words:

> Must the attitude of the evangelist be that Christianity should *supplant* other religions? Or can it content itself with the conviction that Christianity is the *fulfilment* of other religions? Are there still further alternatives — those that hold that in Christ a *transformation* has taken place, or that in Christ *all* religions are brought under judgement?[25]

22 *Ibid.*
23 *Ibid.*, p. 107.
24 Consultation on "Christianity and Non-Christian Religions," Davos, Switzerland, July 21-25, 1955 (WCC Archives: Record of Discussions, Introduction), Box 26.32.10, p. 1.
25 *Ibid.*

The Davos meeting could, however, only suggest some of the directions in which further exploration could proceed. Suggesting that at Tambaram Kraemer's book had primarily been intended to "check the tendency to syncretism," Davos held that the situation had completely changed: "The temptation that besets many of the younger churches at the present time is of a different character. It is the temptation to avoid contact with non-Christians."[26]

It advocated on the one hand a "thorough scientific study of the non-Christian religious systems, in their classical and modern forms," but focussing not on the systems as such but on man in "his faith, his hopes, his fears," as he is shaped by the vital spiritual forces within the non-Christian religions. On the other hand, it called for a "fresh study of the Bible not only to understand what the Bible says about the non-Christian religions, but even more to hear afresh the word of God to man, and to learn to discover the sign of the times in the light of God's word."

The Davos formulation and the programme it suggested were seen by some to be inadequate for reaching the heart of the matter, especially in the context of the resurgent religions to which Christians in younger churches had to relate. Th. van Leeuwen, assessing the meeting, claimed that there had been real confusion on what the issues today should be. "It was, generally speaking, to a large extent a discussion which almost as well could have taken place at the Tambaram conference," for in his view, "real new viewpoints have so far not been introduced into the discussion."[27]

Harry B. Partin, commenting on the struggles to take the study forward, said that people had soon realized that more was required "than a revival of an old debate which had its own setting, terms, and personalities," and that the way forward was to make the debate truly ecumenical by calling on the churches living among people of other faiths to share their experience and struggle:

> ... The problems of this encounter must be a matter of serious concern for the churches in the West and the missionaries from the West, but it must be strongly emphasized that it is primarily the peculiar problem of the churches in Asia and Africa. In an age of ecumenical contact and of theological and cultural exchange, churches and theologians from other parts of the world can render some aid, but it is the churches 'in loco' which must undertake the actual encounter. It is their peculiar God-given task which nobody can take from them or take over from them. ... [28]

---

26 *Ibid.,* p. 4.

27 A. Th. van Leewen, "How Should We Continue the Post-Tambaram Discussions?" (WCC Archives: Division of Studies, 1956), box no. 26.32.10 –mimeographed paper.

28 Harry B. Partin, "The Word of God and the Living Faiths of Men," *Occasional Bulletin* (Research Department, Church Assembly, and Overseas Council, no date),

This was an important moment in the ecumenical movement for this particular insight into the method of carrying the study forward had a decisive impact on the future discussions of Christian relations to people of other faiths. Hitherto in spite of the substantial contribution of Asians to the ongoing discussions, the debate itself had been led by, and based primarily on the experience of, missionaries. Henceforth, at least from the perspective of Hinduism, persons such as S. Kulandran and D. T. Niles from Sri Lanka and P. D. Devanandan and M. M. Thomas from India were to set the tone. The study itself acquired a broad base, enabling the East Asia Christian Conference also to contribute to the ongoing discussions.

The Word of God and the Living Faiths of Men

When the first major consultation on "The Word of God and the Living Faiths of Men" met in Bossey, Switzerland, in July 1958, S. Kulandran of Jaffna, Ceylon, was asked to make the major contribution on "Non-Christian Faiths and Faith — Our Attitude Towards Them." His presentation actually re-opened the Tambaram debate in the context of Hinduism.

Kulandran criticized both the excessive and outright rejection of non-Christian religions and their uncritical acceptance. For him, the Christian–Hindu encounter was a reality of life:

> To us non-Christian systems are not speculative formulations; they are living things pressing hard on us. The attitude to be adopted towards them is to us not academic, but a matter of life and death. We have the advantage, that Western Christians did not have for a long time, of knowing those systems from close quaraters. We do not therefore run the risk of being precipitated into any opinion because of the surprise born of sudden discovery. In spite of what the missionaries were trying to tell our fathers and grandfathers, most of them knew of the austerity of renunciation, the tender piety and the really breathtaking abandon of devotion that may be encountered in non-Christian religions. . . . [29]

From this perspective he criticized the positions taken by J. N. Farquhar and A. G. Hogg on Christian relations to Hinduism. In Kulandran's view, Farquhar's concept of the 'Crown of Hinduism' was undertaking "the risky adventure in the field of comparative religion." For Kulandran was convinced that Farquhar's method "had its conclusions ready before it started the inquiry," as the outcome of comparative religion almost entirely depended on the criteria adopted. His reservations, however, were based

---

pp. 5-6.

[29] Bossey Consultation on "The Word of God and the Living Faiths of Men," S. Kulandran's contribution on "Non-Christian Faiths and Faith — Our Attitude Towards Them" to Section I (WCC Archives) box no. 26.32.10, p. 4.

on the more serious question of whether Farquhar's inquiry really helped a Christian to relate to Hinduism. Kulandran had his doubts:

> The Farquhar school did not reap any of the benefits it had expected. Non-Christians were not greatly impressed by its show of impartiality; neither was the missionary able to secure the establishment of the superiority of Christianity.[30]

Kulandran also denied that one could take elements of a religion to compare or to affirm their closeness to those of another religion for "one tends to forget what the parts add up to." He recalled that underneath apparent similarities lie very deep differences:

> In reference to Christianity, we find that while Buddhism exalts ethics like Christianity, because of this very exaltation it dispenses with God. It exalts its ethics into the place of God ... Islam is monotheistic like Christianity, and because of its very monotheism denies the cardinal Christian doctrine of the Incarnation. In a sense, Vaishnavite Hinduism gladly accepts the doctrine of Incarnation, a little too gladly — but sets at naught what to us is the very point of the doctrine, by teaching a virtually unlimited number of incarnations, and including among the nine main ones, the Buddha, who has no use for God.[31]

"The common elements," he concluded, "may not be very common after all!"

Kulandran was also critical of the shift made at Tambaram from non-Christian religions to non-Christian individuals. Recalling that the Davos meetings had also tended to segregate man from his religion, he rejected A. G. Hogg's notion that the gospel could be in 'continuity' with the faith of the individual yet 'discontinuous' with his religious tradition. Kulandran held that the individual could not be segregated from the system for in spite of all the autonomy, an individual's mind and life were "shaped by the beliefs and systems prevailing in his country." When one broke with any system, Kulandran contended, one entered into another system. And he gave an illustration from Hindu piety, with which he was most familiar:

> Tukaram's sublime piety was bestowed with single-minded determination on the image of Vithoba at Pandharpur, about which it has been said, "to the Western mind it is most incredible that the image of Vithoba could arouse ardent feelings of any kind save that of repulsion." His biographers say that to forget Tukaram's veneration of the image of Vithoba "would be to forget half of Tukaram's spiritual life, wrapped up as it was so closely with the condescending love the god was supposed to have shown in accepting incarnation at Pandharpur."[32]

30 *Ibid.*, p. 5.
31 *Ibid.*, pp. 5-6.
32 *Ibid.*, p. 9

Kulandran did not deny that non-Christians occasionally rose to heights which could be considered 'Christian.' "But," he said, "the heights and depths are usually in the system to which they belong."

Having rejected both the Farquhar and the Hogg options, Kulandran agreed more with Kraemer than with Kraemer's opponents in insisting that Hinduism, being itself a distinctive and total religion, could not be compared with Christianity. He went even further to affirm that since Christians believed that "God saves man in Jesus Christ," it was difficult for them also to affirm that "either the thought systems or the thinking of individuals" in other religions also showed "evidence of the same saving knowledge":

> All that I can say is as far as I can see, non-Christian thinking, both of systems and individuals, seems to be different from what I know to be God's revelation for the salvation of man.[33]

But Kulandran parted company with Kraemer in refusing to draw negative conclusions based on his positive affirmation of the Christian belief that God saves humankind in Christ. He refused to call the other religions 'disbelief' or 'human attempts.'

On the question of whether there was salvation in other religious traditions, Kulandran said that "argument, even theological argument" may not settle the matter. "I am not willing to set bounds to the mercy of God. May not God deal with those who do not accept the gospel of Jesus Christ in love, as he deals with them in justice?" Kulandran believed that He might. "And this," he added, "not because of the non-Christian religion, but in spite of it."[34]

We have dealt with Kulandran's contribution at Bossey in some detail because it was representative of the general position taken by a number of Asian Christian theologians in relation to Hinduism who influenced the thinking within the ecumenical movement. It is significant that they did not take sides with Farquhar or even Hogg. Kulandran, as we have noted, rejected both the concepts of fulfilment and of separating the 'faith' of the Hindu from his religious tradition.

The Davos preparatory documents noted this almost with disappointment, seeking explanation:

> In spite of the Bangalore Continuation Committee, the tendency in India and Ceylon has been more to side with Kraemer than against him. Faced with the massive presence of the classical non-Christian religions like Hinduism, Theravadin Buddhism, and Islam, now mostly in a state of powerful renaissance, the theory of continuity seemed somewhat devoid of

---

33 *Ibid.*
34 *Ibid.*

meaning to the younger theologians. David Moses, P. D. Davanandan, and
D. T. Niles may be cited as representatives of this tendency.[35]

There were, of course, others like Chenchiah and Chakkarai who had great
difficulties with some of Kraemer's positions. But P. D. Devanandan, for
example, was deeply influenced by Kraemer's main thesis and defended the
'Church-centred' approach to mission.[36] D. T. Niles, as a young evangelist
from Ceylon, had attended the Tambaram conference and served as
secretary to Section I. Stephen Neill said that Niles was "at that time
feeling a little overwhelmed at finding himself in such an eminent company
of persons like Henry van Dunsen, Gerogia Harkness, Herbert Farmer,
Hendrik Kraemer, and others."[37] Kraemer did have an important impact
on both Niles and Kulandran.

But there was a fundamental difference in the way the Asian theologians interpreted and applied the insights Kraemer brought to Tambaram.
They looked at the non-Christian world not as something 'out there.' They
were part of it. They shared the cultural heritage of the past and the
present historical reality that shaped their relations. In the post-colonial
situation there was also the task of nation-building. What role should
Christians play in reconstructing the nation? What contributions could they
bring to the building of a community of people who had a variety of
cultures, languages, and religious beliefs and were now called to a life as
a nation? In other words, there were new questions about the relationship
of the Asian churches to their neighbours. These questions raised other
questions about their relationship to the older churches as well. In a
presentation to the World Student Christian Federation, Kraemer himself,
having traced the radical transformation that was taking place, summarized
the challenge faced by the younger churches in the following words:

> The transformation of the world situation outlined above has put the
> 'younger churches' overnight into a totally new environment. The task
> before them, the opportunity and temptations surrounding, beckoning, and
> menacing them, are so tremendous that it is no exaggeration to say that
> they face a superhuman summons. They must work out an entirely new
> relationship with the 'older churches' and Western missions, and with the

---

35 Mimeographed paper given as an introduction to the Davos meeting, author not
cited (WCC Archives), Box 26.32.10.

36 "For Tambaram again brought to the forefront a new sense of the solidarity and
community of the Christian world forces, a consciousness of the ecumenical aspect of
the world community of the Church Universal in which the younger and the older
churches, in whatever part of the world they may be, *function* together in the unity
that comes out of realizing their common compulsion to proclaim the gospel. The
church's chief responsibility is to function: and that church functions which spreads
abroad the evangel," P. D. Devanandan, "After Tambaram — What?" *The Guardian*
(Madras, January 26, 1939): 42.

37 Stephen Neill, *Men of Unity* (London, 1960), p. 131.

ecumenical movement; further they have to find their place in their own new world, usually as minorities surrounded by non-Christian cultures and religions, often under the shadow of not being accepted as truly 'belonging,' because of their origin in Western religious activity. They have to learn the art of Christian citizenship in nations which are going through difficult struggles. They are called to be in their own environment the vanguard of the Christian witness which is essentially the common task of all Christian churches in cooperation and mutual service.[38]

This description was a truer reflection of the context in which the Asian Christian theologians faced their task than was the simple assumption in the Davos preparatory paper that seemed to suggest that the Asians sided with Kraemer almost as a reaction against the resurgent religions. When it is said that Devanandan sided with the 'church-centred emphasis,' one should add that he did so in order to affirm the ecumenical understanding of 'the church' at Tambaram opening up new possibilities for relationship, partnership, and mutual support.[39]

We need to note here that the Asian theologians basically supported Kraemer's position that each religion had its own integrity and should be treated accordingly. Hinduism could not be divided into smaller pieces to see which would fit into a Christian conception of the world, or even to determine which of them could, when interpreted, be seen to be fulfilled by the Christian revelation. These Asians also believed that Christians had a witness to offer and a mission to fulfil within the life of the nation. But how should one serve, and what assumptions should one make about one's neighbour's faith and practice in carrying out this task and, most importantly, how should one find answers to these questions within the context of an ongoing, inevitable and, for the newly independent churches, a decisively significant relationship that had to be developed with neighbours of other faiths? Reality made all the difference to the Asian discussions, for persons like Devanandan, Niles, and M. M. Thomas, however sympathetic to Kraemer, had no option but to go beyond him. M. M. Thomas observed that Devanandan "was never satisfied with the destruction of the idea of fulfilment in the relation between the Christian faith and other religions, and has ever since been in a sense irritated with his Kraemerian self and struggling to get out of it into a more positive post-Kraemer understanding of Jesus Christ. . . ." We could say the same of other Asian theologians on the scene.[40]

---

38 Hendrick Kraemer, "History's Lessons for Tomorrows Missions" in Audrey Abrecht, ed., *Milestones in the History of Missionary Thinking* (Geneva: WSCF, no date), p. 205.

39 Carl F. Hallencreutz, *New Approaches to Men of Other Faiths*, pp. 32-33.

40 M. M. Thomas, *The Christian Response to the Asian Revolution*, p. 100.

As the Executive Secretary in the WCC Department of Evangelism (1953–59) D. T. Niles was also able to make a significant contribution to the development of this issue.

Emphasis on the Mission of God

In a semi-official volume *Upon the Earth*, Niles summarized the positions being taken within the ecumenical movement concerning other religions and offered his own assessment of the way in which the debate ought to move. Lesslie Newbigin says that this was one of the two books that tried to pull together "studies that involved the active participation of a great number of people in the five continents." In his view the moment of their writing marked "both the closing of one stage of the discussion and the initiation to a new stage."[41] In his work, Niles first gave a useful summary of the positions on Christian relations with other faiths taken within the ecumenical movement and their implications for the nature of the contact between Christian and Hindu.

The study showed that there was still a persistent view that Christianity should supplant other religions because they are of purely human origin. "An important variant of this attitude," Niles pointed out, "is that the Christian witness does not need to and, indeed, cannot express a judgement on other religions. Christianity and these religions are of two different kinds. So, what is permissible and effective is to set Christianity over against other religions, making the demand that those of other religions give up and embrace Christianity instead." Here evangelization in the sense of challenging others to accept Christianity is the "one responsibility of the evangelist."[42]

The second point of view saw Christianity as the fulfilment of other religions. There were many strands of this view, but the predominant ones held that "there is in these religions a real yearning for God which is truly a partial response to His approach, and this yearning is truly met by Christ." Niles pointed out that those who held the fulfilment approach had gone beyond Kraemer's idea of 'unexpected fulfilment' of God's wrestling with man in his religious consciousness to the view that the deep yearning in these religions was reflected in their teachings as well and that "these teachings find their full meaning and significance in and are truly construed as pointers to Jesus Christ." This approach supported the study

---

41 Lesslie Newbigin's Foreword to D. T. Niles' *Upon The Earth: The Mission of God and the Missionary Enterprise of the Churches* (London: Lutterworth Press, 1962), p. 7. The other book on *The Missionary Nature of the Church* was written by J. Blauw. Both were written at the request of the Central Committee of the WCC and the Missionary Studies of the IMC to summarize the debate and to take it further.

42 *Upon the Earth*, pp. 227-28.

of comparative religions in order to isolate truths from the whole body of belief to "show that these truths point to the truth in Jesus Christ."[43]

The third position followed the idea of Hogg, maintaining that there was in all religions the possibility of 'faith' between God and man —a possibility which is realized by many persons— yet that in Christianity this possibility had become a free gift to all. A Christian must 'listen' to a person of another religious tradition in order to understand his 'faith' and to acknowledge it. "The Christian Gospel must then be addressed to that faith in order that faith may be made secure."

The dialectic approach to other religions, presented by Niles as the fourth position, maintained that in Jesus all religions were brought to judgement, and that Jesus remained the judge of all religions, including Christianity. As Kraemer had argued, the messenger of the gospel in this view stood alongside his hearers as the emissary of the gospel to them. "The Christian is in the world; the gospel is over against it."[44]

Niles characterized the study's fifth position as the "view which held that the motive of Christian witness should be not one of seeking to make Christians of adherents of other religions, but of so presenting Jesus Christ to them that He Himself will become for them the point of reconception with respect to their own religion."[45] He pointed out that this view implied the belief that in the course of time there would emerge a new religion in which all religions, including Christianity, would be comprehended.

In this view Christianity had to give as well as receive, so that the true method of approach was one of cooperation. "Worshipping and working together, Christians and those of other faiths will help one another to a fuller understanding and a more comprehensive acceptance of all that it means when one says 'I believe in God'." Niles commented that the vastly different attitudes represented among those who were "equally committed to the Church's task of proclaiming the Gospel" raised the question as to whether the participants in this discussion were "sufficiently agreed on what the discussion should be about or on the frame of thought within which the debate should take place."[46]

He attributed the 'sharp disagreement' among the different positions to the fact that they were dealing in one way or another with Christianity and other religions as such, even when the gospel was taken as the centre and content of the Christian component of the discussion. He felt that the

43 *Ibid.*, p. 228.
44 *Ibid.*, p. 229.
45 *Ibid.*
46 *Ibid.*, p. 230.

way forward would be to shift the discussion to a new framework "about the address of the gospel to men in their several homes."[47]

Here we see a parallel between Kulandran and Niles. Both of them wanted to shift the discussion from the religious system to man, but both insisted that man should be seen as a religious person shaped and controlled by the religious belief in which he was immersed. They disagreed with the emphasis of Jerusalem and Evanston that urged Christians to address the Hindu or the Muslim not as a Hindu or a Muslim, but as a fellow man. Instead, they wanted the gospel to be addressed not to Hinduism or Islam but to a Hindu man or a Muslim man; to men in their several 'homes'; a Hindu could not be understood outside Hinduism which was his home; and yet it was to a Hindu we should relate and not to Hinduism.

Niles reached these positions by distinguishing between two components of the discussions, namely, the Christian and the non-Christian. On the Christian side, Niles agreed with Kraemer that what was decisive was the Christian message and not Christianity. He felt that much of the difficulty that non-Christians had with the Christian message had to do with their identifying it with the empirical Christianity which appeared as "an arrogant and aggressive religion" with a body of beliefs, ethical norms, cultic practices, and cultural values. Niles had more problems than Kraemer had with empirical Christianity; seen through Asian eyes, it also had a colonial orientation and a missionary ethos, and was therefore judged to be an alienating and destroying factor by those concerned with preserving Asian culture and community life.[48]

> All this means that the discussion is not about the relation between the religion, or the religious life, of Christians and that of those who are not Christians; nor is it about the relation between the religious beliefs of Christians and the beliefs of those who are not Christians; rather, it is about the operation of the gospel itself among those who are Christians and among those who are not. It is when the gospel is preached that the relation we are seeking to understand is set up. ... [49]

Regarding the non-Christian component of the discussion, Niles again argued for a new framework of understanding. "In the history of the discussion we are speaking about," he said, "the non-Christian factor has been variously defined as a non-Christian faith, non-Christian religions, a non-Christian world." In Niles' view, none of these items could respond

---

47 See pages 230-32 for the full discussion. Niles takes up this question for a fuller discussion in his book *The Preacher's Task and the Stone of Stumbling*, The Lyman Beecher Lectures for 1957 (New York/London, 1958), p. 80ff.

48 Cf. Christopher L. Furtado, *The Contribution of Dr. D. T. Niles to the Church Universal and Local* (Madras: Christian Literature Society, 1978), p. 192ff.

49 *Upon the Earth*, p. 233.

adequately to the complexity of the situation to which the gospel and the Christian had to relate.

When one asks the question "What is the object to which the gospel is addressed?" the answer surely is the "world." "But what is the nature of this world?" Niles asked. To begin with, this is the world over which God rules and which, at the end, he will judge. This is the world that God has loved in Jesus Christ. The world at times rejoices in him and at other times is rebellious against him. In it there is much truth, beauty, and goodness as well as faith towards God and love towards man; it is very much a religious world.[50]

The point Niles wished to make was that the gospel was addressed to a world which was no stranger to God, and to those to whom God was no stranger. There was faith in the world. And therefore Niles agreed with Hogg that it was legitimate to ask, what relation the gospel, when proclaimed, established between itself and such faith. But he rejected the idea that the answer held the key to an understanding of the relation between the Christian gospel and the non-Christian world, for the nature of the non-Christian world was not determined by the presence in it of persons of faith. While agreeing with Hogg that the connection between the gospel and non-Christian faith was an important component to our understanding, Niles also believed with Kraemer that the non-Christian world was determined more "by those complete systems of life and belief which are able to sustain themselves without accepting the gospel of Jesus Christ and, therefore, cannot accept it without being subverted by it."[51]

It is characteristic of Niles, however, that he refused to accept that the gospel was addressed to these totalitarian systems either. "It is addressed to the world of those whose life and thought these religions are a part."

> The Christian message is not addressed to other religions, it is not about other religions; the Christian message is about the world. It tells the world a truth about itself — God loved it and loves it still; and, in telling the truth, the gospel bears witness to a relation between itself and the world. It is this relation which is the subject of our discussion.[52]

Niles elaborated the significance of this understanding not only in the rest of his report, but also in the numerous books that he wrote on reconceiving missions in the post-colonial period.[53] We should, however, limit our

---

50 *Ibid.*

51 *Ibid.*, p. 234.

52 *Ibid.*, p. 235.

53 Of special interest are: *The Preacher's Task and the Stone of Stumbling* (1957), *The Preacher's Calling to be Servant* (1958), *Whereof We are Witnesses* (1965), *The Message and its Messengers* (1967). Also of significance are the reports of the EACC on other religions which he often drafted.

discussion to his specific influence on the ongoing discussion that we are
here tracing.

Niles' major contribution to the debate lay in his insistence on changing the framework of the discussion from 'Christian–Hindu' into 'God-
World.' Though he seems to have drawn his inspiration from Kraemer's
emphasis on 'the Christian message' in a 'non-Christian world,' Niles made
copious use of Kraemer's work, and appropriated from it significant points
to start a new debate. To begin with, Niles looked at the world —the
arena where human life unfolded— as a differentiated, complex, and
ambiguous reality, of which the world of religious systems was an important component. He also refused to regard Christian revelation as totally
unrelated to the religious life of man. Since the world was made by God
and God was actively related to it in love and salvation there was a
mission of God already present in the world before one could begin to
talk about a Christian relationship to other faiths. Since religious life was
part of 'the world,' Niles concluded that God's mission was also active in
the religious life of man, working towards the fulfilment of God's purpose
for the world. "God is *always* busy with *every* man, because each man is
made in the image of God."[54]

Even though Niles recognized that when we deal with man we are
dealing with man in his religion, he maintained a distinction between man
in the totality of his existence and man in his religious system. "There is
a true sense," he claimed, "in which each man's religion can be more or
can be less than his religious system."[55] Each man was less than his
religious system when he could not or did not fulfil the ideals held up by
the system to which he belonged. It was also true to experience that
man's religious life could and did transcend all that could be described
within the religious system, for people had experiences, intuitions, and faith
perspectives that went beyond the narrow confines of their own or any
other religious system. This was true to the experience of both Christians
and non-Christians. In Niles' opinion this 'overspill in the religious life' of
man was an area where there could be much conversation and interaction
between a Christian and a person of another faith.[56]

Niles also examined the implications of the belief that God's love for
the world was expressed in God's act in Jesus Christ, and argued that this
supreme act of God within His mission in the world was also something

---

54 *The Preacher's Task and the Stone of Stumbling,* p. 92.
55 *Ibid.*
56 Furtado points out that this concept of 'overspill' came into the discussion as a
result of a Muslim speaking about an 'overspill' in his religious experience which could
not be accounted for in terms of his own religious tradition. The term however accu-
rately describes what Niles was after. He saw this 'overspill' as the actual 'point of
contact' between Christians and persons of other faith.

that had to be 'already present' in the world before any reflection on the Christian relation to the Hindu or Buddhist could begin. This 'previousness of Christ' or 'the presence of Christ in the history of other faiths' thus became an important concept in Niles' thought. He took this idea to the point of arguing that when one was in conversation with a Hindu one could discern Christ at work and learn more about him.

From all the foregoing we can note that Niles objective was to change the framework of the discussion. He claimed the world for God; he saw the act of God in Jesus Christ as an act within the total mission of God in the whole of human life. The Christian discussion about relationships to the non-Christian world was, in his view, primarily about the 'message and the messengers' and how they were linked to the ongoing mission of God in the world.

What then was evangelism all about? Niles argued that the Christian activity in the world was *to be part* of the mission of God, but an important part of it, for the Christian's task was to announce what God had done in Christ, which had made all the difference to the world. What God had done in Christ was not part of the general way in which God related to the world. It was a special act with an eschatalogical dimension. Christians were that part of humanity which had come under the grip of this mission and they had the task of calling others to become part of a mission which would have a decisive impact on the whole of human life, including religious life.[57]

One of the essential features of Niles' treatment of the question was the eschatalogical framework that he gave to the whole consideration; this did not evoke such questions as "Who will be saved?" or "Does Christ fulfil Hinduism?" to the point of needing an immediate answer to argue for or against a positive relationship to other religions and their adherents. Once Niles had begun with the 'mission of God,' and looked at the world as 'that which God loves and wills to save,' other questions receded in importance and emphasis. Niles was thus able to say that the whole discussion of what happens when the Christian message was set in a non-Christian world had to be "pushed beyond the area of such questions as 'who will be saved?' into the area where the determining question is 'what does God require?' " For participation in the total mission of God and witnessing to it have become the basic rationale of Christian life.[58]

In the same way the whole question of 'fulfilment' must also be set in an eschatalogical context and seen in terms of a process rather than an event:

---

57 Niles develops this idea fully in his *Preacher's Calling to be Servant* (London: Lutterworth Press, 1960).
58 *Upon the Earth, op. cit.,* p. 244.

... the world at present is in the process of fulfilment so that, when we look at the process and precisely because we are looking at the process, it is impossible to describe it in any simple way. We see both the scaffolding and the building, both the work being done and the fruit of it. The very intricacy of the process lends truth to all the various types of assertions made about those relations which are the result of the Christian message being active in a non-Christian world.[59]

Niles' significant contribution to the ecumenical discussions was that by broadening or giving a new framework he enabled the younger churches to make greater sense of their own relation to the non-Christian world, which was no longer a world 'out there' 'to be occupied,' but one they had inherited, and where, together with persons of other faiths, they had to build communities. Niles claimed this world for God not only by citing natural theology, but by arguing that Christ was already present there inviting his church to join him and witness to him. This was the kind of framework that made sense for what others such as P. D. Devanandan and M. M. Thomas wanted to do, namely, to participate with the Hindus and everyone else in the building up of the nation.[60]

Christian Concern within Hinduism

P. D. Devanandan took Niles' argument that God in Christ was already active in the world —and therefore also within the society moulded by Hinduism— and worked out its implications for Christian–Hindu relations in the revolutionary situation in India. He quoted Niles as the basis for the section of his speech on "Witness in a World of Other Faiths" to the Third Assembly of the WCC in New Delhi:

The Christian witness does not grasp the true inwardness of his work where he does not see that God is previous to him in the life of the person whom he is seeking to win for the gospel, and also previous to him in whatever area he is seeking to make the gospel effective.[61]

The fact that the task of the Christian messenger was to witness to the gospel *in* the world where God was already active, Devanandan argued, meant that Christians were called to be *with* their fellowmen in their struggles in both religious and secular life. He therefore rejected such words as 'encounter,' 'confrontation,' and 'approach' as inappropriate to describe the nature of the relation between the Christian and the Hindu in contemporary India. For if we were to regard religious faith also as a

---

59 *Ibid.,* p. 245.
60 *Ibid.*
61 "Called to Witness," Address to the Third Assembly of the WCC, New Delhi, revised and printed in P. D. Devanandan, *Preparation for Dialogue* (Bangalore: The Christian Institute for the Study of Religion and Society, 1964), p. 189.

response to God, "it would be difficult for a Christian to deny that these deep inner stirrings of the human spirit" seen within the Hindu struggle to come to terms with contemporary revolution, "are in response to the creative activity of the Holy Spirit."[62] Addressing the first Assembly to meet in the Hindu context of Asia, he repudiated some of the earlier attitudes that had tended to ignore the work of God in other religious traditions:

> At best we can only confess our inability to understand God's ways with us men; at worst, we must blame ourselves for our blindness in refusing to believe that God is equally concerned with the redemption of people other than us, people who may not wholly agree with our understanding of God's being and His purpose for the world of His making.[63]

But what was new to the situation in Devanandan's view was that our ignorance of the religious environment no longer insulated us from its influence; nor could our indifference to it exclude us from its claims. For the resurgence of Hinduism was not just an attempt to interpret it to the contemporary world, but also a claim for its universal validity and a missionary purpose.[64]

In an earlier pamphlet on "The Gospel and the Hindu Intellectual," Devanandan had challenged the Jerusalem IMC meeting's attitude to secularism. For he was convinced that in the Indian context the rise of secularism had a different effect. "The position seems to have shifted since Jerusalem (1928)," he wrote, "when missionary thinking was inclined to hold secularism was the common enemy of all religion. Today the antithesis between what is described as religious and what is regarded as secular has no longer the same validity."[65] He held that it would look as though modern secularism served the purpose of a much-needed corrective "wherever religion had tended to become other-worldly and pietistic." The real problem confronting the Hindu leaders was how to effect a synthesis between the traditional worldview and contemporary secularism.

This struggle, Devanandan claimed, was the place where the Christian should recognize the work of the gospel. Did the gospel have something to say to this quest to discover the true meaning of human life in India

---

62 *Ibid.,* p. 188.

63 *Ibid.*

64 *Ibid.,* p. 189. In his booklet *Resurgent Hinduism: Review of Modern Movements* (Bangalore: CISRS, 1958), Devanandan characterized the movements within Hinduism as having four fundamental purposes: (a) to relate science and religion, reason and revelation, rationalism and mysticism; (b) to integrate spirituality to the dynamics of contemporary secularism; (c) to redefine man and his place in relation to the nature of things; (d) to integrate Hindu cultural values into the contemporary national and world culture, pp. 25-26.

65 P. D. Devanandan, *The Gospel and the Hindu Intellectual: A Christian Approach* (Bangalore: CISRS, 1958), pp. 22-23.

today? Could Christians recognize the work of God in Christ in the humanization processes taking place in the society in which they lived? More importantly, Devanandan saw in this struggle the real and relevant place for the meeting between the Christian and the Hindu, and their meeting Christ together where he was at work in the world to fulfil God's purpose for his creation.[66]

It was this aspect of God's concern within Hinduism to bring India and the Indian people to himself that Devanandan missed in the Tambaram and post-Tambaram discussions. In his view, these discussions had been overly dominated by Kraemer's distinction between the "biblical view of revelation of God in Christ and the human quest of non-Christian religions for experience of God-realisation." His quarrel with the discussion was that "revelation *from* God has been stressed at the expense of revelation *to and for the world* of man." If the act of God in Jesus Christ was "to seek and to find the lost world of men," then, Devanandan stressed, the theological approach had "tended to overlook the underlying anthropological concern":

> Perhaps the time has now come for us to focus attention on the human aspect in God's redemptive act — on man as he really is, the creature for whose sake Jesus Christ died and rose from the dead.[67]

For Devanandan, the Christian–Hindu relation was therefore always an evangelistic situation, for at that meeting there was also the meeting with Christ who was at work to bring about a new creation, directed at both the Christian and the Hindu. That was why it was not sufficient to study the scriptural foundations of the historical religions in their classical expression. Christians needed "a sympathetic understanding of their present claims as dynamic faiths expressed in the lives of people."[68] Like Niles, Devanandan was convinced that if Christians were in contact with Hindus in the context of the struggles of their daily lives and of the nation, they could not but discern the work of God towards the new creation.

Devanandan was hesitant, however, to apply all the implications of his position to the Tambaram debate on revelation and fulfilment. In his article, "The Younger Churches Look Ahead," he put the issue in the form of questions:

---

66 In his book *Salvation and Humanization: Some Crucial Issues of the Theology of Mission in Contemporary India*, (Bangalore: CISRS, 1971), M. M. Thomas says that "Devanandan was never tired of insisting that it is at these points of the struggle of Hinduism to relate the world to God and historical purpose to eternal salvation and the difficulties it faces in the struggle, that Christ is in dialogue with Hinduism and Hindu."

67 *The Gospel and the Hindu Intellectual*, p. 21.

68 *Preparation for Dialogue*, p. 191.

Can the Christian Church discern in such renewal the inner working of the Spirit of God, guiding men of other faiths than ours, as well as men of no faith, into a new understanding of God's ways with the world of men today? If all 'new creation' can only be of God where else could these 'new' aspects of other beliefs in the thinking and living of people have sprung from?[69]

His own view was that even though "such heart-searching questions will have to be faced" by the Christians of his generation, there was no ready answer, for "we needed to know much more than we do now of the living faiths of other men, and, even more, of faiths whereby we ourselves live." He was convinced that the Christian community at that moment was 'theologically unequipped' to answer these, or indeed to live in the religious plurality of the twentieth century.[70]

At New Delhi, however, he raised the question in a different form, and he was also prepared to attempt an answer:

Is the preaching of the Gospel directed to the total anihilation of all religions other than Christianity? Will religions as religions, and nations as nations continue characteristically separate in the fulness of time when God would "gather together in one all things in Christ, both which are in heaven, and which are on earth; even in him" (Eph. 1:10)?

In facing this question Devanandan distinguished two types of fulfilment. The first had to do with "the gospel proclamation of the fulfilment of God's promise of the Kingdom," and the other with "the hope in fulfilment of all religious faith, wherever it is found." On the second hope, Devanandan would only hint that "all sincere human striving to reach out to God will indeed find favour with Him." But he built his own hope both for the Christian in his faith, and the Hindu in his, in the 'totally assured' hope in the kingdom. "To the discerning eye of faith, the eternal future is being fulfilled in the contemporary present. It is in this sense our Lord declared that He has come not to destroy but to fulfil."[71]

The New Delhi Report

The New Delhi report shows that the Assembly was able to accommodate the fresh thinking that had taken place since Evanston. It took account of both Niles' report on the broad-based study as well as the appeal Devanandan had made to the Assembly reflecting on the situation faced by the younger churches.

[69] "The Younger Churches Look Ahead," compiled in *Preparation for Dialogue*, p. 177.

[70] *Ibid.*, p. 178.

[71] "Called to Witness," in *Preparation for Dialogue*, pp. 192-93.

The report on the Section on Witness made a clear statement on the 'previousness of Christ,' which was central to the thinking of both Niles and Devanandan:

> Christ loves the world, which he died to save. He is already the light of
> the world, of which he is Lord, and his light has preceded the bearers of
> the Good News into the darkest places. The task of Christian witness is
> to point to him as the true light, which is already shining.[72]

The text recognized that the church in every land faced new situations which required "new strategies and new methods, an adventuring into new forms of social relationships"[73], and it spoke of "a renewed sympathy with men in their aspirations and suffering" and a "fresh determination to speak to man the truth of the gospel in the actual situations of life."[74]

The emphasis on the church was less visible at New Delhi for it placed the emphasis on the gospel, and on the presence of Christ in the world as the one who brings "the searching light of his judgement on all men, beginning with us." The report called upon the churches to ask critical questions about themselves as to whether they had "been sensitive to the ceaseless work of the Holy Spirit among men" and whether they thought and acted as though Christ had died for all men and not just for them.[75]

New Delhi, by and large, was keen to affirm the solidarity between Christians and others in the struggle to find and affirm the new humanity towards which nations like India were groping:

> Joyfully we affirm our solidarity with all men, for our Lord has joined
> himself to us by becoming man. Solidarity with all men of every nation,
> class, colour, and faith without distinction in our common manhood is a
> starting point of the renewal of the life and witness of our churches by the
> Holy Spirit.[76]

The affirmation of God's presence and activity among the people of other faiths, however, was not without controversy at the Assembly. The report recognized that while there was agreement that "God has not left Himself without witness even among men who do not yet know Christ," and that "the reconciliation wrought in Christ embraces all creation and the whole of mankind," there was disagreement over the definition of "the relation and response of man" to the activity of God among them.

---

72 *The New Delhi Report: The Third Assembly of the WCC, 1961*, W. A. Visser 't Hooft, ed. (London: SCM Press, 1962), p. 77.

73 *Ibid.*, p. 78.

74 *Ibid.*

75 *Ibid.*, p. 79.

76 *Ibid.*, p. 80.

The Assembly therefore put its seal of approval on the continuation of "The Word of God and the Living Faiths of Men" study and even stressed its urgency, for there was insufficient knowledge in the churches of the "wisdom, love, and power which God has given to men of other faiths and of no faith" and of the changes taking place because of the Christian–Hindu encounter. "We must take up the conversations about Christ with them," the report insisted, "knowing that Christ addresses them through us and us through them."[77]

Christian–Hindu Concern in Humanization

It was M. M. Thomas who picked up the emphasis that Devanandan had made at the New Delhi Assembly and developed it into a serious continuing concern within the ecumenical movement. For him the whole question of Christian–Hindu relationships could only be discussed in the context of the struggle in Asia for the humanization of society:

> It is my conviction that the relation between Salvation and humanization, i. e., between the ultimate destiny of man and his historical destiny, which we saw as fundamental in Christian rethinking, is also the fundamental issue debated within all the religions, and I would add, secular movments, of India. Only the language of discourse varies from one movement to another. My thesis therefore, is that it is the theme of humanization which provides the most relevant point of entry for any Christian dialogue with these movements ... at spiritual and theological depth.[78]

Thomas saw two trends in the Hindu renascence providing two types of neo-Hinduism in India. The first, represented by Raja Rammohan Roy and Mahatma Gandhi, was primarily concerned with the moral regeneration of Indian society. Here religion was considered as a spiritual foundation for social morality. The second represented by Swami Vivekananda and Radhakrishnan, attempted to deal with the philosophical vision characteristic of Hinduism in order to show that the ultimate spiritual liberation advocated in the vision could take serious account of "the human values and secular interests to which modern India is awake and give spiritual support to them." He interpreted both developments as having the same goal of dealing with the question of man's ultimate spiritual destiny and the regeneration of human society within the historical process in modern India.[79]

According to Thomas, these attempts within Hinduism to find a spiritual base for true humanization were "the most fruitful frame of

---

77 *Ibid.,* p. 82.
78 M. M. Thomas, *Salvation and Humanization,* p. 20.
79 *Ibid.,* pp. 20-21.

reference which can illumine the theological dialogue at depth between Hinduism and Christianity."[80] It is significant that like Kulandran, Niles, and Devanandan, Thomas also insisted that the gospel and therefore the Christian mission that witnessed to it were "of tremendous relevance to the Asian revolution." He believed that Christianity had made and still could make a crucial contribution to the search for the spiritual foundations "for the new awakening of Asian people to the personal dimension of life." He also maintained that the Christian gospel, centred as it was in Jesus Christ, had so much relevance to this Asian quest that "it is the Christian mission which makes the life of the Church relevant to the Asian revolution."[81] He also argued the converse of this truth, and maintaining that Asia's awakening to the personal dimension of human existence and its quest for its adequate interpretation and spiritual foundation, were a preparation for the presentation and impact of the gospel.

The church could be a meaningful witness in this situation only if its witness constituted the spiritual counterpart of Christian participation in the Asian revolution.[82] This emphasis on participation as the key word to describe Christian–Hindu relations is most crucial to Thomas' understanding of the church and its mission among Hindus:

> One thing is absolutely clear. Participation in the struggle of Asian peoples for a fuller human life in state, society, and culture, in a real partnership with men of other faiths and no faith, is the only context for realizing the true being of the church and exercising the church's ministry and mission. Whether we speak of the evangelistic mission of proclaiming and in other ways communicating the gospel of Jesus Christ, or of the meaning of the church's social service and prophetic ministry or of the worship and fellowship of the Christian congregation or the larger unity of the church, it has sense and makes sense only within this context of participation and partnership. Therefore the life and mission of the church should be so patterned as to make such participation effective and responsible, and an expression of Christian discipleship.[83]

Thomas thus had an all-embracing idea of Hindu–Christian participation and drew many implications from it.

---

80 *Ibid.*, p. 26. Both Devanandan and Thomas dealt in detail with some of the conceptions within Hinduism and the contemporary Hindu attempts to reinterpret them to show the areas where there was real scope for dialogue between Hinduism and Christianity. This is outside the scope of this study. Also note that M. M. Thomas in his book *Acknowledged Christ of the Indian Renaissance,* gave details of the way the humanization of society had been taken up by movements within Hinduism, partly due to the impact of the Christian message on India.

81 M. M. Thomas, *The Christian Response to the Asian Revolution,* pp. 93-94.

82 *Ibid.*, p. 94.

83 *Ibid.*, p. 104.

Evangelism for him, therefore, had meaning at depth "only as a word coming out of a church engaged with all people in their struggle for personal dignity and social justice." Still it should not to be something directed by the Christians towards others as outsiders. "When whole peoples are awake to the task of building a more human society and culture," Thomas said, "a partnership in nation-building between Christians and non-Christians is the proper context for evangelism."[84]

Here Thomas was supported by Niles' who as the founding General Secretary of the East Asia Conference guided its first Assembly at Kuala Lumpur along the same lines. The report of this Assembly, held in 1959, also emphasized that Christians should go into "every part of the life of our peoples, into politics, into social and national service, into the world of art and culture, to work in real partnership with non-Christians."[85] Only a year earlier Devanandan had interpreted Christian service along the same lines, insisting that "there is also a social and political *diakonia* by which the church interests itself in the wider social issues because it has discovered that only by so doing can it meet the full needs of men." Devanandan had also insisted that these 'secular' aspects of Christian mission were "not designed to hasten the expansion of Christianity"; rather, in such *diakonia* "God's redemptive power is at work in our day-to-day life, liberating the individual and renewing human society."[86]

Thomas also interpreted partnership with Hindus as Christian willingness to enter "the main stream of national life," not with any idea of controlling it but "to serve man's manhood in it." Of course Thomas was not romantic about this for he knew that several studies in Asia had shown that "the churches are living spiritually and socially in what are called mission compounds, 'Christian Ghettoes' of their own creation, inward-looking and concerned with themselves."[87] He also recognized the dilemma facing Christians, who had enjoyed privileges during the imperial rule in the context of the post-independent developments, and especially the crippling minority consciousness of the church in the now liberated, predominantly Hindu, India. But he saw no way out for the church except to relate to the Hindus in partnership:

> It is only as Christians overcome their isolation from the main national stream and shed (*sic*) being minority-conscious that they can affirm their character as a people 'in Christ,' living *for* the larger human community as its *servant*; and it is only thus that the church can become an open community which is the bearer of meaning for *all* men. In fact, the

---

84 *Ibid.,* pp. 105-6.

85 *Witnesses Together,* The Official Report of the Inaugural Assembly of the EACC, held at Kuala Lumpur, Malaya, 14-24 May, 1959.

86 *The Gospel and the Hindu Intellectual,* pp. 24-25.

87 *The Christian Response to the Asian Revolution,* p. 105.

church can recover its prophetic being and ministry only along these lines.[88]

Here Thomas took on those who understood the churches' role among the Hindus as one of a relevant minority that could as such only play a prophetic role. He referred to the current criticism that the Asian churches were too timid to 'speak the truth' to the authorities. Admitting that this might well be so, Thomas said that only a church which had developed a prophetic being could exercise the prophetic ministry of criticism. "Only participants can be prophets," he insisted, "therefore it is important that we take our participation in nation-building more seriously, and build up our right to criticize."[89]

He recognized that partnership with Hindu neighbours did not mean that there would be no situations where Christians, precisely because of who they were, would have no choice but to engage in prophetic criticism. He also allowed for the possibility that a situation might be so judged as to "leave no room for Christians to serve men within the institutional structures through constructive participation," and that Christians might come to the point of discerning that "the time had come for a confession of Christ in total protest, accepting the suffering it involves."[90] His own judgement, however, was that the Asian situation was flexible enough to allow Christians to engage constructively in nation-building as the very expression of the church's prophetic being. In this participation Christian service to the community might not bear the Christian stamp. But Christian participation would mean that even though the discussions affecting human society were necessarily carried out in 'secular' terms, Christians would have an opportunity to introduce insights of the gospel on the nature and destiny of man.[91] For Thomas such cooperation with Hindus in the humanization of society constituted the major task of the church in India.

Moving Towards an Attitude of Dialogue

At the 1961 New Delhi Assembly the International Missionary Council was integrated into the World Council of Churches and became the WCC's Commission on World Mission and Evangelism. When the Commission held its first full meeting in Mexico City in December 1963, S. Kulandran and M. M. Thomas were among those who gave the important opening addresses.

---

88 *Ibid.*, p. 108.
89 *Ibid.*, p. 109.
90 *Ibid.*, p. 110.
91 *Ibid.*, p. 112.

Addressing the conference on "The World in which we Preach Christ," Thomas outlined the contemporary secular challenges, the rise of resurgent religions and the need to come to terms with them. He summarized his own position in the following words:

> Christianity, renascent religions, and secular faiths, are all involved in the struggle of man for the true meaning of his personal social existence — each on its own terms but together. It seems to me that the relation between Christian faith and other living religions and secular faiths is passing to a new stage, because they not only co-exist in the same society but also cooperate to build a secular society and culture. It is within such co-existence and cooperation that we can best enter into dialogue at the deepest level on the nature and destiny of man and on the nature of ultimate truth.[92]

Noting Paul Tillich's comment that the highly developed religions of Asia had not rejected the Christian answer *as answer*, but that the Christian answer was no answer to them because they did not ask the questions which the gospel was supposed to answer, Thomas felt that the changing situation offered a new historical opportunity.[93]

The significance of modern secularism and the modern renascense of ancient religions was precisely that for the first time Christianity could participate, because the questions they were now asking about human existence and salvation were "those for which the gospel has the answer." Man, whether secular or religious, was now asking questions, Thomas maintained, to which the gospel was challengingly relevant. Hence the urgency for participation and dialogue:

> It is only as the Christian missions are patterned to participate in the common agony of articulating these questions and the answers to them within the framework of contemporary life and language, that they can understand in depth the meaning of Jesus Christ for today and communicate the Gospel of Salvation to others.[94]

But what are the nature and limits of this dialogue? On what basis do Christians enter into dialogue with people of other faiths? S. Kulandran took up this issue in his presentation on "Witnessing to Men of Other Faiths." Dealing with 'the why,' 'the what,' and 'the how' of Christian witness, Kulandran spelt out his understanding of dialogue under the 'how' section, interpreting it primarily as a new context for Christian witness.

92 M. M. Thomas, "The World in which we Preach Christ" in Ronald K. Orchard, ed., *Witness in Six Continents,* Records of the Meeting of the Commission on World Mission and Evangelism of the WCC held in Mexico City, December 8-19, 1963 (London: Edinburgh House Press, 1964), p. 18.

93 Thomas refers here to the collection of essays by Paul Tillich, *Theology of Culture* (New York: Oxford University Press, 1959), pp. 204-5.

94 *Witness in Six Continents,* p. 19.

He saw much value in the increase of knowledge about other faiths, for this made it possible to start with a measure of agreement. He saw parallels to this in the preaching of St. Paul who would begin with the promise of a Messiah when he spoke to the Jews and on the common religious quest when he addressed the Athenians. "Our knowledge of the religious context of the other party in the dialogue." Kulandran said, "will teach us where exactly the agreement should be based; but it always has to be a quest common to both parties."[95]

The essence of dialogue is facing the disagreements which one soon encounters. "Disagreements do exist, and hence the need for dialogue," said Kulandran; "our disagreement with the position of Islam differs from our disagreement with the Hindu Advaitin, and our disagreement with an Advaitin from that with a Hindu theist. We may find that our agreements with a Hindu theist or a Muslim will be the basis for our disagreement with the Buddhist."[96]

Kulandran believed that one should not stop at disagreements, for "to stop with disagreements is to lose faith in the possibility of evangelism." To him, "the step from the stage of disagreement to that of ultimate agreement is the most important step in dialogue and the most important act in evangelism; it is to convince the man with views so different from ours that God's offer is being made to him also."[97]

Kulandran was aware that this "ultimate agreement" was not easy and that since one must face different kinds of disagreements the "ultimate agreement may not be the same in all dialogues." He was convinced, however, that "if the evangelist is himself convinced about the truth and the urgency of his message, he will find God working with him and lifting him to the ultimate stage; for it is He who finally bringeth men unto Himself."[98]

The Mexico Report

We noted earlier that there had been some reservations at the Whitby and Willingen conferences about the IMC becoming part of the WCC out of the fear that it might lose its emphasis on evangelism. The Ghana Conference of the IMC, however, made the final decision to join the WCC, and the meeting of the CWME at Mexico City was, in many ways, the testing ground of this new marriage. The report of Section I of the Mexico meeting on

95 S. Kulandran, "Witnessing to Men of Other Faiths," in *Witness in Six Continents,* p. 98.
96 *Ibid.*
97 *Ibid.*
98 *Ibid.,* p. 98.

"The Witness of Christians to Men of Other Faiths" seems extremely cautious.

Commenting on the Mexico meeting, Bishop Anastasios of Androusa said that the issue of relations between Christians and people of other faiths was "presented and treated in such a manner as to avoid the old polarization" and that "the Mexico meeting deliberately tried to steer clear of the reef-infested area of theoretical problems by turning its attention to the personal domain, i. e., to the *man* of another faith." He added that in spite of this attempt, the sharp differences between those who looked upon other religions as something that "must be radically rejected and overcome" and others "who maintained that God works in manifold ways even through them" did surface at the meeting. He felt that the compromise was possible only because the emphasis was placed on the personal level, on meeting persons of other faiths.[99] The report attempted to hold together the need to continue the missions in the non-Christian world and the desire to emphasize partnership with non-Christians in the post-colonial situation where there was little or no choice but to engage with others in nation-building.

At a number of points in its report the Mexico meeting maintained the emphasis on evangelization which had been prominent at Whitby and Willingen:

> Everyone who has experienced the liberating power of Christ is claimed by God to declare His wonderful deeds, in witness to other men. Our proclamation of the Gospel to men of all faiths, or to men of no faith at all is itself a part of the mighty acts of God. Witness is, therefore, a clear and compelling obligation upon every Christian, every congregation, and the whole Body of Christ.[100]

Affirming the emphasis on the church, the report also claimed that "to be a Christian necessarily involves being brought by Christ into the visibly witnessing community of faith."[101]

Of more significance was the unequivocal warning against relativism, made obviously to placate those who were nervous about the increasing pressures for partnership and relationships with people of other faiths:

---

99 Bishop Anastasios of Androussa, "Mexico City 1963: Old Wine into Fresh Wineskins" in the *International Review of Mission* LXVII, no. 267 (July 1978): 356-57. The 'old polarization' meant here is the debate on 'continuity–discontinuity' at Tambaram and after and the different positions taken in the post-Tambaram debates on Revelation.

100 Report of Section I on "The Witness of Christians to Men of Other Faiths," *Witness in Six Continents,* p. 144.

101 *Ibid.,* p. 145.

Christian witness to men of other faiths also calls today for vigilance against religious relativism and syncretism. These may take various forms such as mixing of beliefs and practices, slow absorption into other religious systems, the loss of conviction as to the finality of Jesus Christ, and the sophistication that likes to feel itself at home in every variety of belief. Behind all these forms lies the presumption that it is the wisdom of man that establishes the truth.[102]

In spite of this clear warning, the Mexico report went much further than Whitby and Willingen in calling for an altered attitude to persons of other faiths.

The Section "Our Attitude Towards Men of Other Faiths" began with the affirmation that "The Christian attitude towards men of other faiths is basically one of love for all men, respect for sincerity wherever found, and patience to search for ways to bear effective witness." The report recognized that a person of another faith had his own reasons for believing as he did, and that "many followers of other faiths today find satisfaction and inspiration in the ways their faiths are being reinterpreted to lend added meaning to individual, social, and national life."[103]

The report also had a Section on "The Nature of Dialogue," but dealt with this subject in a rather elementary way, emphasizing the "willingness to listen to what the other is saying and to recognize whatever truth be in it." There was also the call to sensitivity for the "deep sentimental associations" people had for words, doctrines, etc., and to the fact that each person had a different and specific background which moulded his or her perceptions. The report, nevertheless, put dialogue at the service of Christian witness. "Whatever the circumstances may be," the Section concluded, "our intention in every human dialogue should be to be involved in the dialogue of God with men, and move our partner and ourselves to listen to what God in Christ reveals to us, and to answer him."[104]

"The Message" from Mexico, therefore, returned to the spirit of Willingen and made no reference either to partnership or dialogue, but called the church to mission in all "six continents." "Mission," it affirmed, "is the test of faith:"

We affirm that the God whose world this is has revealed himself in Jesus Christ. He who is the head of the church is Lord of all. His is the name above every name. His love is for all mankind. He has died and risen again for all. Therefore we can go to men of other faiths or to men of none in humility and confidence, for the Gospel we preach is the account of what God has done and still does for all men. All men have the right

102 *Ibid.*, p. 146.
103 *Ibid.*, p. 145.
104 *Ibid.*, p. 147.

to know this, and those who do know it are committed to making it known. No one, and least of all Christians, can hold that it does not matter what man believes as long as they (*sic*) believe something. The ultimate issue in human life is precisely who God is, and this we know in Jesus Christ.[105]

A General Evaluation

In tracing ecumenical thinking on Christian relations with people of other faiths during the period between Tambaram (1938) and the first meeting of the Commission on Mission and Evangelism in Mexico City (1963), we have stayed close to events and to persons related primarily to the issue of Christian–Hindu relations. One should recognize that this is only a part of a much wider discussion which lies outside the scope of our present concern. Even so it is clear that a variety of interests, sometimes in conflict with each other, shaped developments during this period.

The most obvious feature of these discussions is the increased and more articulate participation of the leaders from the younger churches, who brought into the discussion their experience of shared life with people of other faiths. Until 1938, ecumenical discussions on Christian relations with people of other faiths were, we repeat, primarily a conversation among missionaries with varying perceptions of other faiths and a variety of views on how Christians should relate to them. The shift after 1938, however, was so radical that even Kraemer's attempts to modify and restate his position in his later volumes had little or no effect on the direction of the ongoing discussions.

The enhanced role of the younger churches was of course facilitated by historical developments. The end of the colonial period was marked by a vigorous resurgence of Asian religions, and this posed a serious threat to some of the assumptions of Christian missions. These religions began to present themselves as universal alternatives to the Christian faith. Locally, they posed a serious challenge to the younger churches who, having been stripped of their colonial power base, had a 'new' experience of being minorities in predominantly non-Christian societies.

The discussions of this period show that the energies of the younger churches were thinly spread over a number of issues which they had to face all at once. One of their major concerns was the question of the relationship between the older and the younger churches that were now no longer a part of the 'mission field,' but churches in their own right in nations that had newly become independent. The 'self-hood' of the younger churches, the discovery of their own mission, and their own

---

105 *Ibid.*, p. 174.

attempts to articulate the new relationship that should exist between them and the older churches absorbed much of the energy of their leadership.

Yet the relationship with people of other faiths was also an existential concern for them. It is this existential pressure that seems to have dominated discussions within the younger churches. Both Devanandan and Thomas looked to Christian partnership in nation-building as the axis of their theological reflections. They saw the task of the church primarily in terms of participation. This was, however, not a participation deriving simply from the existential emergency of post-colonial developments. Both Devanandan and Thomas were convinced that the message of the gospel was challengingly relevant both to the humanization that went with nation-building and the search within the renascent movements of Hinduism for spiritual foundations that would undergird the processes of the humanization of society.

It is significant that both these thinkers refused to continue the Tambaram debate within the theological framework that Kraemer had presented. Such issues as continuity and discontinuity, revelation and religion etc., receded into the background. The *task* and *role* both of the church as a community, and of Christians as fellow-citizens with Hindus and others, became the predominant concern.

Niles shared the same concern, but apparently chose to play the role of interpreting the ideas of the younger churches in theological moulds that could offer some linkage between this new thinking and developments within the wider ecumenical fellowship. By shifting the focus of the discussion from 'Christian and non-Christian' to 'gospel and the world,' Niles provided a wider frame of reference, but he too refused to be dragged into the Tambaram discussions in any significant way. Both he and Kulandran stood firm on the church's task and its calling to present the gosepl, but they understood it within a wider conception of God's ongoing relation with all of humanity. The positions taken by these Asian thinkers were pushing ecumenical discussions towards a dialogue relationship with neighbours of other faiths which would not compromise the general conviction that the gospel message was relevant to the Asian societies undergoing a revolutionary change.

At the level of official meetings within the ecumenical movement, however, there were discernable tensions. Both Whitby and Willingen had reaffirmed the Tambaram stand on presenting the gospel to the non-Christians with the intention of expanding the areas occupied by the church. The Amsterdam Assembly of the WCC, also dominated by the mission-oriented churches, had only reaffirmed the positions taken within the IMC.

It is only after Evanston that one begins to discern the tension between the missionary traditions inherited by the IMC and the 'new' tradition created by the churches meeting in Council, where the younger churches were able to make their voices heard. This can be seen in the marked differences in the attitude to other faiths seen in reports of the New Delhi Assembly on the one hand, and the report of the CWME meeting in Mexico City on the other. The New Delhi report accommodated the challenge of the younger churches and stressed the urgency of carrying forward the study on "The Word of God and the Living Faiths of Men." Mexico City, faced with the same challenges, chose to go the way of Whitby and Willingen and reaffirm the supremacy of the Christian message over other religions and the need to call all men to accept membership in the church.

After the IMC had become part of the WCC, this tension between the traditional concern to convert the non-Christian world on the one hand, and the experience of the younger churches urging a more open, dialogical, and mutual relationship with people of other faiths on the other, came under the same roof, and ironically even became strange bed-fellows within the CWME, for it was there that the study on "The Word of God and the Living Faiths of Men" was located. It is indeed significant that a separate sub-unit on "Dialogue with People of Living Faiths and Ideologies" had to be created within the WCC to provide a new locus to follow up on the results of this study. At the subsequent WCC Assemblies at Nairobi and Vancouver these two sides were locked into deep controversy. To these we shall return later, but now we should pick up "The Word of God and the Living Faiths of Men" study where we left it (at Bossey) and see how this concern developed into a programme on "Dialogue in Community."

CHAPTER VI

Dialogue in Community

Introduction

We noted earlier that the study on "The Word of God and the Living Faiths of Men" had originally been conceived as an attempt to reopen, after the interruption caused by the Second World War, the questions that remained unresolved at Tambaram. What was most significant about the study was the broad base which it eventually received. The Study Centres around the world were asked to take up the theological questions which it raised, and consultations on its various and varied aspects were held in Jerusalem, Burma, Hong Kong, and India. The Indian meeting, held at Nagpur from 10-16 October 1960, was designed as an actual dialogue, where Hindu religious leaders and philosophers joined Christians in a exploration of the "Hindu and Christian Views of Man."[1]

The East Asia Christian Conference (EACC), meeting in Bangkok in 1964, issued a remarkably well-conceived document on the "Christian Encounter with Men of Other Beliefs" which proved to be one of the major inputs to the study.[2] The Asian thinkers considered in our last chapter made substantial contributions to these discussions; P. D. Devanandan played the key role in organizing and setting directions for the Nagpur meeting, and D. T. Niles' views heavily influenced the EACC document. The fruits of the study, which had opened its cautious and tentative first buds at Davos, blossomed at Bossey, and ripened at the New Delhi Assembly, were now ready for harvesting. Responsibility fell on Victor

---

1 A brief report written by J. B. Carman summarizing the major contributions made at this meeting appeared in the *Occasional Bulletin*, published by the Research Department under the title "The Nagpur Colloquium at Work" (no date), pp. 14-22.

2 Printed also in *The Ecumenical Review* XVI (July 1964): 451-55.

Hayward who had been since New Delhi the coordinator of the work of Study Centres around the world. In March 1967 he convened the Kandy consultation on "Christians in Dialogue with Men of Other Faiths," which proved to be one of the major meetings in the history of the discussions that we are tracing here. An important feature of the Kandy meeting was the significant participation of Roman Catholic theologians.[3]

It would be appropriate to pause here to note some of the developments within the Roman Catholic Church which affected thinking within the WCC.

The Impact of Vatican II

Relations between Roman Catholics and Hindus have a complex history, especially in India. Even though the Roman Catholic missions shared some of the negative features of other colonial missionary enterprises, such as ignorance, antagonism, and outright intolerance of Hinduism, there had also been some noteworthy attempts to relate to Hinduism in a positive way. In the field of Hindu–Christian relations we should recall such names as Roberto De Nobili, Constance Beschi, and Hippolito Desideri. Throughout the history of the Roman Catholic Church in India there were many lesser known persons and movements that kept alive the vision of an open, dialogical approach to Hinduism, and especially to the culture that derived from it.

The most significant change, which also influenced the outcome of the Kandy meeting, resulted from the more open attitude to other faiths advocated by the Second Vatican Council. In 1963 a special Secretariat was created to deal with Catholic relations with non-Christian religions. Also important was the promulgation of a "Declaration on the Relationship of the Church to Non-Christian Religions" at the end of the Council.

This Declaration did not deal with the theological issues involved in relating to people of other faiths, but it advocated openness to other religions along with an uncompromising stand on the uniqueness of Christ. It made the following statements on Hinduism:

> From the ancient times down to the present, there has existed among diverse peoples a certain perception of that hidden power which hovers over the events of human life. . . . Such a perception and such a recognition instill the lives of these people with a profound religious sense. . . .

3 C. F. Hallencreutz notes that this was the first time the Roman Catholic theologians entered the debate within the WCC on interfaith relations. Details of this meeting are considered later in this chapter. Since a large number of Orthodox churches had joined the WCC at the New Delhi Assembly in 1961, this meeting also had significant Orthodox participation. See S. J. Samartha, ed., *Living Faiths and the Ecumenical Movement* (Geneva: WCC, 1971), p. 66 ff.

Thus in Hinduism men contemplate that divine mystery and express it through an unspent fruitfulness of myths and through searching philosophical inquiry. They seek release from the anguish of our condition through ascetical practices or deep meditation or a loving, trusting flight toward God.[4]

On the overall attitude to other faiths, the Declaration drew mainly on natural theology, the doctrine of the sacramental nature and life of the church, and the need to be open and loving in Christian relations to others, which was also expressed in a willingness to "acknowledge, preserve, and promote the spiritual and moral good" found in other faiths:

The Catholic Church rejects nothing which is true and holy in these religions. She looks with sincere respect upon those ways of conduct and of life, those rules and teachings which, though differing in many particulars from what she holds and sets forth, nevertheless often reflect a ray of that Truth which enlightens all men. Indeed she proclaims and must ever proclaim Christ, "the way, the truth, and the life" (John 14:16), in whom all men find the fullness of religious life, and in whom God has reconciled all things to Himself (Cf. II Cor. 5:18-19).[5]

While affirming Christ as 'The Truth,' the Declaration advocated an open attitude to other religions:

The church therefore, has this exhortation for her sons: Prudently and lovingly, through dialogue and collaboration with the followers of other religions, and in witness to Christian faith and life, acknowledge, preserve, and promote the spiritual and moral goods found among these men, as well as the value of their society and culture.[6]

A more precise position regarding the Catholic Church's attitude to non-Christian religions, however, is to be found in the "Dogmatic Constitution of the Church":

Those also can attain to everlasting salvation who through no fault of their own do not know the Gospel of Jesus Christ or His Church, yet sincerely seek God and, moved by grace, strive by their deeds to do His will as it is known to them through the dictates of conscience. Nor does divine providence deny the help necessary for salvation to those who, without blame on their part, have not yet arrived at an explicit knowledge of God, but who strive to have a good life, thanks to His grace. Whatever goodness or truth is found among them is looked upon by the church as

---

4 "Declaration on the Relationship of the Church to Non-Christian Religions" (*Nostra Aetate*), Walter M. Abbott, S. J., ed., and Joseph Gallagher, translations editor, *The Documents of Vatican II* (New York: America Press, 1966), para. 2, pp. 661-62.

5 *Ibid.,* p. 662.

6 *Ibid.,* pp. 662-63.

preparation for the Gospel. She regards such qualities as given by Him who enlightens men so that they may finally have life.[7]

Roman Catholic theologians like Karl Rahner, Raimundo Panikkar, Hans Küng, and H. R. Schlette developed the seminal ideas present in these documents into more elaborate theological positions. To this we shall return in our last chapter. For the present we should also note the encyclical *Ecclesiam Suam* which Pope Paul VI issued on 6 August 1964 to present a model of the Roman Catholic Church's relationship to the world. Part III of the encyclical described this relationship in a series of concentric circles, the outermost representing the Church's dialogue with humanity in general. The next circle was the Roman Catholic Church's dialogue with non-Christian religions. Then came the 'separated brethren' and the inner dialogue within the Roman Catholic Church. The statement on the Roman Catholic Church's dialogue with people of other faiths exhibited the same double tone, of affirming the finality of Christ on the one hand, and openness on the other:

> Indeed, honesty compels us to declare openly our conviction that there is but one true religion, the religion of Christianty. It is our hope that all who seek God and adore Him may come to acknowledge its truth.
>
> But we do, nevertheless, recognize and respect the moral and spiritual values of the various non-Christian religions, and we desire to join with them in promoting and defending common ideas of religious liberty, human brotherhood, good culture, social welfare and civil order. For our part we are ready to enter into discussion on these common ideals, and will not fail to provide every opportunity for such discussion, conducted with genuine mutual respect, where it would be well received.[8]

The documents of the Vatican Council did not offer much theological reflection on Christian relationships with other faiths. But the positive recognition of the other faiths and the affirmation of the possibility of salvation through them suggested in "The Dogmatic Constitution on the Church," along with the invitation to dialogue addressed in *Ecclesiam Suam,* opened the flood gates within the Roman Catholic Church. With a strong tradition of natural theology, and a sacramental understanding of the role of the Church in salvation, the Roman Catholics after Vatican II were theologically much better positioned to tackle the question of relationships between Christianity and other faiths. Their participation at the Kandy consultation, therefore, had a significant impact on both the conduct and the outcome of the meeting.

---

7 "Dogmatic Constitution of the Church" (*Lumen Gentum*), Chapter II, "The People of God," *Documents of Vatican II,* para. 16, p. 35. The text in this edition has been mixed up in the printing process. It is corrected by comparing with other translations.

8 *Ecclesiam Suam,* Part III, Section III, p. 112.

Dialogue Affirmed — Kandy 1967

So far we have been tracing the ways in which the debate on relations between Christians and people of other faiths, which had begun at Tambaram, was continued, particularly in those parts of the world where Christians lived in close proximity to Hindus. The Kandy meeting, to which we now turn, could be characterized as the 'summit' of these discussions, for it was there that the underlying theological assumptions of Tambaram were directly challenged and an attempt was made to give an alternate vision. Kandy marked a new departure regarding relationships between Christianity and other faiths.[9]

The theological challenge to the Tambaram thesis was best articulated in Kandy by Kenneth Cragg, who questioned some of the basic assumptions that Barth and Kraemer had made in shaping what had already come to be identified loosely as the 'Protestant view' on Christian relations with other faiths. Cragg's first quarrel with Barth had to do with the latter's absolute and wholly transcendental interpretation of revelation, which in his view was the primary cause for a non-dialogical, self-assertive understanding and presentation of the Christian message. "Missionary theology in its proper awareness of the 'givenness' of the faith and a concern for its 'uniqueness'," said Cragg, "has tended to high-handed and distant attitudes in presenting it. ..."[10] Cragg was alluding to Barth's concept of total discontinuity in the relation between religion and revelation. He respected Barth's concern for the gospel as a counter-force to "the sanguine, naturalistic, complacent hopes, and notions" of natural man. But he did not believe that revelation could be "so new, so unheard-of, so unexpected," as Barth had put it, as to be wholly in contradiction with "the hunger and thirst" expressed in man's religion. Otherwise it could not present itself as "good news."[11]

Cragg contended that the "newsworthiness" of the gospel had to do not only with what it "declared" but in its ability "to relate itself to the hearer's situation." The news becomes 'good' only insofar as it was confirmed to be so by the hearer. He had serious difficulties, therefore, with the position that gave absolute transcendence to the good news as

---

9 The consultation on "Christian Dialogue with Men of Other Faiths" at Kandy, Sri Lanka, was organized by the WCC Department of Studies from 27 February–6 March, 1967. It brought together Protestants, Orthodox, and Catholics who had been working on the issues involved. Among those who presented the main papers were Kenneth Cragg, Lyn de Silva, and J. Blauw.

10 Kenneth Cragg "The Credibility of Christianity," Papers of the Kandy consultation published in *Study Encounter* III, no. 2 (1967): 57.

11 *Ibid.*

something that did not "mediate with unbelief" and stood in need of "no collaborative support outside of itself."[12]

As Farmer had at Tambaram, Cragg also held that this kind of interpretation of the relation between the gospel and man in his religious life violated another aspect of the New Testament witness:

> The incarnation may be defined as truth undertaking whatever its comprehensibility requires. "The Word was made flesh": that *to* which God speaks is that *in* which he speaks. Ministry must follow the same pattern. For "as he is, so are we in the world." "Behold I stand at the door and knock." "He that hath ears to hear let him hear." These are the patterns of the New Testament — a willingness to be credibly pondered and credibly related to men where they are, so as to enlist and elicit, not their capitulation but their embrace; to stir and invite them to inward recognition and obedience.[13]

Cragg's concern here was of course to lay the foundation on which he could argue for a dialogical stance both in relating to persons of other faiths and in assessing their faith and experience. But would such a sympathetic interpretation compromise the 'uniqueness' or 'decisiveness' of the gospel? Cragg disagreed with Kraemer's interpretation of the uniqueness of the gospel primarily as the supreme 'act' of God in the world of biblical realism. He could not accept that the 'uniqueness' or 'decisiveness' of the gospel could be a matter for assertive claims. For him the uniqueness of the gospel was "discernable only in the wake of recognition":

> The incomparability of Christ is not an independent conviction, a belief in a claim that can or should exist arbitrarily or dictatorially. It only enters into credence with the entry of Christ; it is a *post facto* experience of faith and not a sanction for it.[14]

In Cragg's view a dialogical attitude to other faiths would add credence to the gospel rather than imperil it; an assertive attitude would only betray insecurity. "Evangelism is nothing if it is not a willingness for relationship."[15]

But Cragg saw a more serious issue in the assertive attitude towards other faiths arising from the unwillingness of the Christian partner to affirm the common humanity of all men. This, he said, was coupled with the "general neglect of, or retreat from, the whole significance of nature." He felt that the neo-orthodox theology had exalted the 'historical' as the definitive area of Divine self-disclosure almost to the point of a total neglect of natural theology. He himself failed to understand how concepts

---

12 *Ibid.*
13 *Ibid.*
14 Cragg takes the example of Paul's metaphor of the 'Ambassador' which carried for him the double stance of inward obligation and outward relationship.
15 *Ibid.*, p. 58.

of 'salvation history,' 'election,' etc., which formed the back-bone of neo-orthodox theology could have meaning outside God's purpose in creation:

> We need a much more patient theology of nature. For nature is after all, the ground of culture, the habitat of history. There is no significant exodus where there is no significant 'ecology.' God is not in the exile, if he is not evermore in the harvest and the seasons. God is not in the Incarnation, if he is not within the mystery of the natural order. ... [16]

Cragg made a passionate plea for a revision of the Protestant attitude to nature and to natural theology. Loyalty to nature, he claimed, had to do with loyalty to the Incarnation, for the "revelatory feasibility of Incarnation presupposes the revelatory quality, in part, of all experience: a world into which we believe God has been born is nowhere irrelevant either to Him or for Him. ..."[17]

It was not Cragg's intention to minimize the challenge of the Christian message or to take away the 'offence of the cross' which was important in Kraemer's presentation at Tambaram. He recognized that the message of the gospel did confront man in a radical way as Kraemer and Barth emphasized it. But he maintained that it was not for the Christians to sharpen or exaggerate this offence. Rather it was their duty to translate the mystery of Christ into universally acceptable terms, taking the side of the hearers in the humanity that Christ had also embraced. "We are not town-criers of the grace of God, but would-be guests at every man's home for its sake."[18]

We have focussed on Kenneth Cragg's presentation to the Kandy meeting because he was able to summarize some of the points which, in the view of many of the participants, required fundamental theological rethinking in order to move towards a dialogical frame of reference in the understanding of relations between Christians and people of other faiths. This, in fact, was the thrust of the Kandy statement.

The Kandy Statement

According to Victor Hayward, who had organized the meeting, this statement was "based on the general acceptance that God's love and purpose of salvation extends to all people of every century, country, and creed; that it pertains to this world as well as to the coming age, that it is corporate as well as individual, and that it embraces all aspects of man's existence."[19] In fact, the statement approved the Vatican Council's affirmation,

---

16 *Ibid.*
17 *Ibid.*, p. 59.
18 *Ibid.*, p. 60.
19 Cf. Report of the meeting, *Ibid.*, p. 53.

in the Dogmatic Constitution on the Church, that those who sincerely seek God according to the dictates of their conscience were within God's salvic purposes.

We have already observed that the New Delhi Assembly had recognized the importance of a dialogical relationship to people of other faiths, especially as something relevant to the life of the younger churches. The CWME meeting at Mexico City had also recognized the need for dialogue, even though it remained within the theological framework erected at Tambaram. Kandy's objective was to spell out some of the presuppositions that the churches would have to accept if dialogue was to become the principal idea in defining the Christian attitude to other faiths. It achieved this by articulating a basis for dialogue and its implications for proclamation and conversion.

(a) The Basis of Dialogue

The Kandy statement appealed to the solidarity which Christians shared with all others in the one humanity as the fundamental basis for dialogue, affirming that God alone had "made every nation of men." It was significant that all mankind was "caught up in one universal history, and made increasingly aware of common tasks and common hopes" that brought them together. But the report also spelt out the participants' idea of a more specifically 'Christian' basis for the affirmation of common humanity:

> For the Christian, a deep sense of community is given by his belief that all men are created in the image of God, by his realization that Christ died for every man, and by the expectation of His coming kingdom. Here is the foundation of the Christian approach to any human being.[20]

Significantly, the statement did not go beyond this affirmation of common humanity and the universal appeal to the importance of Christ as its basis for dialogue. Notably absent was any theological statement on other faiths apart from the recognition that "as our dialogue with men of other faiths develops, we may gain light regarding the place held by other religious traditions in God's purposes for them and for us." This question, the study maintained, "cannot be answered *a priori* or academically, but must continue to engage our earnest study and reflection."[21]

20 Statement on the Basis of Dialogue, Report of the Kandy Consultation, *Study Encounter,* p. 53.
21 *Ibid.,* p. 53.

(b) The Nature of Dialogue

The Kandy statement took Incarnation as the model for the nature of dialogue. "Love always seeks to communicate" it said. "Our experience of God's communication with us constrains us to communicate with men of other beliefs." It affirmed further the belief that Christ is present whenever a Christian sincerely enters into dialogue with another man. In an apparent reference to the New Delhi statement, it added that "the Christian is confident that Christ can speak to him through his own neighbour, as well as to his neighbour through him":[22]

> Dialogue means a positive effort to attain a deeper understanding of the truth through mutual awareness of one another's convictions and witness. It involves expectation of something happening — the opening of a new dimension of which one was not aware before. Dialogue implies a readiness to be changed as well as to influence others. Good dialogue develops when one partner speaks in such a way that the other feels drawn to listen and likewise when one listens so that the other is drawn to speak. The outcome of dialogue is the work of the Holy Spirit.[23]

(c) Proclamation and Conversion

The participants at the Kandy meeting were aware that an open, humble, and friendly attitude to other faiths had been generally advocated in the discussions on mission. Dialogue, therefore, when understood primarily in relational terms and as something based on the common humanity of all people in creation, was no longer too controversial for ecumenical discussions. They intended to go further but were unable to incorporate some of the theological implications of Cragg's call for a reappraisal of natural theology and a fresh look at the assumptions undergirding the church's ministry of evangelization. The consultation did comment, however, on two matters of practical importance to interfaith relations, namely, proclamation and conversion leading to baptism.

The report observed that dialogue and proclamation were not identical, but related, for at any time during the course of a living dialogue "moments of proclamation of the gospel may be given." Admitting that proclamation could be made in other ways than dialogue, the report suggested that it should nevertheless always be made "in the spirit of dialogue." Similarly, any dialogue might include proclamation, for Christians would participate in a dialogue "in the spirit of those who have good news to share."[24]

---

22 *Ibid.,* p. 54.
23 *Ibid.*
24 *Ibid.,* p. 55.

On the question of conversion, the Kandy report reflected some of the deep continuing controversy, not least in India, over whether all who had come to believe in Jesus Christ should accept baptism and church membership as marks of their conversion to Christ. Gandhi, among others, had raised objections in India to 'converts' leaving the fold of Hinduism. The whole question of conversion had also become a sensitive matter for people of other faiths, and it was easy for them to interpret the new Christian interest in dialogue as the latest device for the expansion of the church. This had been one of the sensitive issues at the CWME meeting in Mexico City in 1963, where the report on Witness had finally insisted that notwithstanding the sensitiveness of the issues involved, "to be a Christian necessarily involves being brought by Christ into a *visible,* witnessing community of faith,"[25] and that "our intention in every human dialogue should be ... to move the partner and ourselves to what God in Christ reveals to us, and to *answer him.*"[26]

There were also disagreements over this matter at Kandy. "We recognize that there is often confusion, within the church and outside of it," the report said, "between conversion as an innner spiritual and moral rebirth, a radical turning to God, and conversion as a change of cultural and sociological affiliation."[27] The conference also registered disagreement over whether it was part of God's redemptive purpose to be savingly involved through Christ in other systems of belief, and recognized that here there were a number of questions "that needed further study." The best that the Kandy statement could do was to leave conversion as one question on which individuals had to make their own decision, for one could not determine how God worked in the lives of individuals and communities:

> This very fact is one of the reasons which should make us leave it to the conscience and inner illumination of those who within other systems take up Christian discipleship whether or not it is God's will for them that they should leave their own social and religious community. The spirit of dialogue should anyway prevent us from dogmatism on this subject.[28]

In an obvious attempt to satisfy those who insisted on the 'visible' community, the report said that "normally conversion leads to baptism and incorporation into the church." And then it added: "There may, however, be situations —personal or social, spiritual or practical— in which the church may support the individual in his decision to postpone or abstain from baptism. Baptism is an invitation and a gift, not an imposition."[29]

25 Ronald K. Orchard, ed., *Witness in Six Continents,* p. 55.
26 *Ibid.,* p. 147.
27 Kandy Report, *Study Encounter,* p. 55.
28 *Ibid.,* p. 56.
29 *Ibid.*

(d) The Significance of Kandy

In his introduction to the Kandy statement, Victor Hayward recalled that both at the WCC's Third Assembly at New Delhi and later at the Mexico meeting of the CWME, "very worthwhile and stimulating" discussions had taken place at the Sectional meetings on Christian relations with and witness to people of other faiths. "When it came to drafting and subsequent discussions in plenary sessions, however," he lamented, "the outcome on both occasions was very unsatisfactory and frustrating."[30]

This comment pointed to a deep division within the ecumenical movement over the theological approach to people of other faiths and its implicit significance for the Christian understanding of mission. In the tension between those who had an exclusivistic understanding of the Christian faith and therefore viewed other faiths primarily as 'mission fields,' and those who wanted to understand the phenomenon of other religions as somehow within the salvic purposes of God, the more mission-oriented group had almost always prevailed. The strength of this position had been somewhat shaken at Jerusalem, but Tambaram had restored it with more credence than ever to its pre-eminence in the ecumenical theology of missions. Every subsequent ecumenical event, despite the passionate plea on the part of some of the churches that lived in religiously plural societies, and despite the accommodation made in certain parts of the reports to their views, reinforced the overall impression that for all the humility in which the statements were clothed and the openness to which the churches were called, the prevailing theology was exclusivistic. The appeal to the uniqueness of Christ and the call to evangelize the people of other faiths somehow gained precedence among the many current interpretations of the changing situation.

Even though it was only the report of a consultation and not an official statement, the Kandy document was important because it was the first to submit 'dialogue' as a new basis for Christian relationships with people of other faiths to the official consideration of the Central Committee of the WCC. It had the added advantage of being the fruit of a study initiated officially by the WCC.

Of course, this report was inadequate in many ways. It did not take a definitive stand on the question of the theological basis of the Christian relationship with people of other faiths. Carl Hallencreutz has observed that Kandy "applied both the typically Roman Catholic view of the relationship between non-Christian religions and the church as between the 'ordinary' and the 'extra-ordinary' ways of salvation and the more familiar emphasis within the World Council on 'common humanity' as both the

---

30 *Ibid.,* p. 51.

starting point and a basis for a common hope."[31] If this was the case, it was so by implication and not through a clear theological synthesis of the two approaches.

The conference had also shown an interest in positive appraisals of secularism and indigenization, but it did not delve at all deeply into the questions of 'dialogue and proclamation,' or 'conversion and baptism.' It would be too much to expect it to have gone any further, for the meeting had in fact succeeded in identifying many theological issues on which there was still deep disagreement within the ecumenical fellowship.[32] Kandy had, however, put 'dialogue' firmly on the ecumenical map, and its report was well received by the Central Committee of the WCC at its August 1967 meeting in Crete.

The Uppsala Response

Even as it welcomed the Kandy report, however, the Central Committee decided that the time was not yet ripe for a major discussion of its contents at the Fourth Assembly of the WCC at Uppsala, then only a year away. Instead, it recommended that the report be referred for a full discussion to the next meeting of the Commission on World Mission and Evangelism.[33]

The impact of the Kandy statement was nevertheless felt both in the Uppsala preparatory process and in the final report of the Assembly's Section II, on "Renewal in Mission." This report emerged as a neatly balanced statement incorporating the findings of Kandy without dealing with any of the underlying theological controversies, over some of which the Section meeting itself seemed to have had 'heated discussions.'[34] It affirmed dialogue as a way of life for the Christian:

> The meeting with men of other faiths or no faith must lead to dialogue. A Christian dialogue with another implies neither denial of the uniqueness of Christ, nor of any loss to his own commitment to Christ, but rather that a genuinely Christian approach to others must be human, personal, relevant, and humble. In dialogue we share our common humanity, its dignity and its fallenness, and express our common concern for that humanity.[35]

31 *Living Faiths and the Ecumenical Movement*, S. J. Samartha, ed. (Geneva: WCC, 1971), p. 66.

32 The Kandy Report, *Study Encounter, op. cit.*, p. 73.

33 *Ibid.*, p. 51.

34 Cf. Carl Hallencreutz in *Living Faiths and the Ecumenical Movement* (Geneva: WCC, 1971), p. 67.

35 Norman Goodall, ed., *The Uppsala Report 1968: Official Report of the Fourth Assembly of the WCC,* Uppsala, 4-20 July, 1968 (Geneva: WCC), p. 29.

Those who drafted the Uppsala report seem consciously to have chosen 'common humanity' with people of other faiths as the basis of dialogue, thereby suspending any judgement on the theological significance of other faiths for Christian self-understanding and mission. They also affirmed the previousness and presence of Christ in dialogical situations:

> As Christians we believe that Christ speaks in dialogue, revealing himself to those who do not know him and correcting the limited and distorted knowledge of those who do. Dialogue and Proclamation are not the same. The one compliments the other in a total witness.[36]

A Historical Note

As already stated, our primary aim is not to repeat the history of the ecumenical movement or of the World Council of Churches but to trace the evolution of thinking within the ecumenical movement, and especially within the World Council of Churches, about Christian relations with other faiths.

We must presently turn to consider the ways in which the Kandy statement stimulated a discussion of "Dialogue in Community," and an assessment of the theological merits of this idea for contemporary Christian–Hindu relations. But first, to facilitate our understanding of this discussion we should briefly review the historical events following the Kandy meeting which eventually resulted in the formation of the sub-unit on Dialogue with People of Living Faiths and Ideologies (DFI) as a crucial leader and partner in these discussions.

After Uppsala, the WCC's interest in the question of relating to people of other faiths experienced a rapid and far-reaching evolution. Kandy had given a strong profile to the study on *The Word of God and the Living Faiths of Men*. In August 1968, Stanley J. Samartha, who would later become the first director and chief architect of the sub-unit on Dialogue, was invited by the Studies Department of the Commission on World Mission and Evangelism to follow up on 'The Word of God and the Living Faiths of Men' study.[37] In August 1969, the Central Committee received a progress report and authorized a consultation, which met in March 1970 at Ajaltoun, Lebanon, bringing together adherents of a number of religious traditions for an actual dialogue on relations between their

---

36 *Ibid.*

37 Stanley J. Samartha became the first director of the sub-unit on Dialogue with People of Living Faiths and Ideologies when the Central Committee meeting in Addis Ababa in 1971 decided to set up the new sub-unit.

peoples. This marked a new departure, for the emphasis had changed from conversation *about* dialogue to engagement *in* it.[38]

The Ajaltoun experience was evaluated theologically at a further meeting in May 1970 in Zurich, Switzerland and the findings were summarized in an important document known as the Zurich aide-mémoire. This set out some of the basic principles for a dialogical relationship with people of other faiths.[39] During this period dialogue with people of other faiths gained recognition as a major concern within the WCC. The 1971 Addis Ababa meeting of the Central Committee issued "An Interim Policy Statement and Guidelines" on the WCC's dialogue with people of living faiths and ideologies, and in so doing it also created a new sub-unit on Dialogue.[40]

Preparations for the WCC's Fifth Assembly (Nairobi, 1975) included a serious consideration of the sub-unit's experience of actual dialogue with people of other faiths, along with some reflection on its theological implications. For the first time at Nairobi, five members of other world faith groups were guests at a WCC Assembly.[41] Dialogue nevertheless attracted much controversy at Nairobi, so a consultation was planned to bring together persons representing a range of viewpoints: This took place at Chiang Mai, Thailand in April 1977, and its most important achievement was the elaboration of *Guidelines on Dialogue*. These *Guidelines*, which identified both the areas of agreement and disagreement in the churches and raised the theological issues needing further reflection, were commended to the churches for study and action.[42]

The reflections that had transpired since Nairobi were gathered in their turn into the preparatory process for the WCC's Sixth Assembly (Vancouver, 1983), where the Commission on World Mission and Evangelism and the sub-unit on Dialogue now under the leadership of John Taylor who had succeeded Stanley Samartha, attempted to present a common statement on 'Witnessing in a Divided World.' At Vancouver, dialogue as a way of relating to people of other faiths aroused no objection, but the

---

38 The Ajaltoun meeting (16-26 March 1970), brought three Hindus, four Buddhists and three Muslims together with a number of Christian participants to explore the possibility of an ongoing dialogue between religious communities. The full report and the papers presented are published in S. J. Samartha, ed., *Dialogue Between Men of Living Faiths* (Geneva: WCC, 1971).

39 First published in the *International Review of Mission* LIX 236 (October 1970). Also in *Living Faiths and the Ecumenical Movement, op. cit.,* pp. 33-43.

40 First published in *The Ecumenical Review* XXIV, no. 3 (July 1971). Also in *Living Faiths and the Ecumenical Movement, op. cit.,* pp. 47-54.

41 The resolution to invite guests of other faiths was passed at the Second Meeting of the Dialogue Working Group which met in New Delhi, September 1974. See *Minutes,* p. 19.

42 For responses to the Chiang Mai meeting see *Minutes of the Third Meeting of the Working Group on Dialogue* (1978), p. 96 ff.

attempt to speak of God's relation to people of other faiths provoked great controversy, reminiscent of some of the disagreements we have mentioned in the early chapters of this study.[43] In the following paragraphs we shall draw on the discussions of the period which we have just outlined. We must, however, limit our purview to the main lines of thought, so that we may devote our final chapter to a consideration of Hindu–Christian relations in the context of recent developments.

Dialogue in and for Community

In the course of our discussions we have noted three significant shifts in the conduct of Christian relations with people of other faiths within the ecumenical movement. The first shift related to the 'content of other faiths' as the focus of discussion. At Edinburgh, Jerusalem, and Tambaram the emphasis was on the content of belief in the other religious systems and on how the gospel message related to them. The issue was posed in terms of the challenge of the gospel message to the non-Christian world which defined itself differently. After Tambaram the discussions shifted to 'religions' in general, and the specificity of religious traditions and their belief systems was more or less ignored.

The second shift had to do with the the scope of the problem and the process of dealing with it. Asian thinkers pressed for a new framework wherein the gospel message as well as other religious traditions was understood to be addressing a complex world, in which religious traditions were only one important set of components. This shifted the issue from the theology of religions to missiology and focussed attention on the way the gospel related to the religious as well as to the secularized man *in the world,* at least in theory. But it pushed the reality of religions as religions to the background. This new focus opened fresh possibilities for cooperation and relationships with people of other faiths and ideological persuasions.

The third shift was consequent to the second one and focused on the goal or purpose, namely, the discussions moved away from theological issues to questions of human relationship. This emphasis on relationships raised questions about their theological foundations, but the main concern was how Christians could *live* with people of other faiths in community.

The Zurich aide-mémoire on "Christians in Dialogue with Men of Other Faiths" offered an excellent illustration of these changes in the context it provided for its statement on dialogue:

---

43 Cf. *Minutes of the Sixth Meeting of the Working Group* (1985), pp. 23, 32.

We are at a time when dialogue is inevitable, urgent, and full of opportunity. It is inevitable because everywhere in the world Christians are now living in a pluralistic society. It is urgent because all men are under common pressure in the search for justice, peace, and a hopeful future and all are faced with the challenge to live together as human beings.[44]

Significantly, almost all the important documents on dialogue tended to give this sociological, existential necesssity as the primary basis for a dialogical relationship with people of other faiths. The official "Interim Policy Statement and Guidelines" drawn up by the Central Committee also followed the Zurich aide-mémoire and spoke of the 'urgency' of dialogue due to the 'common pressures' for justice and peace.[45]

Often this sense of oneness that arose from historical necessity was complemented by the sense of oneness in 'common humanity.' Generally speaking, the need for the different sections of human society, religious and otherwise, to live in community became the axis of the argument for relationships during this period. This idea was developed fully at the multilateral dialogue meeting in Colombo (1975) on "Towards World Community," where there was a recognition of past failures and an affirmation of the search for community as the goal for the future.

Towards World Community

Admitting that they had different worldviews and different interpretations of the times, the Colombo participants nevertheless affirmed that they had sensed together something of their common humanity:

> We also acknowledged real common links based on a sense of universal interdependence and responsibility of each and every person with and for all other persons; we together recognized the fundamental unity of human beings as one family and committed ourselves to strive and, if necessary, to be ready to pay a price to realize the equality and dignity of all human beings.[46]

Those present had no illusions about the feasibility of a world community for they clearly recognized the part religious communities played in disrupting and dividing community life. They declared in their memoran-

---

44 "Christians in Dialogue with Men of Other Faiths: The Zurich Aide-Mémoire," in S. J. Samartha, ed., *Living Faiths and the Ecumenical Movement, op. cit.,* p. 33. The document was first published in the *International Review of Mission* LIX 236 (October 1970).

45 "The World Council of Churches and Dialogue with People of Living Faiths and Ideologies — An Interim Policy Statement and Guidelines," *Living Faiths and the Ecumenical Movement, op. cit.,* p. 47. The document was first published in *The Ecumenical Review* XXIV, no. 3 (July 1971).

46 S. J. Samartha, ed., *Towards World Community: The Colombo Paper* (Geneva: WCC, 1975), p. 116.

dum that they were "conscious of compromise and lack of responsibility on our part and on the part of our neighbours," and they admitted that religions and ideologies were sometimes "arrogantly self-sufficient"; finally, they stressed the need to avoid such self-sufficiency.[47]

In spite of the stress on the importance of community and unity in most of the documents, there was apparently no attempt to conceive of a universal religion or an integration of religions consonant with the vision of Hocking. In fact, the Hindu participant at the Colombo meeting, K. Sivaraman, made the strongest statement against any such idea, even arguing for the necessity for religions to make absolute claims, but within a pluralistic frame of reference:

> Is religions' claim to a final truth and absolute truth a local and dispensible feature of religion, so that we can look forward to a day when all religions pointing beyond their particularity, will be reconciled? Will the emerging world community be marking the day of the liberalists' paradise?
> Let me answer with an emphatic 'no'. The claim to final truth is an integral part of religion and must be experienced existentially.[48]

Sivaraman contended that liberalism and syncretism lacked the enthusiasm of commitment on which religions, including Hinduism "were founded and grounded." Ecumenicity within a religion and between religions, in his view, "should entail religious co-existence of the kind that preserves the character of religion as man's ultimate commitment."[49]

He rejected the idea that the emphasis on 'world community' or 'one humanity' should lead to claims that religions were "equally valid paths leading to the same goal, as mountain paths leading to the same summit." The definition of the Ultimate Truth a religion embodies has its own integrity, and such core definitions are by no means interchangeable. In this sense all religions are not equal; nor were they relative.[50]

Sivaraman held that religions were 'alternate absolutes' mutually exclusive except in a transcendental sense. For him, the ecumenicity of religions lay in the 'object' or goal of religions which is not divided, even when there were many possible ways of reaching it. He took the example of the circle, whose only common reference point is the centre: "There are infinite approaches to the centre from the periphery which may be described as alternative lines of approach in the sense that they are incommensurable. To each line the centre is surely, 'its' centre, the

47 *Towards World Community*, p. 117.
48 K. Sivaraman, "Resources in Hindu Morality and Religion" in *Towards World Community*, p. 27.
49 *Ibid.*, p. 29.
50 *Ibid.*

terminus of its length. But who can deny that the periphery in its entirety is the periphery of one centre."[51]

It is of interest that in this particular encounter it was the Hindus who insisted on the necessity of respecting the integrity of each religion, opposing general concepts like 'all religions lead to the same goal' without necessary qualifications of their meaning. They insisted that religions are different and must be treated so, not only as socio-cultural entities but also as belief systems defining the ultimate goal and its way. Significantly, however, they insisted that despite all the differences in the description, the centre in which all existence is rooted has indeed to be the centre of all existence and of all attempts to relate to it. Precisely because of this common centre, the different religions, treated as such, still provide enormous scope for cooperation, mutuality, and inter-relationships.

K. L. Sheshagiri Rao, another Hindu participant in several WCC dialogues, argued on the same lines as Sivaraman:

> Since differences are important, and in some cases unbridgeable no uncritical syncretism (*dharmasankara*) is entertained. While marvelling at the uniqueness of each religious tradition, Hindus appreciate the enrichment that comes from religious diversity. Each tradition is valued for the differences it brings to the human community. It makes them humble and prevents a sense of complacency and self-sufficiency in their own beliefs and practices.[52]

This examination of the documents from the period of the WCC's actual engagement in dialogue with Hindus shows that by and large the Hindus were clear on the premise on which dialogue was taking place, namely, the acceptance of religious plurality as a necessary reality. In the Hindu view this plurality could not be removed, and should in fact be respected, for while absolute claims would always emerge from the perspective of human apprehension, the truth to which all claims pointed must be one. A careful reading of the Hindu presentations shows that there was no general view that 'all religions lead to the same goal,' traditionally defended by Hindus, as is sometimes believed to be the case; there were not two centres to human existence, so all religions must point to or be in relationship with one centre. There might still be differences, distortions or even, from the perspective of different standpoints, wholly inadequate definitions of the goal and the way. Religions were different, not the same. But no religion should reject plurality, which was of the essence of the nature of human relationships with the 'centre.' In his assessment of his experience

51 *Ibid.*

52 K. L. Sheshagiri Rao, "Human Community and Religious Pluralism in Hindu Perspective" in *Dialogue in Community,* C. D. Jathanna, ed. (Mangalore, India: The Karnataka Theological Research Institute, 1982), p. 166.

at the Ajaltoun dialogue, the Hindu participant said that this sense of the 'otherness' of the other was vital for any enrichment through dialogue:

> Our dialogue during these days brings home to us a new sense of 'incompleteness,' a sense of the need for the truly other — the 'other' in the way of thinking and feeling that I cannot simply assimilate to my own, but which I confront inescapably, in other words, 'encounter.' It is the 'other' which comes with the demand to be understood in terms of its incommunicable 'otherness.' This does not mean confessing to a theological deficiency in one's position. On the contrary, it speaks for recognition of a new source of strength, hitherto remaining undetected. By virtue of its very adequacy and relevance, it opens itself for looking beyond itself, and evokes in one a creative need for the other.[53]

On the Christian side, however, there was too much diversity over the theological basis for seeking community with the Hindu or with any other religious person. This is best illustrated by the document on "Seeking Community" of Section III of the Nairobi Assembly, which lists some of the positions that Christians had taken on this issue both at Nairobi and at earlier meetings with Hindus and other religious partners.[54]

Besides the affirmation of the socio-political necessity for dialogue, the most popular view was the acceptance of 'common humanity' in creation, sometimes expressed in the general affirmation that 'God loves all His creatures.' This position was challenged from the perspectives of human sin, the relevance of the work of God in Christ and, especially, 'Christ's demand' to preach the gospel to all the nations.

Another thesis stressed the incarnation and the message of reconciliation as the bases for seeking community and being in dialogue with people of other faiths. This, however, also proved to be inadequate for the discussion because it always led to a consideration of 'attitudes' toward people of other faiths rather than a theological basis for th Christian–Hindu search for community. Both Metropolitan George Khodr and Fr. Paul Varghese (now Metropolitan Mar Gregorios) had already argued at the Central Committee meeting at Addis Ababa (1971) that the search for community and interfaith relations should have a trinitarian basis. Khodr stressed the concept of the cosmic Christ illumining people of all religions.[55] This was one of the possibilities offered at Nairobi as well, but it was not developed, nor was it accepted by many. Other Christians had

---

53 "Dialogue Between Men of Living Faiths" — The Ajaltoun Memorandum, p. 18.

54 David M. Paton, ed., *Breaking Barriers, Nairobi 1975: The Official Report of the Fifth Assembly of the WCC,* Nairobi, 23 November–10 December 1975 (WCC; London: SPCK, 1976), p. 76f.

55 See *Central Committee of the World Council of Churches: Minutes and Reports of the Twenty-Fourth Meeting,* Addis Ababa, Ethiopia, 10-21 January 1971 (Geneva: WCC, 1971), pp. 18-22, 130-35.

looked to a dynamic interpretation of the work of the Holy Spirit as the way forward in the quest for community.[56]

At Nairobi, another question further complicated the whole discussion: Should there be a mutually acceptable common basis between Christians and people of other faiths in order to seek community? "Considerable difficulty was experienced and no conclusion was reached," said the report.[57] We are not suggesting here that Nairobi's pointers towards a theological basis for seeking community were all inadequate. But none of them was sufficiently developed and, furthermore, there was no general agreement among Christians about the components of such a basis.

The confusion among Christians came out during the plenary debate, where a "Preamble" had to be added to the report on "Seeking Community" to make it acceptable to most of its opponents. Defending the dialogical attitude and the search for community, Russell Chandran spoke of the controversy as being between 'the Kraemerian approach' and 'the approach of dialogue.'[58] He put his finger on the heart of what has since come to be known as the 'Nairobi Controversy' over dialogue; it was a conversation, or rather a conflict, between 'Tambaram' and 'Kandy' for, all appearances to the contrary, the 'Tambaram debate' was not over, and in Chandran's opinion had not really begun in earnest within that part of the ecumenical family dominated by the Protestant and Orthodox member churches of the World Council of Churches. Let us illustrate our case with some passages from the "Preamble" attached to the Nairobi Report on "Seeking Community":

—We all agreed that the *skandalon* (stumbling block) of the gospel will be always with us. . . .
—While we do seek wider community with people of other faiths, cultures, and ideologies, we do not think that there will ever be a time in history when the tension will be resolved between belief in Jesus Christ and unbelief. . . .
—We should make a proper distinction between the division created by the judging Word of God and the division of sin. . . .
—We are all agreed that the great commission of Jesus Christ which asks us to go out into all the world and make disciples of all nations, and to baptize them in the Triune name, should not be abandoned or betrayed, disobeyed or compromised, neither should it be misused. . . .
—We are all opposed to any form of syncretism, incipient, nascent or developed, if we mean by syncretism conscious or unconscious human attempts to create a new religion composed of elements taken from different religions. . . .

56 *Breaking Barriers*, p. 76.
57 *Ibid.*
58 *Ibid.*, p. 71.

—We view the future of the church's mission as full of hope for it is not upon human efforts that our hope is based, but on the power and promise of God. ... [59]

The ideas of the Preamble could be traced point by point to the issues defended at Tambaram, and they rendered ineffective whatever else the report said about Christian relations with people of other faiths. Nothing in the Preamble was unacceptable in substance to those who had defended the dialogical approach, but it was deeply disturbing that the theological frame of reference, the presuppositions about other faiths, and the stance from which one looked at the issue had not changed since 1938. The charges against the dialogical approach were exactly the same as those levelled against liberalism at Tambaram — syncretism, loss of mission, and compromise of the uniqueness and finality of Jesus Christ.

The Nairobi debate also reflected a controversy between the churches that lived in religiously plural societies and those which did not. Arguing that the concern for dialogue derived from a full commitment to one's faith and offered a valid safeguard against uncritical syncretism, Lynn de Silva of Sri Lanka pleaded that dialogue with other faiths was needed to liberate Christians from the "closed or cloistered" system to which they belonged, and "to repudiate the arrogance, aggression, and negativism of our evangelistic crusades which have obscured the gospel and caricatured it as an aggressive and militant religion," making "proclamation ineffective and irrelevant" for the people of Asia.[60]

Russell Chandran begged the churches from predominantly 'Christian' countries to exercise more patience and understanding with those who had to deal with the concrete realities of their life situation:

> We would like our brethren who are concerned about the commitment to the Great Commission of our Lord and the dangers of syncretism to be willing to listen to the testimony and insights of those who have more knowledge of other faiths and are in no way less committed to Jesus Christ and his mission. We plead that they avoid the mistake of making judgements on the basis of traditional doctrines, without the knowledge of other peoples and their faiths, and thus failing to grow into the fullness of Christ.[61]

These interventions at Nairobi were also reminiscent of the pleas made in Asia following the Tambaram meeting.

David E. Jenkins (now Bishop of Durham) said that the attempt of the churches living in religiously plural societies to make claims at Nairobi for dialogue led "to an outcry about syncretism and betrayal of the gospel."

---

59 *Ibid.,* pp. 73-74.
60 *Ibid.,* p. 72.
61 *Ibid.*

He said further: "The response of the drafting committee to this outcry
left many Asians and others feeling that their insights and convictions were
being trampled on and betrayed."[62]

Guidelines on Dialogue

The Nairobi controversy over dialogue has been interpreted in many ways.
Stanley J. Samartha, then director of the WCC sub-unit on Dialogue, interpreted it as an inevitable clash of attitudes between those for whom
dialogue had become a matter of daily experience and others who did not
live with religious plurality in any significant way. Pointing out that the
Fifth Assembly had to deal with "more countries, more languages, and
perhaps more controversial issues than previous assemblies," he felt that
it was significant that "Nairobi succeeded in providing ecumenical space"
for the confrontation between the various views. In Samartha's view, the
significance of the debate was that it rendered the question of Christian
relations with other religious communities "a live issue for the churches in
the post-Nairobi period."[63]

In his critical analysis of the debate, Lukas Vischer observed that the
difficulty lay in moving away from concrete involvement in living dialogue
as the focus of theological discussions to a preoccupation with the systematic concept of dialogue and abstract theories about it.[64] The moderator
of the Dialogue sub-unit, D. C. Mulder, attributed the controversy at
Nairobi to the lack of unanimity among the churches on the whole question of dialogue and the basis for seeking community with people of other
faiths. Noting that there was "much hesitation and some suspicion,"
Mulder pointed out that the report at Nairobi quite often "could do no
more than summarize a whole range of differing opinions."[65]

The Central Committee of the WCC therefore authorized the sub-unit
on Dialogue to convene a theological consultation in Chiang Mai, Thailand
in April 1977 to allow a fuller consideration of some of the theological
issues raised at Nairobi. T. K. Thomas, who participated on behalf of the
Christian Conference of Asia, has helpfully summarized the purpose and
issues of the consultation:

---

62 David E. Jenkins, "Nairobi and the Truly Ecumenical: Contribution to a Discussion about the Subsequent Tasks of the WCC," *The Ecumenical Review* XXVIII 3
(July 1976): 281.

63 "Courage for Dialogue: An Interpretation of the Nairobi Debate" in S. J. Samartha, *Courage for Dialogue — Ecumenical Issues in Inter-religious Relationships* (Geneva:
WCC, 1981), p. 51.

64 Quoted by Paul Löffler in "Representative Christian Approaches to People of
Living Faiths: A Survey of Issues and its Evaluation" in *Faith in the Midst of Faiths:
Reflections on Dialogue in Community,* S. J. Samartha, ed. (Geneva: WCC, 1977), p. 21.

65 *Faith in the Midst of Faiths,* pp. 5-6.

The purpose of the consultation was threefold:

—to clarify the Christian basis for seeking community by focusing theological
reflection on specific issues and particular contexts;
—to indicate the nature of the Christian community within the human
community in a pluaralistic world; and
—to suggest 'guidelines' to Christian communities in pluralist situations to be
communities of service and witness without diluting their faith or compro-
mising their committment to Christ.

The issues discussed were the following:

—What is the nature of the community Christians are committed to seek?
What are the impediments to seeking community and what are the insights
from within the Christian faith that help them to relate themselves as
'communities of service and witness' to their neighbours?
—What is the theological significance of other faiths and cultures in the
Christian perspective? Is God at work among people of other faiths and
ideologies?[66]

Thomas remarked that Chiang Mai did not resolve the issues: "The old
questions remain not because they are not answered, but because the
answers are 'many and various'." He noted, however, that Chiang Mai
enabled the questions to be posed "with more clarity and greater integrity."[67] The Chiang Mai statement, later adopted with a number of modifications as the *Guidelines on Dialogue,* dealt primarily with the three
questions that had provoked theological controversy at Nairobi: The nature
of the Christian community within the human community, the bases and
goals of dialogue, and the consequences of these for Christian faith.
(Would they move the churches in the direction of syncretism?)

On the question of 'community,' Chiang Mai was able to affirm what
had always been possible at earlier discussions: The primary basis for
seeking community was rooted in the common humanity which Christians
shared with all others in creation and in God's overall purpose for it.
"Christians begin their reflection on community from the acknowledgement
that God as they believe Him to have come in Jesus Christ is the creator
of all things and of all humankind; that from the beginning He willed
relationships with Himself and between all that He has brought to life;
that to that end He has enabled the formation of communities, judges
them, and renews them."[68]

Emphasizing the reality of ongoing day-to-day life in community with
those who live by different faiths, Chiang Mai echoed Devanandan and
M. M. Thomas by recalling the challenges which Christians faced in such

---

[66] T. K. Thomas, "Report on Chiang Mai," in *Faiths in the Midst of Faiths,* p. 181.
[67] *Ibid.,* p. 182.
[68] *Guidelines on Dialogue with People of Living Faiths and Ideologies* (Geneva: WCC,
1979), p. 3.

common tasks as nation-building. Communities once closed to each other were "being thrown into relationship with others with which they find themselves engaged in the task of nation-building." The report called on Christians to recognize the cultural and religious pluralism into which they were being drawn and to which they needed to respond.[69] While affirming the richness of the diversity within humankind "as created and sustained by God in His love for all people" the *Guidelines* also warned that this diversity had often been abused in situations where one was "tempted to regard one's own community as the best; to attribute one's own religious and cultural identity an absolute authority."[70]

In this self-critical analysis the *Guidelines* seemed to be close to affirming that religious and cultural diversity was within God's purpose. But where they sought to give a more reasoned theological basis for religious plurality and the place of the Christian community as a community in itself in relationship with others, the document could do no more than list the theological differences which emerged. It offered four different bases for the "experience of communion":

–Our communion in the church as a sacrament of the reconciliation and unity of humankind recreated through the saving activity of God in Jesus Christ;
–our communion with God who, in the fulness of His Trinity, calls humankind into unity with Him in His eternal communion with His entire creation;
–our communion in fellowship with all members of the Body of Christ through history, across distinctions of race, sex, caste, and culture;
–a conviction that God in Christ has set us free for communion with all peoples and everything which is made holy by the work of God.[71]

The first type reflected the view of the Roman Catholic participants, who emphasized the sacramental nature of the Christian community within the human community. The second, held predominantly by the Orthodox participants, emphasized the glorification of the whole creation in God, and sought to understand the life and relationship of the Christian community to the world in eschatological terms. The third and fourth positions represented the views of the Protestant participants.

Given this diversity of views, the *Guidelines* could only affirm both the need to seek community and the ambiguity involved in the search:

As Christians we are conscious of a tension between the Christian community as we experience it to be in the world of human communities, and as we believe it in essence to be in the promise of God. The tension is fundamental to our Christian identity. We cannot resolve it, nor should

69 *Ibid.,* pp. 4-5.
70 *Ibid.,* p. 5.
71 *Ibid.,* pp. 7-8.

we seek to avoid it. In the heart of this tension we discover the character of the Christian church as a sign at once of peoples' need for fuller and deeper community, and of God's promise of a restored human community in Christ.[72]

Like earlier consultations, Chiang Mai could thus only draw ethical and moral implications about Christian relationships with other faiths. The report said:

> Our consciousness of the tension must preclude any trace of triumphalism in the life of the Christian church in the communities of humankind. It should also preclude any trace of condescension towards our fellow human beings. Rather it should evoke in us an attitude of real humility towards all people since we know that we together with all our brothers and sisters have fallen short of the community which God intends.[73]

Even though the Chiang Mai meeting experienced considerable difficulty in finding a theological basis for relating to people of other faiths, it had an easier task in dealing with the purpose of dialogue and its relationship to Christian witness. It emphasized that dialogue had to be "described, experienced, and developed as a life-style."[74] Dialogue was necessary in order "not to disfigure the image of your neighbours" and to create an atmosphere of "trust and respect" in mutual relationships. The report went further to affirm dialogue as an expression of Christian love and service:

> Dialogue, therefore, is a fundamental part of Christian service within community. In dialogue Christians actively respond to the command to "love God, and your neighbour as yourself." As an expression of love, engagement in dialogue testifies to the love experienced in Christ. It is a joyful affirmation of life against chaos, and a participation with all who are allies of life in seeking the provisional goals of a better human community. Thus "dialogue in community" is not a secret weapon in the armoury of an aggressive Christian militancy. Rather, it is a means of living our faith in Christ in the service of community with our neighbours.[75]

For those who feared that dialogue would lead to the loss of the sense of mission, the Chiang Mai report insisted that in a dialogue one could "speak the truth in love." Recognizing that in all witnessing situations "the spirit of dialogue" was indispensable, the paper denied that there could be any need to see "dialogue and giving witness as standing in contradiction to each other," and it affirmed dialogue as an activity in which Christians could often find opportunities for "authentic witness":

72 *Ibid.,* pp. 8-9.
73 *Ibid.*
74 *Ibid.,* p. 10.
75 *Ibid.,* pp. 10-11.

Thus, to the member churches of the WCC we feel able with integrity to commend the way of dialogue as one in which Jesus Christ can be confessed in the world today; at the same time we feel able with integrity to assure our partners in dialogue that we come not as manipulators but as genuine fellow-pilgrims, to speak with them of what we believe God to have done in Jesus Christ who has gone before us, but whom we seek to meet anew in dialogue.[76]

The consultation rejected syncretism as Nairobi had understood its meaning — "conscious or unconscious human attempts to create a new religion composed of elements taken from different religions,"[77] and it noted that most dialogue partners also rejected syncretism in this sense. There was affirmation, however, of the "positive need for a genuine 'translation' of the Christian message in every time and place," although there was always a risk that such translation of the message for different cultural settings and Christian approaches to other faiths might "go too far and compromise the authenticity of Christian faith and life." A similar danger, the consultation said, lay in "interpreting a living faith not in its own terms but in terms of another faith or ideology," for such interpretation would be "illegitimate on the principles of both scholarship and dialogue."[78]

Responding to the fact that fears of syncretism were expressed at Nairobi predominantly by the delegates of Western churches, the consultation noted that the wrong type of syncretism was not "a risk endemic only in certain continents," but could be recognized also in the "compromise of the Gospel in the so-called 'civil religions' of the West."

The burden of the argument was that the risks of syncretism "should not lead Christians to refrain from dialogue"; rather, they should become an "additional reason for engaging in dialogue so that the issue may be clarified."[79] Noting that "within the ecumenical movement the practice of dialogue and the giving of witness have sometimes evoked mutual suspicion," the *Guidelines* pleaded that there was a need within the ecumenical fellowship to give everyone "space and time" to explore the riches of the gospel in different social, political, and cultural contexts.[80]

For us, the major significance of the Chiang Mai consultation and the *Guidelines on Dialogue* does not lie in their attempt to define community or in the comments they made on dialogue and syncretism. These, as we have noted, had been matters for discussion since the Kandy meeting. Chiang Mai affirmed some of the earlier findings but in a discussion that

76 *Ibid.,* p. 11.
77 See discussions on the Preamble added to the Nairobi report on Seeking Community.
78 *The Guidelines on Dialogue,* pp. 14-15.
79 *Ibid.*
80 *Ibid.*

gathered a broad spectrum of theological positions from a group of persons representing all the major branches of the Christian faith. This enabled the Central Committee to 'receive' the guidelines, to 'adopt' the recommendations made to the churches, and to affirm the programme of dialogue as a priority within the Council.

Of greater significance for our present discussion is the matter on which the participants at Chiang Mai could not agree, and which they therefore placed within quotation marks, namely, the issue of the "theological significance of other faiths and ideologies." It was here that Chiang Mai was trying to deal with the theological issues unresolved since Tambaram. The controversy at Nairobi was by no means new, but improved methods of mass communication and media interest highlighted the controversy and gave it wider publicity. In essence, the Nairobi debate manifested Christians' inability to agree on the question of God's relationship to people of other faiths.

The *Guidelines* admitted that when Christians are engaged in dialogue they cannot "avoid asking themselves penetrating questions about the place of these people in the activity of God in history." Such questions were not theoretical for they arose from a Christian desire to know "what God may be doing in the lives of hundreds of millions of men and women who live in and seek community together with Christians but along different ways."[81]

The document therefore noted some of the questions on which agreement was "more difficult and sometimes impossible" and commended these for "further fruitful discussions" in the future:

—What is the relation between the universal creative/redemptive activity of God towards all humankind and the particular creative/redemptive activity of God in the history of Israel and in the person and work of Jesus Christ?

—Are Christians to speak of God's work in the lives of all men and women only in tentative terms of hope that they may experience something of him, or more positively in terms of God's self-disclosure to people of living faiths and ideologies and in the struggle of human life?

—How are Christians to find from the Bible criteria in their approach to people of other faiths and ideologies, recognizing, as they must, the authority accorded to the Bible by Christians of all centuries, particular questions concerning the authority of the Old Testament for the Christian church, and the fact that the partners in dialogue have other starting points and resources, both in holy books and traditions of teachings?

—What is the biblical view and Christian experience of the operation of the Holy Spirit, and is it right and helpful to understand the work of God outside the church in terms of the doctrine of the Holy Spirit?[82]

---

81 *Ibid.*, p. 11.
82 *Ibid.*, p. 13.

The Chiang Mai consultation was aware that the debate would ultimately turn on these theological points, but the participants could not join this debate in any significant way.

An Ecumenical Affirmation

Discussions within the CWME after the meeting at Mexico City also showed that while the need for a positive relationship was affirmed, there was a reluctance to deal theologically with the reality of religions as such. The 1973 Bangkok meeting on "Salvation Today," for example, was held in a predominantly Buddhist milieu. Emilio Castro has said that two attitudes were represented as this conference. The first of these found expression in the description of the church's task in Thailand, as it was explained to the conference by its representative:

> ... the main concern of the Church of Christ in Thailand was church growth; their goal was to double the membership of the church in four years. So they preached to the people and invited them to become Christians and to join the church.[83]

The second attitude was typified by the invitation for dialogue extended to Buddhist monks; this "illustrated an approach that pointed to the need to respect other religions and to learn from them." Castro observed, however, that "the report of the conference makes only a passing reference to the encounters with Buddhists." His concluding remarks on this aspect of the Bangkok gathering underlined the indecision on plurality that has plagued ecumenical discussions:

> When the delegates at Bangkok talked about salvation, they were all aware that they were surrounded by millions of people who too were seeking salvation, though their lives were centred in a totally different set of values. The challenge of other religions remains an open question in the missionary task of the church. What is the place of other religions in God's Kingdom?[84]

The focus of the next CWME world conference (Melbourne, 1980), was on the poor. The question of other faiths as a theological issue played little role in the discussions, although it was recognized that the majority of the poor of the earth were also people who lived by other faiths. Melbourne decided, however, to approach people of other faiths "not so much in terms of their religious convictions but in terms of their local human condition."[85]

---

83 Emilio Castro, *Freedom in Mission: The Perspective of the Kingdom of God* (Geneva: WCC, 1985), p. 19.
84 *Ibid.*
85 Cf. *Freedom in Mission*, p. 33.

The CWME's official document, *Mission and Evangelism: An Ecumenical Affirmation*, picked up the work on dialogue begun at Mexico City and went much further in affirming a dialogical relationship to people of other faiths. "True witness follows Jesus Christ in respecting and affirming the uniqueness and freedom of others" the statement said, confessing that Christians "have often looked for the worst in others and have passed negative judgement upon other religions."[86]

On the question of God's relationship to people of other faiths, the Affirmation could go only as far as the earlier statements, affirming God as the "creator of the whole universe" and as one who "has not left himself without witness at any time or any place." It would not draw any theological implications from this belief beyond noting that the "Spirit of God is constantly at work in ways that pass human understanding and in places which to us are least expected." In entering into a relationship of dialogue with others, therefore, "Christians seek to discern the unsearchable riches of God and the way God deals with humanity."[87]

The inability of the ecumenical discussions within the CWME in particular and within the WCC in general to affirm pluralism more consciously, received fresh articulation in paragraph 42 of the *Ecumenical Affirmation*:

> The Word is at work in every human life. In Jesus of Nazareth, the Word became a human being. The wonder of his ministry of love persuaded Christians to testify to people of every religious and non-religious persuasion of this decisive presence of God in Christ. In him is our salvation. Among Christians there are still differences of understanding as to how this salvation in Christ is available to people of diverse religious persuasions. But all agree that witness should be rendered to all.[88]

The statement thus attempted to accommodate the emphasis on accepting and respecting people of other faiths as partners in dialogue, and it appealed to the cosmic 'Word' active in every human life as the basis of such relationship. To those who would say "In him is Salvation," the statement responded, "In him is *our* salvation." Yet there was an admission of deep disagreement as to whether God was savingly active in other religious traditions. We shall return to a fuller consideration of this text again at a later stage.

The Guidelines on Dialogue was intended to give only a broad framework of agreement about Christian relationships with other faiths to facilitate further theological work on the issues of interfaith dialogue. It is therefore significant that the *Ecumenical Affirmation*, which was primarily concerned with mission and evangelism could incorporate so much from

---

86 *Mission and Evangelism: An Ecumenical Affirmation*, para. 41.
87 *Ibid.*, para. 43.
88 *Ibid.*, para. 42.

the Guidelines about dialogue and God's relationship with people of other faiths. The initiation of the theological discussions recommended in the *Guidelines* nevertheless became the task of the sub-unit on Dialogue. Let us look at some of the ways in which Stanley Samartha developed this theological work through the addresses and articles he offered as the Director of the Programme.

Courage for Dialogue

"Religious pluralism today is not just an academic issue to be discussed, but a fact of experience to be acknowledged," said Samartha. Noting that religions have traditionally been "moats of separation rather than bridges of understanding between people," he asked:

> How can men and women, committed to different faiths, live together in multi-religious societies? In a world that is becoming a smaller and smaller neighbourhood, what are the alternatives between shallow friendliness and intolerant fanaticism? What is the Christian obligation in the quest for human community in a pluralist situation?[89]

In many ways, these questions reflect the sub-unit's overall preoccupation: the promotion of an actual encounter between people of different religious traditions with a view to opening up new possibilities for relationships. Theological reflection was to take place only in the context of this encounter.

The work of the sub-unit thus moved away from sponsoring Christian discussions on theology to promoting actual bilateral and multilateral meetings between Christians and persons of other faiths. The sub-unit also encouraged dialogue at regional and local levels, primarily through study centres and dialogue centres in different parts of the world. It was necessary, therefore, to spell out the nature and consequences of dialogue, and the sub-unit gave this matter much attention. Here are some of Samartha's criteria for a dialogical relation between Christians and people of other faiths:[90]

> —There can be no dialogue between religions; dialogue can take place only between people of living faiths. While concepts and ideas are important, the first step in real dialogue is "to realize that religion is much more than its creeds formulated in particular categories."[91]

89 S. J. Samartha, "Religious Pluralism and the Quest for Human Community" in *No Man is Alien: Essays on the Unity of Mankind,* J. Robert Nelson, ed. (Leiden: E. J. Brill, 1971), p. 129.

90 Cf. my own summary in "Some Glimpses into the Theology of Dr. Stanley Samartha" in *Dialogue in Community: Essays in Honour of S. J. Samartha,* C. J. Jathanna, ed. (Mangalore, India: The Karnataka Theological Research Institute, 1982), p. 231 ff.

91 See S. J. Samartha, "The Progress and Promise of Interfaith Dialogue," *Journal of*

—Dialogue is for building community. It should lead to the strengthening of relationships between religious communities. "Informed understanding, critical appreciation, and balanced judgement of each other's faith" should eventually lead to trust, openness, and mutual commitment.[92]

—Dialogue should not lead to an uncritical mixture of religions. It would be foolish to eliminate fundamental differences between religions in the interest of shallow friendliness.[93]

—Interreligious dialogue should not be used by any of the partners as "a subtle tool for mission," or to promote the interests of one particular faith to the detriment of others.[94]

—In many situations of dialogue there is an authentic and inescapable commitment to share and witness. This should not take the form of "unilateral self-projection," but lead to open hospitality whereby each may share in what is most precious to the other.[95]

—Dialogue does not lead to superficial concensus, dilution of conviction or false harmony. It should lead to the re-examination and furthering of one's understanding of one's own faith and the discovery of new dimensions of Truth.[96]

But the more significant aspect of Samartha's work lies in the way he sharpened theological issues for ecumenical consideration. Taking up the relationship between God's universal, creative, and redemptive activity towards all humankind and His redemptive work in Jesus Christ, Samartha said that there were strong reasons for reviewing the prevailing Christian understanding of particularity itself, for Christians could "no longer talk of God's work in the lives of neighbours of other faiths in purely negative terms." If we do take God's relationship to all people seriously, "the particularity of Jesus Christ to other particularities should be considered not in terms of rejection but in terms of relationships."[97]

> Two possibilities are obvious. One is to regard universality as the extension of just one particularity. To the Christian this would mean the conquest of other 'lords' by Jesus Christ; it would mean the extension of the church and the extinction of other communities of faith. To the Muslim it would mean the extension of his particularity with similar

---

Ecumenical Studies 9 (Nov. 3, 1972).

92 "Dialogue as a Continuing Christian Concern" in John Hick and Brian Hebblesthwaite (London: Collins, 1979), p. 164 ff.

93 Cf. the Introductory article in *Towards World Community: The Colombo Papers*, S. J. Samartha, ed. (Geneva: WCC, 1975).

94 Cf. "More Than an Encounter of Commitments" in *Living Faiths and the Ecumenical Movement* (Geneva: WCC, 1971), p. 103 f.

95 See a fuller discussion on Missions in "Missions and Movements of Innovation" in *Courage for Dialogue*, p. 78 ff.

96 "The Lordship of Christ and Religious Pluralism" in *Courage for Dialogue*, p. 98 ff.

97 *Ibid.*, p. 97.

consequences to neighbours of other faiths. This seems neither desirable nor possible.[98]

Samartha also rejected the other extreme, which held that all particularities were "equally valid" and that "no particularity should claim universal validity." This attitude, said Samartha, could lead to a "sterile co-existence or an unseemly competition."

His own view moved towards a qualified relativization of all religions:

The other possibility, however, may be to recognize God alone as Absolute and to consider all religions to be relative. Religious particularities are not denied, but the ambiguity of religions as historical phenomena is recognized. The relativisation of religions would liberate their respective adherents from a self-imposed obligation to defend their particular community of faith over against the others, in order to be free to point to the ultimacy of God, who holds all things and all people in his embrace.[99]

Samartha was quick to point out that this did not mean that there was a neutral or objective ground or height from which one could relate to the world of religions. "There is no theological helicopter that can help us to rise above all religions and to look down upon the terrain below in lofty condescension" he said; "*our* standpoint, therefore, has to be Christian; but by the same token our neighbours are also free to have *their* particular standpoints."[100] More significantly, Samartha held that there could also be moments of dialogical relationship "where particular labels that partners wear lose importance and that which is behind and beyond them breaks through in spiritual freedom, offering a vision of the ultimate which holds them together":

We should of course be critically loyal to our own community of faith, the church which is our spiritual home. But our final obligation as Christians today is not to Christianity as a religion, nor to Western forms of Christianity which some of us have inherited, nor even to African or Asian expressions of Christianity which some of us —perhaps with a mixture of national zeal and religious enthusiasm— are trying to promote, but to God, who at the very point where he reveals himself in Jesus Christ, liberates us from our particular bondages in order to have new relations with our neighbours in the larger community. Only then do we become fully free to share with our neighbours the inestimable riches of God in Jesus Christ.[101]

Samartha insisted that only dialogue in community could be the focus for Christian witness in a plural world. Witness in its true sense could not be offered without an admission that it was offered not because there was no

---

98 *Ibid.*
99 *Ibid.*
100 *Ibid.*
101 *Ibid.,* p. 98.

truth in other religions, but because Christians had come under obedience to the truth revealed in Jesus Christ as the focus of their "doing the truth in love."[102] "There are different faiths, there are alternate ways of salvation, there are different hopes about human destiny, there are different affirmations as to what happens in the end," said Samartha. He concluded that "in the last analysis religions should be recognized as having responded to the mystery of the Ultimate."[103]

In Samartha's view, Christian witness has to do not with taking truth anywhere but with the belief that "in Jesus Christ the Ultimate has become intimate with humanity," and that nowhere else has "the victory over suffering and death manifested so decisively as in the death and resurrection of Jesus Christ."[104]

On the basis of his affirmation of plurality, Samartha rejected attempts to understand other faiths and their religious experience purely in terms of an expanded Christology:

> In the last analysis, religious pluralism means that there are fundamentally different answers to the problem of existence. There seems to be no way out of this plurality. One may enlarge the boundaries of the church to accommodate 'anonymous' Christians. One may extend the lineage of Christ back before Abraham to relate him to larger humanity. One may emphasize the 'cosmic' Christ to include principalities and powers and even nature in his domain. But this kind of 'cooption' may be regarded as patronizing by our neighbours of other faiths. It may satisfy an uneasy Christian conscience, but cannot cancel the persistent fact of religious pluralism. It is certainly not acceptable to our neighbours who are 'listening in' to us.[105]

In Samartha's view people of different religions should admit their 'interim' character, the fact that they are different responses to an Ultimate Mystery that is beyond total comprehension, and acknowledge that they are 'on the way,' in this common pilgrimage and that they need each other.

Samartha thus interpreted the Hindu and Christian religious faiths as two responses to the Truth "which transcends differences in human understanding." What was important to Hindu–Christian relations was not "whether one or other is false, but the distinctiveness of each of the responses." Samartha held that "In the core of any religion, including Hinduism and Christianity, there is something which belongs to it alone, separately, distinctively, decisively." It was this something which made each

---

102 Samartha develops this idea of truth as something that receives concrete manifestation of life in his article "Ganga and Galilee: Two Responses to Truth." We shall return to this shortly.

103 "The Lordship of Jesus Christ and Religious Pluralism," p. 103.

104 *Ibid.*

105 *Ibid.*

religion 'unique' and precluded any one from claiming 'uniqueness' to the exclusion of the other.[106] From this perspective Samartha made an important response to the Nairobi debate on decisiveness:

> ... a particular religion can claim to be decisive for some people, and some people can claim that a particular religion is decisive for them, but no religion is justified in claiming that it is decisive for all. The Hindu and the Christian have their own particular, distinctive contributions to make to the common quest for truth. 'Relativity' in this sense does not undermine religious life, but strengthens and mutually enhances the quality of the quest.[107]

Following Howard Burkle, Samartha claimed that religions were relative *because* they were 'special and distinctive.' The very qualities which 'disqualified' their claim to absoluteness made "each religion precious and irreplaceable."[108] To say that the Christian revelation is relative was "not to deny the absoluteness of the divine truth which is revealed therein. It is to deny the absoluteness of what any creature apprehends of divine truth."[109]

In any case, Truth in relation to human apprehension was never understood in either Christianity or Hinduism in "static" terms as something "out there for the people below to look and respond." In Hinduism *dharma* and *satya* were closely related and in Christianity the emphasis was on obedience to the Truth which was more decisive than speculations about God as The Truth. So what should be emphasized in Hindu–Christian relations was a dialogue 'into truth' about concrete social realities; this would also help us to see how the Truth beyond all claims was understood by the partner.

> Dialogue into truth should also mean growth in truth in the sense that through dialogue opportunities for participation in truth are enhanced, openings to further dimensions of truth are increased, and the obligation to be committed and loyal to what has been received becomes more compelling.[110]

Observing that Hinduism and Christianity had "developed separately during the centuries and shaped their own profiles without much mutual influence," Samartha claimed that the pressure to live in community and the willingness of the Hindu and the Christian to be in dialogue offered "immense possibilities" for the future. "Therefore," he said, "in spite of

---

106 "Ganga and Galilee: Two Responses to Truth," article included in *Courage for Dialogue*, pp. 152-53.

107 *Ibid.*

108 Here Samartha is referring to Howard R. Burkle's article on "Jesus Christ and Religious Pluralism," *Journal of Ecumenical Studies* XVI 3 (Summer 1979).

109 *Courage for Dialogue*, p. 152. Here too Samartha is following Howard Burkle.

110 "Ganga and Galilee: Two Responses to Truth," p. 153.

difficulties and setbacks we should confidently work together in community, hoping to grow together in truth."[111]

Conclusion

In the opening paragraphs of the next chapter we shall summarize our findings and draw some general conclusions about furthering the ecumenical discussions. Here we need only note that, despite the serious setback at Nairobi, discussions since the Kandy meeting have taken 'dialogue' as the primary frame of reference for understanding Christian relationships with people of other faiths. Much work has been done in defining and refining the meaning, purposes, and goals of dialogue, as well as the attitude that should go with it.

At Kandy, Kenneth Cragg had already raised the theological issues involved in a dialogical relationship, both for a Christian theological understanding of other faiths and for the concept and practice of mission. By taking up the theological issues listed in the *Guidelines,* Samartha provided a more direct link between the continuing discussions within the structures of the World Council and the contemporary debates about the Theology of Religions.

What are some of the implications of these developments, and what suggestions can we make for Christian–Hindu relations? It is to these questions that we turn in our final chapter.

111 *Ibid.*

Part 3

The Quest for a Future

CHAPTER VII

Towards a Theology in Relationship

As we approach the concluding stages of our discussion it will be useful to have a bird's eye view of the developments outlined thus far and to restate more precisely the specific issues on which we need to concentrate in this concluding chapter.

A Summary of the Developments

Our consideration of the 1910 meeting of the IMC has shown that Christian–Hindu relations are not a new issue for ecumenical discussion. The content and presentation of the Christian message, the presuppositions of the Christian missions, and Christian attitudes to the Hindu and to Hinduism were all matters for specific attention at Edinburgh. The records of the meeting indicated three reasons why this had become an important issue. First, the missionaries themselves were deeply challenged by the religious reality that confronted them, which they could not simply set aside as 'unbelief' or 'superstition.'[1] Second, the missionaries found that the whole of Hindu society was so closely knit together and organized around the assumptions of Hinduism that it was very difficult to find a point of entry that would not ultimately challenge the whole social system, provoking strong resistance and challenge from the Hindu side.[2] Third, the continued existence of Hinduism as a living reality alongside Christianity raised questions about attitudes to and relationships with those who had

---

1 Most of the respondents to Commission IV's questionnaire confirmed this in their reports. See Discussion in Chapter II, p. 21 f.

2 It was Macnicol that spoke about the Hinduism 'proud of itself' and wanting to defend itself as the religion of the land. See Chapter III, p. 34 ff.

heard the gospel but not responded to it by changing their religious identity.[3]

We noted that the challenge of religious plurality, and of Hinduism in particular, was taken up for serious consideration by Commission IV, but missionary confidence at that period was so strong that the pleas of this Commission were set aside; instead, a programme for the evangelization of the world was emphasized.[4] Jerusalem, 1928, witnessed the crisis of this unbridled confidence. This was caused partly by the revival and reformation of Hinduism (mainly in response to the missionary movement), an aggressive posture towards missions and conversions on the part of many Hindus, and the rise of nationalism linked to the affirmation of 'the religion of the land.' Of even greater significance were the rise of secularism in the West and the deep questioning, from within the liberal wings of the church, of the presuppositions of missions.[5]

It appeared that the church was willing to cooperate with the other religious traditions against the 'common enemy,' but still maintaining the specificity of the Christian message and witness. There were attempts to look to the 'values' in Hinduism that could be enriched by the presentation and 'entry' of Christ within the Hindu religion as such.[6]

Tambaram, 1938, however, proved to be the culmination of the resistance within the missionary movement to the liberal ideas about Christian relations with Hinduism. Kraemer's interpretation of Hinduism as a "primitive apprehension of reality" that was naturalistic and vitalistic, and as a religion that began and ended with man, reversed the trends of 1928. His view that Hinduism constituted a "human attempt" and a "groping after God," his closely argued position on the need for Christian mission, and his emphasis on the planting of the church in non-Christian societies were to become major influences in determining Christian–Hindu relations for decades to come.[7]

Kraemer's insistence that empirical Christianity fell within the category of 'unbelief' in the dialectical understanding of the gospel and religion did not have the effect he had hoped for on Christian–Hindu relations. Instead, the superiority of Christianity over all other religions, as the one

---

3 *Ibid.*

4 The sharp contrast between the discussion and report of Commission IV on the one hand, and the Edinburgh Report on the other, is an evidence of this confidence. See Chapter II, p. 28 ff.

5 Cf. Chapter III, p. 48 ff.

6 Here there was a difference between Macnicol and the final report. Macnicol spoke of Christ 'entering' the Hindu spiritual Home; the Report called on the non-Christians to consider the claims of Christ. Discussion in Chapter III, p. 39 f. and p. 44 ff.

7 We have maintained that this view put forward by Kraemer using Barth's and Brunner's theology has become the theological formation of most Protestant congregations on the question of other faiths. See Chapter IV, pp. 58-65.

which carried the gospel message, and of the church as the community
that had responded to the gospel, became the controlling forces in determining the overall attitude of the church to the Hindus. Kraemer had of
course argued for a deeply personal, truly humble, and genuinely self-
giving attitude to the Hindu as the only 'point of contact' between the
Christian and the Hindu. He also revised his position on the status of
Hinduism in the economy of salvation, but these changes did not diminish
the essentially triumphalistic attitude of Christians in their relations with
Hindus. Tambaram interpreted the church as both the primary instrument
and the fruit of the gospel message. The supplanting of other religions by
the church was thus the inevitable implication of the Tambaram emphasis.[8]

It was the post-colonial revival of India that enabled a shift in Hindu–
Christian relations. To the younger churches, which had by now become
independent, the Hindu world was no longer a 'mission field' of the
Western missionary movement. Devanandan, Kulandran, Niles, and Thomas
helped to shift the emphasis from 'Christian–non-Christian' to 'the Gospel
and the World' so they could address the issue of Christian participation
with others in the building of the nation and the pluralistic society that
constituted it. Of more significance was their insistence on placing the
Christian mission within the larger 'mission of God,' which included God's
active dealing with Hindus and Hinduism.[9] Devananadan and Thomas
emphasized the need to understand the renewal and humanization of
Hindu society as the locus of meeting the risen Christ and of witnessing
to him. Persons like Chenchiah went further to suggest that the Christians'
goal was not the conversion of the Hindu but the transformation of
Hinduism.[10]

The discussions within the WCC, now concentrated on the post-Tambaram studies on the "Word of God and the Living Faiths of Men," came
under the influence of developments within Roman Catholicism following
the Second Vatican Council. Vatican II affirmed a broader understanding
of God's salvific will and the need for cooperation and collaboration with
people of other faiths. With regard to Hinduism, the Council affirmed
both the spiritual quest and the many ways of salvation to which the
tradition bore witness as matters for serious theological appraisal.[11] The
influence of Roman Catholic thinking, Orthodox participation in the
ecumenical movement and the developing historical situation combined to

8 See Chapter IV, pp. 65-68 and pp. 83-88.

9 See our discussion on Devanandan, Niles, and Thomas in Chapter V, pp. 106-120.

10 For Chenchiah's position see D. A. Thangasamy, *The Theology of Chenchiah*,
op. cit., p. 195 ff.

11 See Chapter VI, p. 129 ff. See also the Vatican documentation, "The Attitude of
the Church Towards the Followers of Other Religions" (Vatican City, Pentecost 1984),
pp. 7-22.

bring a new emphasis to 'dialogue' as the primary mode of Christian–Hindu relations.

Even though the emphasis on dialogue had played a crucial role in the WCC's relations with people of other faiths, theological hesitations and controversy continued within its ranks and eventually erupted in a significant way at its Assemblies in Nairobi and Vancouver. The ecumenical movement was deeply polarized at Nairobi between those who represented what might be called the 'Tambaram position' and others who stood by the implications of the 'dialogical attitude' developed at Kandy.[12]

Our purpose in retracing these developments is to highlight some of the areas where the ecumenical movement may need to concentrate attention in the coming years if it is to help Christians in their search for relationships with people of other faiths. The Nairobi debate and the Vancouver discussions, which we shall briefly review in the following pages, showed that much more theological work was needed if, for example, the Christians in India were to come to grips with their life in a multi-faith society where Christian–Hindu relationships have reached a critical stage.[13] Here we shall identify two areas where further ecumenical reflection is necessary. We shall also show the relevance of the contemporary discussions in the field of theology of religions to this concern and, finally, we shall indicate some directions in which we might proceed in the future.

Issue I:

Is Religious Pluralism Within God's Purpose?

The underlying issue in all the ecumenical discussions in our view could be reduced to the question of Christian attitude to religious plurality itself. Is religious plurality within God's purpose? Is pluralism a blessing or a curse? Should the Christian attitude to other faiths, however humble, loving, and open, aim primarily at supplanting them?

In the ecumenical discussions which we have traced, religious plurality was not itself the subject of discussion; rather, all positions taken could be shown ultimately to take one side or the other on the issue of plurality. The discussions were primarily about the validity of specific religious traditions, often wondering whether God was revealingly active in their

---

12 Discussion of these two Assemblies will follow.

13 Stanley J. Samartha in "Interreligious Relationships in the Secular State," *Current Dialogue* II (December 1986) points to a number of areas of tension in interfaith relations in India, pp. 22-28.

history, or whether the religious experiences to which the adherents of different faiths testified could have any ultimate meaning.[14]

Both at Edinburgh and Jerusalem some persons had wanted to affirm plurality, at least partially. Edinburgh's Commission IV had pleaded that the religious experience of the Hindu should not be set aside. It had argued that the depth of understanding of Reality as seen in Hinduism and the testimony of those who were in contact with devout Hindus witnessed to a 'two-way communication' between God and man that should be a challenge to any Christian exclusivism that would consider Hindu religious experience as 'false' or 'invalid.'[15]

Nicol Macnicol's stand at Jerusalem (on the 'spiritual values' of Hinduism as those that could be 'enriched' and 'fulfilled' by the entry of Christ into the Hindu spiritual 'home') came nearest to the full affirmation of religious plurality in keeping with the mood of Jerusalem.[16] The positions taken by Devanandan, Niles, and M. M. Thomas implicitly affirmed plurality, but these were based on the conviction that the whole of religious life was renewed and redeemed by the risen Christ.[17] Such viewpoints were strengthened by the emphasis on the 'Cosmic' Christ within Roman Catholic theology after Vatican II[18].

It is important to note that it was only Tambaram that actually worked out a theologically argued position on other religions and their theological 'status' in relation to the gospel. Kraemer had analyzed all the major religious traditions of the world and drawn the conclusion that the gospel was in discontinuity with them. The implication of the Tambaram position for plurality was that it must be fought and overcome.[19]

It is our conviction that all the discussions which have taken place within the WCC since its formation have never radically challenged Tambaram's position on religious plurality. Indeed, the emphasis on 'dialogue' avoided the question of religious plurality by concentrating on the issue of relationships. There was of course an implicit affirmation of plurality in the dialogical attitude, but wherever pressed on the issue, the *Guidelines* attempted not to take sides. The theological issues that had to do with plurality, as seen earlier, were stated with a question mark behind them.[20]

---

14 This was the focus of the Jerusalem and Tambaram meetings. While Jerusalem was open to see 'values' in other faiths, Tambaram rejected it. (Chapters III and IV).

15 Chapter II, p.21 for example.

16 Chapter III, p. 39ff.

17 Discussed in Chapter V. For a fuller treatment see M. M. Thomas, *Man and the Universe of Faiths, op. cit.,* pp. 129-57.

18 See below where we deal with the theology of Karl Rahner and Raimundo Panikkar as the development of cosmic Christology.

19 See discussions under "Tambaram and Missions" in Chapter IV, pp. 83-86.

20 *Guidelines,* p. 13f.

The Nairobi controversy was thus the necessary consequence of the fundamental theological inadequacy of the discussions within the WCC. Indeed, the report on "Seeking Community" affirmed many dimensions of Christian relationships with other faiths that had not been undergirded by the prerequisite theological positions on plurality itself. The outstanding illustration of this problem, however, was to appear in the equally divisive discussion at the WCC's Sixth Assembly at Vancouver (1983): Here, the Section on "Witnessing in a Divided World," which dealt with the question of Christian relations with people of other faiths, aroused so much controversy that it had to be referred back to committee. The Section report's comments on God's relation to other faiths created an uproar not dissimilar to that in Nairobi seven years earlier.[21]

The report presented to the Vancouver plenary read as follows:

> While affirming the uniqueness of the birth, life, death, and resurrection of Jesus to which we bear witness, we recognize God's creative work in the religious experience of people of other faiths.[22]

A number of interventions raised serious objection to the recognition of 'God's creative work' in the religious experience of the people of other faiths. The deep disagreement induced the majority of the Assembly to vote to refer the report back to the drafting committee. And the drafting committee received no fewer than sixty-eight written proposals, all relating to that one sentence. Finally the Central Committee meeting that immediately followed the Assembly accepted the following formulation:

> While affirming the uniqueness of the birth, life, death, and resurrection of Jesus to which we bear witness, we recognize God's creative work in the seeking for religious truth among people of other faiths.[23]

"What is recognized here as belonging to God's creative work," commented Emilio Castro, "is not the achievement of other religions, but the searching for truth within those religions. Many were dissatisfied with the statement, but it illustrates how controversial the dialogue concern continues to be."[24]

To sharpen the issue, we must observe that the real controversy centred much more on the theological assumptions behind dialogue than on the dialogical relationship itself. It is indeed significant that the WCC

---

21 For the full section report see David Gill, ed., *Gathered for Life: Official Report, VI Assembly, World Council of Churches,* Vancouver, Canada, 24 July–10 August 1983 (Grand Rapids: Wm. B. Eerdmans; Geneva: WCC, 1983), pp. 31-42.

22 *Monthly Letter on Evangelism* 11 (WCC: Nov. 1983), describes the different formulations attempted and the objections raised, p. 1 ff.

23 *Ibid.*

24 Emilio Castro, Editorial for the Issue on "Dialogue: An Ecumenical Concern," *The Ecumenical Review* XXXVII 4 (Oct. 1985): 384-85.

Assembly in 1983 could not agree to speak of "God's creative work in the religious experience of people of other faiths" but could only "recognize God's creative work in the seeking for religious truth" among people of other faiths. It is our contention that the root of the problem lies in the absence from the ecumenical movement of a considered theological position on religious plurality, and this argument is aptly illustrated by the close similarity between the last Vancouver formulation and the position taken at Tambaram in 1938:

> We believe that Christ is the way for all, that He alone is adequate for the world's need. . . . Men have long been seeking Him all through the ages. Often this seeking and longing have been misdirected. But we see glimpses of God's light in the world of religions, showing that His yearning after His erring children has not been without response.[25]

Had the theological understanding of Christian relationships with other faiths not moved since 1938? Our study of the developments since Tambaram does show that it had. But the reluctance of the WCC discussions to take a more explicit stand on the theological significance of religious plurality has plagued, and will continue to plague, any serious ecumenical consideration of these relationships. We are convinced that the time is ripe for the ecumenical movement to develop a set of theological convictions about religious plurality along the same lines which it has already followed in relation to mission and evangelism, and to dialogical relations between Christians and people of other faiths. Without a contemporary theological response to religious plurality, future discussions on the issue are bound to result in the selfsame stalemate as at Nairobi and Vancouver, and yet again concerned Christians will have to fall back on Tambaram, which adopted the only clear position vis-à-vis other faiths and a theology of mission to sustain it.

In an article entitled "The WCC and the Academy: A Memorandum," Krister Stendahl bemoaned the increasing distance that had crept between the WCC's work and the academic disciplines since 1948. "Academic theologians of our time were few and far between at Vancouver," said Stendahl, "not only among delegates but also among advisers," noting that the WCC had thus lost a heritage that it had once cherished. Stendahl agreed with the emphasis on participation and strongly believed that the academic input must come from a variety of cultural contexts. But the scholars' presence was essential, "for they have a way of addressing the questions behind the questions." They can be masters of the "hermeneutics of suspicion," and "they can often ask: Why are we doing what we are doing — rather than something quite different?"

---

25 "Findings of Tambaram Meeting," in *The Authority of the Faith*, p. 200.

But more importantly, Stendahl worried that the absence of a serious attempt to incorporate contemporary thinking into the WCC's work had lulled the WCC into settling down with an unchallenged, neo-orthodox variety of 'received theology' from the mid-twentieth century. Stressing that many of the major moral and spiritual questions confronting the churches were already on the academic agenda, he concluded: "So it is not 'we and them.' It is a troubled humanity seeking light wherever it can be found."[26]

During the last decade there has been enormous soul-searching among theologians of religion on the whole issue of pluralism and relationships between religious communities. We are convinced that this self-examination is of challenging relevance to the WCC's occasional hesitation between the security of its 'received theology' and the impulse to further exploration. So we must now turn our attention to the contemporary discussion of the theology of religions in order to assess its contribution to the issue we have indicated.

Attempts in Contemporary Discussion to Deal with Pluralism

In recent years, there have been a number of attempts to analyse contemporary discussions of the theology of religions. In a useful volume, Alan Race has typified patterns of Christian theology of religions as tending towards 'exclusivism,' 'inclusivism' or 'pluralism.'[27] A similar classification is also used by the Church of England study-book, *Towards a Theology for Interfaith Dialogue*,[28] while Gavin D'Costa's *Theology and Religious Pluralism* refers to 'pluralist,' 'exclusivist,' and 'inclusivist' paradigms.[29]

In an examination of the various ways in which each of the world religions has responded to religious plurality, Harold Coward characterizes Christian approaches as 'theo-centric,' 'Christo-centric,' or 'dialogical.'[30] But Paul Knitter offers a much more extensive and comprehensive treatment of Christian attitudes towards world religions, using four models: 'conservative' (one true religion), 'mainline Protestant' (salvation only in Christ), 'Catholic' (many ways, one Norm), and 'theo-centric' (many ways to the centre).[31] It is beyond our scope either to examine these systems or to

---

26 Krister Stendahl, "The WCC and the Academy: A Memorandum" in *Faith and Faithfulness: Essays on Contemporary Ecumenical Themes, A Tribute to Philip A. Potter,* Pauline Webb, ed. (Geneva: WCC, 1984), pp. 74-75.

27 Alan Race, *Christians and Religious Pluralism: Patterns in the Christian Theology of Religions* (London: SCM Press, 1983).

28 *Towards a Theology for Inter-Faith Dialogue* (London: CIO Publishing, 1984).

29 Gavin D'Costa, *Theology and Religious Pluralism: The Challenge of Other Religions* (London/New York: Basil Blackwell, 1986).

30 Harold Coward, *Pluralism: Challenge to World Religions* (New York: Orbis, 1985).

31 Paul F. Knitter, *op. cit.*

develop a new taxonomy, or even to consider them in any detail. It is important, however, to note the relevance of some aspects of these discussions to the issue at hand and to see how they take up questions that have already appeared in the ecumenical debate and develop them in the light of contemporary realities.

We noted that the Barth—Brunner—Kraemer position on the discontinuity between the gospel and religions had dominated the Protestant discussions. The most radical challenge to this stance came from John Hick. But Hick shifted from a theological to a philosophical, moral framework for understanding Christian relations with people of other faiths, claiming that it was unlikely that at any time "all religious men will think alike, or worship in the same way, or experience the Divine identically." He held that the contrary would be the case:

> ... So long as there is a rich variety of human cultures —and let us hope that there will always be this— we expect there to be correspondingly different forms of religious cult, ritual, and organization conceptualized in different theological doctrine. And so long as there is a wide spectrum of human psychological types —and again let us hope that there will always be this— we should expect there to be correspondingly different emphases between, for example, the sense of the divine as just and as merciful; between *karma* and *bhakti*; or between worship as formal and communal and worship as free and personal. Thus we may expect the different world faiths to continue as religious-cultural phenomena, though phenomena that are increasingly interpenetrating one another.[32]

We have quoted Hick here at length to show the difference between his starting point and Kraemer's. Kraemer began with biblical realism and looked upon religious diversity as evidence of 'misguided' attempts that must be challenged and corrected by the presentation of the gospel, but Hick recognized diversity not only as an empirical reality to be dealt with, but also as something inevitable and necessary. In his essay, "Whatever Path Men Choose is Mine," he ruled out the possibility that all people could belong to a single religion as not only unlikely but also "not a consummation to be desired." Here again he argued that it was in the nature of religious life that there would "always be the more mystical and the more prophetic types of faith, with their corresponding awareness of the Ultimate Reality as non-personal and personal," and so on.[33]

It is in the context of this affirmation of plurality that Hick made his well-known call for a Copernican revolution in our understanding of the

32 John Hick's concluding article, "The Outcome: Dialogue into Truth" in John Hick, ed., *Truth and Dialogue — The Relationship between World Religions* (London: Sheldon Press, 1974), pp. 151-52.

33 "Whatever Path Men Choose is Mine" in *God Has Many Names* (London: Macmillan, 1980), p. 58.

relationship between different religious traditions. Hick described the Kraemerian understanding of the Christian relationship to other faiths as belonging to the Ptolemaic model, with Christ considered as the centre of the religious universe, but with Christianity becoming its centre in actual fact.[34] It is significant that for Hick the call for a Copernican revolution in the relationship among religions was based on 'new observations' of the past hundred years, just as in astronomy:

> The traditional dogma has been that Christianity is the centre of the universe of faiths, with all other religions seen as revolving at various removes around the revelation in Christ and being graded according to their nearness to or distance from it. But during the last hundred years or so we have been making new observations and have realized that there is deep devotion to God, true sainthood, and deep spiritual life within these other religions; and so we have created our epicycles of theory, such as the notions of anonymous Christianity and of implicit faith.[35]

There is a striking parallel here to the responses to the questionnaire sent by Edinburgh's Commission IV and to Nicol Macnicol's presentation to the Jerusalem meeting. But Hick drew different conclusions. "But would it not be realistic," he asked, "to make the shift from Christianity at the centre to God at the centre, and to see both our own and the other great world religions as revolving around the same divine reality?"[36]

The members of Commission IV, and Macnicol after them, had seen the reality of religious life in other faiths primarily as a theological challenge to Christian faith. Hick, however, pointed out that in a pluralistic world it was not appropriate for one religion to set itself as the only unique and universal revelation. This raised for him questions of morality of relationships and he sought to resolve the problem by bringing God to the centre:

> ... We have to realize that the universe of faiths centres upon God, and not upon Christianity or upon any other religion. He is the sun, the originative source of light and life, whom all the religions reflect in their own different ways.[37]

---

34 John Hick, *The Second Christianity* (SCM Press), 1983, p. 81. (Earlier editions published as *Christianity at the Centre*, 1968, and *The Centre of Christianity*, 1977.) Hick defines epicycles as "imaginary circles centering on the circumferences of other circles, thus forming new and more complex paths which were closer to the actually observed orbits of the planets." He says that by postulating ever more complex arrangements of epicycles, it might have been possible to maintain the Ptolemaic dogma indefinitely. "But," he adds, "sooner or later the human mind calls a halt to such an artificial procedure" (p. 81).

35 *Ibid.*, p. 82.

36 *Ibid.*

37 *God Has Many Names*, p. 52.

In an article entitled "Does Copernicus Help?", J. J. Lipner criticized Hick, among other things, for using the 'God' language. "Where do those religions which accord no final standing to 'God' in the minimal sense of a transcendant, unconditional, existent reality, fit into the Copernican reconstruction?" he asked.[38] Harold Coward had the same difficulty, but was quick to surmize that Hick meant by 'God' what he later described as 'the real,' which may or may not be described in personal terms.[39]

Even though Hick's suggestion opened up the search for a pluralistic model for inter-faith relations, a question remained for many about the nature of truth in religion, especially as it stood in relationship to the 'centre.' Alan Race remarked that Hick's proposal had raised issues of the relative validity and adequacy of the images of God held by the religious traditions and for criteria for evaluating differences.[40] From the perspective of Christian theology, Hick would have to reinterpret Christology to fit the scheme of any new relationships. "None the less," said Race, "one can defend the Copernican revolution insofar as it is submitted as a possible Christian theology of religions for today's 'one world' "; Race is convinced that Hick's suggestion has arisen from the belief that religious experience represents *genuine* encounter with the one ultimate divine reality.[41]

Paul Knitter agreed with Race that the Copernican revolution had in fact introduced the theocentric emphasis as an important way forward in the theology of religions. "I believe," said Knitter, "that this model both addresses the inadequacies and preserves the values of all other models. ... Although I have reservation about some of the individual arguments used by its various proponents, I feel that this model holds the greatest promise for the future inter-religious dialogue and for the continuous evolution of the meaning of Jesus Christ for the world."[42]

Knitter's interest in affirming pluralism derived from a recognition that today we can speak about religious questions only against the background of all the world religions. He further argued that this situation was a result of the increase of knowledge not simply about other religions but also about the adherents of other religions. "It is one thing to confront a religious truth in the abstract — on the printed page or in a classroom lecture," said Knitter. "It is quite another to see it enfleshed in the life

---

38 Julius J. Lipner, "Does Copernicus Help? Reflections for a Christian Theology of Religions" in *Inter-religious Dialogue*, Richard W. Rousseau, ed. (Scranton, USA: Ridge Row, 1981), p. 167f. Reprinted from *Religious Studies* 13 (1977), pp. 248-58.

39 Harold Coward, *op. cit.*, p. 26. Coward, however, is critical of *all* theocentric models.

40 Alan Race, *op. cit.*, p. 83.

41 *Ibid.*

42 Paul Knitter, *No Other Name?* pp. 166-67.

of a friend."[43] Building on this 'new awareness' of plurality, he asked searching questions about the adequacy of the traditional response to plurality as represented by the 1910 call to the 'evangelization of the world,' reclaimed at Tambaram and reaffirmed implicitly in much of the subsequent ecumenical discussion. In Knitter's view, the need for a new response to pluralism became "more pressing" when we looked "carefully at what nineteen centuries of Christian missionary activity have actually accomplished." He noted that in one sense the achievements were "extensive and laudable," for the "blood and sweat of generations of missioners" had resulted in the church's being "planted" in all continents and in almost every nation. He also recognized the overall impact of the gospel message on many cultures.[44] "But if we consider the goal of Christian mission to be conversion," said Knitter, "the picture becomes less impressive, in fact quite disheartening."

> After two thousand years of missionary labours, Christians number only about 31 percent of the world population. If the present demographic trends continue, with the bulk of the population explosion taking place in non-Western, non-Christian nations, some experts predict that by the year 2000, Christians will number only 16 percent of the world population.[45]

Knitter's predictions may be questioned by others who see the future of Christianity precisely in its growth in the non-Western cultures. We have noted this point here because Knitter's concern is shared by many others who feel a need to come to grips with plurality because of their sense that a purely 'missionary response' to plurality will take the church nowhere. Such an awareness is based not on the loss of nerve with regard to missions, but on the question whether it is within God's purpose that the plurality of religions should be abolished: this is the question with which we began our discussion of this issue.

Knitter's own view is that the new perception of religious pluralism is "pushing our cultural consciousness towards the simple but profound insight that *there is no one and only way*" [emphasis Knitter's], but that plurality is of the essence of reality:

> The new awareness of multiplicity, of pluralism, is being felt not just as a provisional situation or a stop-gap admission that we have to tolerate until we can come up with a master plan that will herd all these 'other' sheep into one corral. Pluralism does not result simply from limitations of the

43 *Ibid.*, pp. 3 ff.

44 *Ibid.*

45 *Ibid.* Knitter here follows the predictions of Walbert Bühlmann in *The Coming of the Third Church* (Maryknoll, N. Y.: Orbis, 1977). He notes that although David B. Barratt's *World Christian Encyclopedia* predicts that the Christian population by the year 2000 will remain at the level of 32.3 percent, the number of Christians is actually declining.

human mind to 'get it all together.' Rather, pluralism seems to be the very stuff of reality, the way things are, the way things function. . . . Reality is essentially pluriform: complex, rich, intricate, mysterious. "Pluralism is not the mere justification of opinions, but the realization that the real is more than the sum of all possible opinions."[46]

Knitter's own contribution, however, lies not in the affirmation of plurality along the lines traced by Hick but in the promotion of another view of the inter-relationship between religious traditions within the pluralistic reality. This he called 'Unitive Pluralism.'

The concept of 'unitive pluralism' is built on the assumption that the 'many' affirmed in the pluralistic understanding "cannot exist in splendid isolation." Knitter holds that in the contemporary pluralistic world there cannot be just one religion, but neither can there be many that exist in "indifferent tolerance." Taking his cue from the processive-relational view of reality, Knitter argues that there is a growing relationship and unity between religions, which should be seen as a movement, not towards absolute or monistic oneness, but towards a new kind of unity:

> Unitive pluralism is a *new* understanding of religious unity and must not be confused with the old, rationalistic idea of 'one world religion' in either of its alternate brand names. The new vision of religious unity is not *syncretism*, which boils away all the historical differences between religions in order to institutionalize their common core; nor is it *imperialism*, which believes that there is one religion that has the power of purifying and then absorbing all the others. Nor is it a form of lazy tolerance that calls upon all religions to recognize each other's validity and then to ignore each other as they go their own self-satisfied ways. Rather, unitive pluralism is a unity in which each religion, although losing some of its individualism (its separate ego), will intensify its personality (its self-awareness through relationship). Each religion will retain its own uniqueness, but this unique-ness will develop and take on new depths by relating to other religions in mutual dependence.[47]

Knitter is aware that the concept of unitive pluralism makes a number of assumptions about 'Truth' in religion, a concept which has played an important role in the Christian exclusivist attitude to other faiths. During the Tambaram debate, T. C. Chao, and D. G. Moses had pointed to those inadequacies in Kraemer's understanding of revelation and truth that had

---

46 *No Other Name?* p. 6. Knitter here quotes Raimundo Panikkar's article "The Myth of Pluralism: The Tower of Babel — A Meditation on Non-Violence," *Cross Currents* 29 (1979): 217.

47 *Ibid.,* p. 9. Knitter originally proposed the concept of 'Unitive Pluralism' as one of the possible options within process thinking for dealing with pluralism. At the conclusion of his books (see pp. 220 ff), however, he himself opts for this particular option as the most convincing.

led to his negative conclusions about other religious traditions.[48] Picking up the question within the dialogue debate, Samartha had argued that a new approach to truth in relational terms was a prerequisite for the continuing debate.[49] Knitter affirmed this by questioning the traditional method of arriving at truth *through exclusion,* which method tended to give an absolute quality to the truth that one 'finally' arrived at. "For something to be true" in this scheme, Knitter pointed out, "it has to be, in its category, the only, the absolute truth. One can know it is true by showing how it *excludes* all other alternatives — or, more recently, how it absorbs and includes all other alternatives."[50]

A new understanding of truth in relational terms, Knitter argued, would not compromise a truth as one holds it in its 'uniqueness' but it would enable people to see it in its essential relationship to other truths. "Each religion contains something that belongs to it alone, separately, distinctively, decisively; its particular grasp of divine truth. The truth it contains is uniquely important: It must not be lost," maintained Knitter, but the very sureness about truth relieves that religion of the burden of having to be founded on "the absolutely certain, final, and unchangeable possession of divine truth." Rather, it will be rooted in "the authentic experience of the divine that gives one a secure place to stand and from which to carry on the frightening and fascinating journey with other religions into the inexhaustible fullness of divine truth."[51]

Knitter concluded that the relational understanding of truth helps to clarify both the diversity of religions and their essential unity. "Although there are real and important differences among religions, differences that must be affirmed and confronted if dialogue is to bear fruit," these differences are fundamentally not contradictions, but "dialogical tensions and creative polarities." The world religions, in all their amazing differences, are more complementary than contradictory.[52]

We have dealt so extensively with Knitter's interpretation of plurality and religious truth because he echoes a growing number of voices that call for a reassessment of Christian attitudes to pluralism and to the question of truth. Not all these voices necessarily advocate a theo-centric model of relationships. John Cobb Jr., who also speaks from the tradition of process theology, denies that religions are "modes of experiencing the one transcendent God." He also denies that each religion's identity is unique and that what happens in a dialogue is an encounter of commitments and

---

48 See *The Authority of the Faith, op. cit.,* pp. 25-89

49 See especially his article on "Ganga and Galilee: Two Responses to Truth" in *Courage for Dialogue,* pp. 142 ff.

50 *No Other Name?* p. 217.

51 *Ibid.,* p. 220.

52 *Ibid.*

mutual witness that does not necessarily threaten each other's identity. The very title of his book, *Beyond Dialogue: Towards a Mutual Transformation of Christianity and Buddhism,* shows how he envisions an open encounter between religions that would transform and transfigure each of them.[53]

In his preface Cobb, regrets that there is a widespread feeling that the pluralistic situation demands that either we "continue our belief in Christian superiority" or "see Jesus as one saviour among others." The former position, in his view, turns Christ into an "instrument of our arrogance" and the latter abandons the "universal meaning and truth of Christ so central to our historic faith."[54] Cobb's own view is that religious communities must be in an encounter with others as communities with a mission to each other. Thus for Cobb, the purpose of authentic dialogue is to go 'beyond dialogue':

> That Christians hope to make a difference in others through dialogue should not be concealed. The difference between dialogue and more conventional forms of witness, it is now clear, is that dialogue is associated with making a contribution to religious communities as communities rather than with the conversion of individual members of the community to Christianity.[55]

Cobb's thoughts have strong parallels to the position taken by Chenchiah in the post-Tambaram debates. For, as we have seen, Chenchiah rejected mission as an enterprise for increasing the numerical strength of the church but spoke of a Christian mission to Hinduism as such. He looked on Hinduism as the 'spiritual home' for the Christian message and on Christ as one who would transform and transfigure Hinduism.[56] As Eric Sharpe has rightly observed, Chenchiah saw in the meeting of Christians and Hindus a meeting between East and West, a meeting to which the East had much to contribute.[57]

John A. T. Robinson argues along the same line in his contribution to the discussion, *Truth is Two-Eyed.* Admitting that truth has in fact to be many-eyed, Robinson interprets the particular meeting between Western and Eastern religions as, broadly speaking, a meeting between the prophetic and the mystic approaches to the Ultimate. He does recognize that both tendencies do occur in both types of religions, but he holds that the

---

53 John Cobb, Jr., *Beyond Dialogue: Towards a Mutual Transformation of Christianity and Buddhism* (Philadelphia: Fortress Press, 1982), pp. 44 ff.

54 *Ibid.,* p. vii f.

55 *Ibid.,* p. 50.

56 Chenchiah's position has been considered earlier. For a fuller statement see D. A. Thangasamy, *The Theology of Chenchiah* (Bangalore, India: Christian Institute for the Study of Religion and Society, 1966), pp. 33 ff.

57 Eric J. Sharpe, *Faith Meets Faith,* p. 120 f.

East and the West represent two dominant types of religious experience, each in itself representing a one-eyed view.[58]

Robinson shows that Western Christianity with its emphasis on the personality of God, the historicity of faith and the importance of the material world has been looking into the mystery of God with one eye, whereas the East, using the other eye, has concentrated on the mystical dimensions of reality. What is significant to Robinson is that the one-eyed perceptions, distorted as they are, have not prevented these religions from grasping the truth. "The God who discloses himself in Jesus and the God who discloses himself in Krishna must be the same God, or he is no God — and there is no revelation at all."[59] Robinson sees in developments both within Western Christianity and Eastern religions a move towards correcting the one-eyed versions, and he foresees the future relationship between the two in terms of mutual correction and complementarity.

We shall have to return to both Cobb and Robinson to see how they hold this open attitude to religious plurality in the light of their Christological commitments. But what is important to note at this stage is the swelling tide of opinion, among those who have given some consideration to religious plurality, that some fundamental shift in the Christian assessment of other religious traditions has become a critical necessity.

It is Wilfred Cantwell Smith, however, who takes these developing ideas to their logical conclusion and argues for what he calls a 'world theology.' In Smith's view, the gradual convergence of the different religious communities has now reached the period of 'a common religious history' of humankind. There was a time when one could speak of a Christian, Islamic, or Hindu religious history, but now they are all becoming 'strands' in the total human religious history, for we are now being pushed to a stage in which every religious person has been opened to the possibility of learning from all the religious traditions:[60]

> However incipiently, the boundaries segregating off religious communities radically and finally from each other are beginning, just a little, to weaken or to dissolve, so that being a Hindu and being a Buddhist, or being a Christian and not being a Christian, are not so starkly alternatives as once they seemed.[61]

---

58 J. A. T. Robinson, *Truth is Two-Eyed* (London: SCM Press), 1979, pp. 1-18.

59 *Ibid.,* p. 98.

60 W. C. Smith, *Towards a World Theology* (London: Macmillan, 1981). See especially his chapters on: "A History of Religions in the Singular," and "Religious Life as Participation in a Process."

61 Quoted by Alan Race, *op. cit.,* p. xii, as the governing theme of his treatment of pluralism.

Interestingly there is a close correspondence between Smith's ideas and those which A. G. Hogg had advocated at the Tambaram meeting and after. We noted how Hogg had challenged Kraemer's understanding of Hinduism merely as a naturalistic and vitalistic apprehension of reality, insisting rather that one should distinguish between 'faith' as a personal response to God, and the religious system in its cultic, historical, and social manifestations. He had no quarrel with Kraemer's position that the gospel message was in discontinuity with the religious traditions of the world, but he took enormous exception to Kraemer's unwillingness to accept the reality of personal faith evident in the lives of the people of other faiths, some of which had been a matter of daily experience for him in his relationships with Hindus.[62] Smith's call for a revision of the Christian attitude to religious pluralism is also based on his distinction between 'faith' as a personal response and the 'cumulative religious tradition' that expresses itself in religious phenomena.

In his penetrating study on *The Meaning and End of Religion* Smith argues that the whole concept of 'religion' as a complete system of belief is of comparatively recent origin. According to him, the use of the word 'religions' in the plural came into currency in the middle of the seventeenth century and became popular only by the eighteenth century. Only the intellectual tradition of the West began to classify human religious behaviour into 'types' and persons as belonging to them. This development poses a new difficulty for Smith, because one can really speak of religions only in abstraction, through a reference to the external phenomena which constitute the religion of an individual.[63]

By 'cumulative tradition,' Smith means:

> ... the entire mass of overt objective data that constitute the historical deposit, as it were, of the past religious life of the community in question: temples, scriptures, theological systems, dance patterns, legal, and other social institutions, conventions, moral codes, myths, and so on; anything that can be and is transmitted from one person, one generation, to another, and that an historian can observe.[64]

Faith, on the other hand, is that aspect of the religious life which is beyond the observation of the historian. In Smith's view, "faith cannot be precisely delineated or verbalized," for it is "too profound, too personal,

---

62 Hogg's position has been discussed in an earlier chapter. Eric J. Sharpe, who has studied Hogg's theology in detail, believes that his two books *Karma and Redemption* and *Redemption from this World* are of immense importance and deserve much more attention than they have had. For a fuller treatment of Hogg's position see Eric Sharpe, *Faith Meets Faith*, pp. 37-44.

63 W. C. Smith, *The Meaning and End of Religion* (1962; rpt. New York: Mentor, 1964), pp. 70 ff.

64 *Ibid.*, p. 141.

and too divine for public exposition. ... It lies beyond the sector of
religious life that can be imparted to an outsider for his inspection."[65]
Admitting that faith can be expressed more historically and observably "in
words, both prose and poetry; in patterns of deeds, both ritual and
morality; in art, in institution, in law, in community, in character; and in
still many other ways," Smith insists that these are still "expressions" of
faith and not its substance, for in his view faith in its true essence is in
the "inner religious experience or involvement of a particular person":

> Faith is an orientation of the personality to oneself, to one's neighbour, to
> the universe; a total response; a way of seeing the world and of handling
> it; a capacity to see at a more than mundane level; to see, to feel, to act
> in terms of a transcendent dimension.[66]

The cumulative religious tradition grows and is in constant change and
development, but it remains the milieu that sustains and nourishes the
faith. When a tradition is no longer able to nourish the adherents in their
faith it dries up and eventually dies.

By insisting that "faith is a fundamental category for all religious life
and indeed for all human life," Smith has, like Hogg, elevated faith to a
level different from the cumulative tradition. Insofar as it is a response, an
attitude, an orientation, a way of relating to the transcendent, it can have
no religious label:

> My faith is an act, *I* make, myself, naked before God. ... So there is no
> generic Christian faith, no 'Buddhist faith,' no 'Hindu faith,' no 'Jewish
> faith.' There is only my faith, and yours, and that of my Shinto friend, of
> my particular Jewish neighbour. We are all persons clustered in mundane
> communities, no doubt, and labelled with mundane labels but, so far as
> transcendence is concerned, encountering it each directly, personally, if at
> all. In the eyes of God each of us is a person, not a type.[67]

Smith's universalist understanding of faith and his call for a 'world theology' thus raise the strongest challenge yet to Christian unwillingness to face
religious plurality.

Race believes that Smith has performed a useful service in his "dis-
mantling of the terms in which the problem of conflicting truth-claims
between religions was conceived." for he notes that theologians are
beginning "to talk of religion less as an abstract concept, and more as a
way of 'seeing' the universe and its relation to the divine."[68] But the
major criticisms of Smith's view have been directed against his central
thesis, and Race summarizes these in the form of questions: "Is it poss-

---

65 *Ibid.,* p. 154.
66 *Towards a World Theology,* pp. 113-14.
67 *The Meaning and End of Religion,* p. 172.
68 *Christians and Religious Pluralism,* p. 101.

ible to drive a wedge through the complex reality we call 'religion' and separate a person's 'faith' from the 'cumulative tradition' which has formed him or her? If Cantwell Smith has set aside the important part played by the form of religious tradition in order to develop a pluralist theory around the notion of 'faith,' may he have ignored an essential element in the problem?"[69] It is not our purpose to explore these questions or to make a fuller assessment of Smith's interpretation. From his theory, Smith drew a number of implications for Christian theology and doctrine, implications which are laden with relevance for our present discussion.

Smith made no final difference in principle between the 'doctrinal' and the artistic, moral, communal, and other expressions of faith. Even though this made perfect sense within his framework of understanding, he himself was aware that it would present some problems to many Christian theologians. Particularly since the enlightenment, many Europeans have (in Smith's understanding), "tended to treat intellectual statements of religious faith, whether other peoples' or their own, as though they were straightforward, immediate, and independent descriptions of a metaphysical realm."[70]

Taking his distance from such an understanding of doctrine and theology, Smith points to strands within the Christian tradition that "have been at pains to emphasize that the Christian revelation is not a revelation of propositional truths." His own interpretation of faith and cumulative traditions would, in agreement with these strands, describe doctrinal systems and creeds as derived historical human constructs:

> Doctrinal formulations, theological systems, creeds, and the like, in their historical profusion, variety, consequence, and seriousness, can be understood, and I would feel can be understood only, as statements by and for persons — and also, in a primary and immediate sense, about persons. ... Theology is part of the traditions, is part of this world. Faith lies beyond theology, in the hearts of men. Truth lies beyond faith, in the heart of God.[71]

Smith notes the possible difficulties in this kind of assessment of Christian doctrine and theology. One could call this 'sheer relativism,' implying that theology cannot be true or false, but Smith contends that the real question should be whether a person's faith —and not theology— was true or false, for a theological statement "cannot be badly true in itself, but rather, can become true in the life of persons, when it is interiorized and lived."[72]

From this premise he also infers that man's religious life "is liberated, not devastated," when it is recognized that a religion cannot in itself be true or false:

69 *Ibid.*
70 *The Meaning and End of Religion,* p. 166f.
71 *Ibid.,* p. 167.
72 *Ibid.,* p. 331.

The notion that a given religion may be true, or even more, that it may not be true, has caused untold mischief. Or again, that one religion is true while another is false; or, equally misleading, that all religions are equally true (which is of course, nonsense). We must learn that this is not where truth and falsity lie, and especially not where religious truth and religious falsity lie. Religions, either singly or together, cannot be true or false. .... What a deal of sorrow has flowed from asking a wrong question, and trying desperately but impossibly to answer it. .... [73]

Smith's dissatisfaction with comparing religious traditions on the basis of propositional truths is shared by George A. Lindbeck in his recent study on *The Nature of Doctrine — Religion and Theology in a Post-liberal Age.* Even though Lindbeck's first purpose is to serve inter-confessional dialogue within the church, he develops a theory of human communication that he also applies to dialogue between different religious traditions.

He speaks of three types of theological theories of religion and doctrine current in Christian thinking. The first, which he identifies as the 'cognitive-propositional,' emphasizes the cognitive aspects of religion and regards doctrines as "informative propositions or truth claims about objective realities." The second approach focuses on what Lindbeck calls the 'experiential–expressive' dimension of religion, interpreting doctrine as "noninformative and nondiscursive symbols of inner feelings, attitudes or existential orientations." This approach highlights the resemblances be-tween religions and aesthetic enterprises. The third approach in Lind-beck's analysis, favoured by ecumenically inclined Roman Catholics, attempts to take both the 'cognitive–propositional' and the 'experiential–expressive' dimensions of religion and doctrine as significant and valid.[74]

Lindbeck finds all three of these approaches to religion and doctrine to be inadequate for dealing with the denominational and religious plural-ity of the present age, where the ecumenical imperative has become urgent. He points out that for the propositionalist, if a doctrine is once true, it is always true, and if it is once false, it is always false. In such an understanding it is difficult either to alter a doctrinal position or to reconcile it with others.

The contrast is true for the experiential–expressive approach, where there is an emphasis on the primacy of experience and doctrine playing only a symbolic role. It is possible for the meaning to vary while the doctrine remains the same. Similarly, doctrines can alter without change of meaning. Since doctrines are seen as nondiscursive symbols many meanings are drawn from them, subjecting the doctrines to changes that can lead as far as total meaninglessness.

---

73 *Ibid.,* p. 332.
74 George A. Lindbeck, *The Nature of Doctrine, Religion, and Theology in a Post-liberal Age* (Philadelphia: The Westminster Press, 1984), pp. 16 ff.

The third type, which seeks to combine the first two, is better equipped to account for the variable and invariable aspects of religious tradition, but those who adopt it have never succeeded (in Lindbeck's view) in realizing a satisfactory combination.[75]

Questioning the adequacy of all three approaches, Lindbeck points to the rising body of anthropological, sociological, and philosophical literature which eschews both the cognitive and the experiential–expressive aspects of religion, placing the emphasis not on doctrines themselves, but on their *use*. Doctrines do not preserve truth claims; nor are they expressive symbols. They are "communally authoritative *rules* of discourse, attitude, and action." In this respect they are similar to languages and cultures which also find their significance in their *use* in the community. Lindbeck calls this theory the 'cultural-linguistic' approach. It is not our intention to go into the details of how Lindbeck develops his theory. But it is important to note the implications of his understanding of doctrine for religious pluralism. The 'cultural-linguistic' understanding of religion and doctrine enables us to deal with pluralism by relating the doctrines of different religions to the 'regulative' function which they have in specific communities.

Lindbeck illustrates the point clearly with one example. The rules 'Drive on the left' and 'Drive on the right' are unequivocal in meaning and are unequivocally opposed. But both are binding, one in Britain and the other in the United States, both are intended for the purpose of regulating traffic and avoiding accidents. The position between these two rules can be resolved not by altering one or both of them, but by specifying when or where they apply, or by specifying the situation in which one would take precedence over the other. When doctrines are seen to have this kind of 'regulative' function they can be reconciled with other positions that are seen to be in opposition.[76]

What is significant to our discussion is that Lindbeck's theory of religion and doctrine is yet another attempt to understand and relate religions in the pluralist milieu. Drawing inferences for inter-faith relations Lindbeck says that a propositional approach can only lead to conflicting truth claims, and the experiential–expressive approach to a search for a shared experienced core in religion, both of which have already presented too many problems. In the cultural-linguistic outlook, religions are thought of as "primarily as different idioms for constructing reality, expressing experience, and ordering life."[77] This allows for the possibility "that different religions and/or philosophies may have incommensurable notions of truth,

75 *Ibid.,* cf. p. 17.

76 Lindbeck develops this idea fully in Chapter 4. Here we have attempted only to outline his theory in order to show yet another approach to religious plurality.

77 *Ibid.,* pp. 47-48.

of experience, and of categorical adequacy."[78] The lack of common foundations between religions is seen both as a weakness and a strength:

> It means . . . that the partner in dialogue does not start with the conviction that they really basically agree, but it also means that they are not forced into the dilemma of thinking of themselves as representing a superior (or inferior) articulation of a common experience of which the other religions are inferior (or superior) expressions. They can regard themselves as simply different and can proceed to explore their arguments and disagreements without necessarily engaging in the invidious comparisons that the assumption of a common experiential core make so tempting.[79]

The Challenge

In drawing conclusions from our study of the understandings of, and attitudes to, other faiths discussed within the wcc, we noted that the first issue lay in the absence of any attempt to deal theologically with religious plurality. We have interpreted the controversies at the Nairobi and Vancouver Assemblies as the indications of a serious necessity to deal with this issue in the theological depth it deserves.

In the foregoing pages we have dealt with the ways in which some contemporary scholars have addressed the subject. This list was by no means exhaustive, for we could also have mentioned such well-known Roman Catholic theologians as Raimundo Panikkar, Karl Rahner, Hans Küng, and Aloysius Pieris, all of whom, along with many others, have been seeking a meaningful theological framework for understanding the Christian faith in a multi-faith milieu. We have not discussed some of these here because we will consider their views later, when we come to the implications of pluralism for the discussion of Christology and mission. In any case, most Roman Catholic theologians have been operating largely within the affirmations of Vatican II which, as we have seen earlier, took a positive attitude to the reality of pluralism and saw it as the arena where God would accomplish his salvific will for all of creation.[80]

We should of course recognize that religious plurality is not a new experience for the church. The church was born into a Jewish milieu and had soon to come to terms with the Roman world. Graeco-Roman cults, Hellenistic philosophy, and the many religions with which Christianity came into contact each exerted some influence on the development of the

---

78 *Ibid.,* p. 49.

79 *Ibid.,* p. 55.

80 M. Amaladoss argues in his essay "Dialogue and Mission: Conflict or Convergence?" *Vidyajyoti* L 2 (Feb. 1986): 62 ff, that the Roman Catholic position since Vatican II constitutes a 'new paradigm' which attempts to hold together the universal significance of creation, the Paschal Mystery, and the final fulfilment.

Christian faith and its attitude to other faiths. The early church fathers had themselves taken sides for more exclusivist or inclusivist ways of understanding religious plurality.[81] A detailed consideration of these are of course outside the scope of this study, but it is nevertheless important to be aware of the historical roots of the question.

In a manuscript to be published shortly, M. M. Thomas rightly points to the Roman Catholic–Protestant theological conflict within Western Christianity as one of the important keys to the understanding of the issue. Noting the importance of the relationship between 'nature' and 'grace,' he refers as well to other manifestations of this tension "like the relation between religion and revelation, or between nature and history, or between the realms of the sacred and the secular."[82]

This rivalry was evident of course in the discussions which we have traced. During the preparation of the Jerusalem 1928 meeting, J. H. Oldham recognized the rising importance of the world of other religions and he had tried to put the emphasis at Jerusalem on a comparison between different religions rather than on the 'missionary study' of non-Christian religions as a means to facilitating the spread of the gospel.[83] W. H. T. Gairdiner has shown how Oldham's views were strongly challenged by the Germans, who represented the hard-line 'grace' position of the Reformation churches which began its theological reflections with the depravation of man and insisted that the hearing and responding to the gospel message was the only way of salvation for people who in their ignorance clung to misguided and all-too-human religious traditions.[84] When the Jerusalem committee attempted a compromise between the liberal and conservative positions, the German delegation asked for their minority report to be printed. It was this uncompromisingly evangelistic attitude towards other faiths, often referred to as the 'Continental view,' which finally established itself at Tambaram as the predominant view of the mainline Protestant churches, and it has continued to find expression in the reports of the Commission on Mission and Evangelism within the WCC and in the evangelical voices from outside the WCC symbolized by the Lausanne Covenant.[85]

---

81 Harold Coward gives a useful summary of this development in *Pluralism: Challenge to World Religions*, pp. 15-22. He follows here the more detailed work of K. S. Latourette, *A History of Christianity* (Eyre and Spottiswoode, 1955).

82 M. M. Thomas, typescript "A Concluding Comment" (WCC Publications Office), pp. 16-17. Thomas' work is soon to be published under the title *Risking Christ for Christ's Sake*.

83 Cf. C. F. Hallencreutz, *Kraemer Towards Tambaram*, pp. 169 ff.

84 W. H. T. Gairdner, *JMR*, I, p. 266 f.

85 Here we refer to the positions taken by the IMC meetings at Whitby and Willingen as well as the CWME's first Commission meeting at Mexico City. The subsequent meetings of the CWME have paid little theological attention to religious pluralism, but always

There is an urgent need for a fundamental reassessment of the bases and assumptions of the theology of mission and evangelism within the WCC. Such an assessment will show great advances in theological thinking within the CWME about relating the gospel to the secular challenge, to the quest for liberation, to the poor of the earth, etc. But it will also show a dismal failure in addressing the question of religious pluralism. The formation of the sub-unit on dialogue, which acutally branched out of the CWME, was of course one of several responses to the challenge of pluralism. Since dialogue developed into a programme that concentrated primarily on relationships, the question of the theology of religious pluralism still did not receive the attention it deserved.

It is ironic that Per Lonning, who led the 'attack' both at Nairobi and Vancouver on the presumed theological inadequacies of the reports dealing with dialogue, has recently written in the *Ecumenical Review,* stressing the need to tackle the theology of religions in a more conscious manner.[86] Describing himself as "a veteran 'fighter' from Nairobi (1975) and Chiang Mai (1977) and in the sub-committee on dialogue at several WCC Central Committee meetings in the Nairobi–Vancouver era," Lonning has affirmed that what the "present situation requires above all is a discovery of our unconscious theology of religion(s)":

> Our ecumenical reluctance to undertake a real rethinking of our theology of religion(s) may have to do with the bad luck of 'religion' in Western Protestant theology during the period 1930–70. Also a young ecumenical movement was heavily under the influence of the persistent Christo-centrism of Barthian neo-orthodoxy and of the missiological thinking of Hendrik Kraemer. Religion was interpreted as basically nothing but human self-assertions. ... [87]

Tracing further developments and recent attempts to correct the imbalance, Lonning concluded that "Interfaith dialogue can be adequately adapted and motivated only through a theology of religion developed prior to all programme, as an integral part of our Christian identity."[88]

M. M. Thomas suggests that an adequate theology of religions within the ecumenical movement may well come about when we have a truly

---

maintained an evangelistic thrust in keeping with the IMC's line of thinking. The Lausanne Committee represents the major evangelical groups outside the WCC (although many member churches of the WCC support and participate in its work). The Lausanne Covenant reflects an exclusivistic theological position vis-à-vis other religions.

86 Per Lonning, "Dialogue: A Question about 'Religiology'," *Ecumenical Review* XXXVII (Oct. 1985): 420 ff.

87 *Ibid.,* p. 421.

88 *Ibid.,* p. 427. Lonning holds that "such a 'religiology' (which would include also human orientations of life which do not claim the label 'religion'), while relating to all the various themes of theology, would have to direct its initial considerations to the long neglected theme of creation."

'ecumenical ecumenism' integrating in some way the Protestant, Catholic, and Orthodox views on the issue.[89] The contemporary thinkers we have considered give various possibilities that may usefully be explored. Behind the thoughts of most of these thinkers lies the realization that the world itself is moving towards a 'wider ecumenism' or an ecumenism that, in the true meaning of the word, includes the *whole* inhabited earth — an ecumenism of religions. Thus while Kraemer spoke of the 'Coming Dialogue,' Cobb asks us to move 'Beyond Dialogue.'[90]

It is certainly significant that a number of themes taken up by contemporary theologians of religion have been mirrored in the Tambaram debate. Wilfred Cantwell Smith's deeply researched and profoundly thought-provoking distinction between personal faith in its universalist dimension and cumulative tradition had been Hogg's case in the post-Tambaram debates, but then it had gone largely unnoticed. A deeper study of the implications of Nicol Macnicol's presentation on Hinduism would show that he was advocating a combination of Knitter's 'unitive pluralism' and Cobb's 'mutual transformation' in interfaith relationships. Chenchiah certainly would have agreed with Robinson's concern for a two-eyed view of reality, for he had been among those who, like Lindbeck, had argued that doctrinal formulations about Christ were in fact in the 'linguistic-cultural' idiom of the Western Christians. He contended that God did not reveal 'propositions' but became incarnate so that all cultures could express the mystery in their own idioms.[91]

There is no intention here to say that nothing new has emerged from recent discussions about the theology of religions. Far from it. But we do

---

89 The unpublished manuscript cited above, footnote 82.

90 In *Religion and the Christian Faith,* Kraemer did a historical survey of the 'meeting' between the Western Christian and Eastern non-Christian worlds, at the levels of religion and culture and spoke of the 'coming dialogue,' for which the Western churches should prepare. Cobb urged that dialogue between Christianity and Buddhism should not simply aim at mutual respect and understanding, but also have a 'missionary' dimension, and so he entitled his volume *'Beyond Dialogue.'* For a review of Kraemer's book by M. M. Thomas and the ensuing correspondence between Kraemer and Thomas, see *Some Theological Dialogues Based on the Correspondence of M. M. Thomas,* Indian Christian Thought Series no. 14 (Bangalore: CISRS, 1977), pp. 22-33.

91 In a 1947 letter to *The Guardian* on "Our Theological Task," Chenchiah dealt with the problem of 'translating' theological systems from one cultural community to the other. Noting that concepts and ideas have a 'home' where they carry meaning, Chenchiah wrote "Our object in translation (of theological systems) is to evoke a kind of feeling, emotion akin to the one which the original writers felt. This can never be done by words and meaning alone. ... It calls for ... a capacity to identify oneself with the mind of the original speaker and the mind of the latest hearer, divided from each other by centuries of time and by cultural modes of thought. Can any undertake this task except those inspired by the Holy Spirit alone who can span the first and twentieth centuries in a living way?" Reprinted in D. A. Thangasamy, *The Theology of Chenchiah,* pp. 232-33.

want to underline that what had been rudimentary notions, ideas, and 'hunches' in the Tambaram controversy have now been fleshed out for serious consideration within the ecumenical debate. Hick's call for morality in interfaith relations, Smith's challenge to analyse the true nature of religious life, Lindbeck's analysis of the nature of doctrine, Knitter's and Race's call to respond to life in a pluralist milieu are all elements that must inform any serious ecumenical thinking on this issue.

But are they enough to exorcise Kraemer's ghost, which has so possessed the Protestant strand within the ecumenical movement? Our answer is: No. At the very least, one should say that the theology of religions approach will not by itself be sufficient to make the necessary fundamental shift for dealing with religious plurality within the ecumenical movement. Kraemer arrived at his particular attitude towards people of other faiths not by philosophical, moral, social or any other argumentation, but through his concept of 'biblical realism' and his interpretation of the meaning of the gospel in that context. We must recognize that Kraemer was no unsympathetic theoretician in these matters. He had great respect for, and knowledge of, other faiths and he had lived and worked among people of other faiths for prolonged periods; he had even engaged in actual dialogue. He was critical of the negative approaches of missions and had argued for a loving and humble attitude towards people of other faiths. The understanding of, and the attitude to, other religions which he advocated *was the only position open to him* from the perspective of his commitment to the Christian faith. It was, in his view, a proper understanding of the 'original faith' of the Christians that had led him to his views. It was, as it were, even though the words were not used, a 'Here-I-stand-I-cannot-do-otherwise' position that Kraemer took. Little wonder he has had such a hold on the Protestant tradition that had ensued from this declaration. Our task can be no smaller, nor easier.

Our contention, therefore, is that only a radical reappraisal of Christian theology taking full account of the reality of religions as we have come to know and experience them in our day can produce a theology of religions that would make a fundamental difference to Christian attitudes to, and relationships with, people of other faiths. What lies ahead, therefore, is a task of doing Christian theology in full cognizance of all the new data and the various options for Christian relationships to other faiths. This is the true magnitude of the challenge that faces ecumenical discussions of the future.

Implications for Hindu–Christian Relationships

What then, we ask, are the implications of these proposals for Hindu–Christian relationships? It is neither possible, nor necessary, to trace here the negative side of Christian–Hindu relations within the history of missions. In his recent volume, *Towards a New Relationship,* Kenneth Cracknell includes a well-researched chapter, "About the Old Relationships." Without denying any of the positive aspects of mission, Cracknell acknowledges that "the entails of the historical developments within the Western Christian tradition," "the legacies of earlier missionary theologies" and the "prejudices stemming from the assumption of cultural superiority by colonizers" have rolled into "one single sad tangle" and make it "truly difficult for Western Christians to think in new ways." We must, says Cracknell, "unravel some of these unblessed ties that bind us in knots."[92]

The attempts to develop a new theology of religions belongs partly to this task of undoing the 'sad tangle' that has done so much harm to Hindu–Christian relations. In his thought-provoking essay on "Western Christianity and Asian Buddhism," Aloysius Pieris maintains that "each religion is a *singular* phenomenon and is in a way a *judgement* passed on every other religion." He maintains as well that religions are "so many alternative configurations of basic human values," and it is therefore in "their nature to provoke *comparison* and mutual *criticism, confrontation,* and reciprocal *correction.*" He sees them as intermediary stages between the mere tolerance with which dialogue begins and the positive 'participation' in which it should culminate.[93]

But, he continues, it is most unfortunate that "Christianity, especially Western Christianity, has been passing judgement on other religions, generously offering them criticisms and corrections and indulging in comparisons that were ultimately meant to articulate its own uniqueness." Much that has in the past been called 'The Philosophy of Religion' has also been affected, in Pieris' view, by the apologetic interests of Christian faith. "Even in their most objective and honest studies, Christian professors did not fully renounce their evangelizing role, which consisted not only in proving rationally the wholeness of Christianity but in neutralizing, by means of subtle philosophical explanations, the challenge that other faiths threw at Christian belief. . . ."[94] Analysing the reasons for this Pieris says:

---

92 Kenneth Cracknell, *Towards a New Relationship: Christians and People of Other Faith* (Epworth Press, 1986), p. 9.
93 Aloysius Pieris, "Western Christianity and Asian Buddhism: A Theological Reading of Historical Encounters," *Dialogue,* New Series VII 2 (1980): 49. (Pieris' emphasis.)
94 *Ibid.,* p. 50.

This is because the major part of Western Christianity has not for centuries been confronted by the inner dynamism of other religions. Since the Christianization of Europe, the West had one sole paradigm at its disposal to understand the religious phenomenon: namely, its own Christian experience. Thus "the philosophy of *one* religion became 'Philosophy of Religion'," as Pannikar has bitingly remarked.[95]

What is important to our discussion is that Pieris, discerning a subtle form of apologetic interest in most contemporary forms of 'Philosophy of Religion,' 'Comparative Religion' and 'Phenomenology of Religion,' has raised the questions whether the contemporary forms of 'Theology of Religions' are not also the fruit of a 'new Apologetics,' and whether these are directed towards the "vindication of Christianity's absolute claims in the context of a new awareness of religious pluralism. . . ."[96]

This warning should be taken very seriously as we look to the future of Christian–Hindu relations. For it would be all too easy to develop a theology of religions that addressed the contemporary need for religions to live together and cooperate, but had no roots in the essentials of the Christian faith. Hence we must insist that the new attitude towards Hindus should follow from an attempt to restate the Christian faith in the awareness that Hindus can no longer be kept out of this conversation.

When Farquhar published *The Crown of Hinduism* in 1913, the burden of his message was that it was not Christianity but Christ himself who was the 'crown' of Hinduism. It was in many ways an affirmation of Hinduism with the rider that Christ brings to fulfilment its desires and longings. Farquhar had based his position on a life-long study of Hinduism; indeed, Eric Sharpe has described Farquhar's study of Hinduism (which also produced his *Modern Religious Movement in India*) as a "standing refutation" to "bias and superficiality."[97] More importantly Farquhar had repeatedly insisted that the fulfilment hypothesis was "an item in the Christian advocate's personal intellectual equipment . . . not intended to be used as a homilitical weapon."[98]

As Sharpe has noted, Farquhar's book could not escape the scrutiny of Hindus, for these

---

95 *Ibid.*, pp. 50-51. Pieris' here refers to the essay by Raimundo Panikkar, "Philosophy of Religion in the Contemporary Encounter of Cultures" in *Contemporary Philosophy: A Survey*, R. Klibansky, ed. (Florence, 1971), p. 228f.

96 *Ibid.*, p. 52. Pieris suggests that in the absence of a genuine 'Philosophy of Religion' to complement the 'scientific' studies of religion, the theology of religion has taken the necessary apologetic role.

97 Eric J. Sharpe, *Faith Meets Faith*, p. 28.

98 This is Eric Sharpe's description of Farquhar's position. *Ibid.*, p. 30.

could not be prevented from reading books like *The Crown of Hinduism* on the grounds that they were intended for Christian eyes only. Reading Christian apologetical literature of this type must, one feels, have been an annoying experience to many Hindus. To be provided with a scholarly presentation of various aspects of the Hindu tradition, only to be told at the end that the tradition is either in error or in an incomplete state, certainly appeared to many Hindus to be pure condescension.[99]

One's mind immediately turns to the contemporary debate over the 'Unknown Christ' and 'Anonymous Christianity,' but these should await consideration at a later stage.

What is advocated here is not a call to politeness that would disregard the fundamentals of one's own faith, but a reconsideration of the fundamental presuppositions involved. We noted earlier the position taken by the Saiva Hindu participant at the WCC multi-lateral dialogue in Colombo, K. Sivaraman. In proposing a model for interfaith relationships he rejected the liberalist attitude that by reaching out to the "other" across the gulf "ends up by espousing a religious relativism which is tolerant of everything and intolerant only of intolerance." He went even further to affirm that a "claim to final truth is an integral part of religion and must be experienced existentially"; in his view religions are "alternative absolutes."[100] In the same breath, Sivaraman insists that it is still of the essence of Hinduism to affirm without compromise that there is no one way to the ultimate, given that "there are no goals to the religious quest in the plural."[101] In other words, Sivaraman's attitude to religious plurality arises not out of historical or ecumenical necessity, nor out of a liberalist attitude, but out of a conception of the Ultimate and of humanity's relation to it that allows for, indeed necessitates, plurality.

From the Vaishnava tradition the Hindu guest at the Nairobi Assembly (K. L. Sheshagiri Rao) makes precisely the same point. Noting that "the conception of unity behind diversity has been a fundamental factor in the Hindu religious consciousness"[102], Sheshagiri Rao argues that the theology of pluralism is of the essence of the Hindu conception of the Ultimate and the Hindu understanding of spirituality:

Hinduism teaches the unity of being, which implies that all the things in the universe are knit together in that which is the common basis for all existence. Spirituality probes this underlying unity of life and aims at universal well-being. It gives the philosophical root of non-violence and

---

99 *Ibid.,* pp. 30-31.

100 S. J. Samartha, ed., *Towards World Community,* pp. 26-27.

101 *Ibid.*

102 K. L. Sheshagira Rao, "Human Community and Religious Pluralism — A Hindu Perspective" in *Dialogue in Community: Essays in Honour of S. J. Samartha,* C. D. Jathanna, ed. (Mangalore, India: The Karnataka Theological Research Institute, 1982), p. 166.

love. It encourages a way of life where the individual is enabled to live
in tune with the infinite. It asks people to transcend the barriers that their
little egos have erected around themselves.[103]

We are not asking that Christian theology should adopt the Hindu attitude
to plurality, but we expect such an attitude to plurality to arise, like
Kraemer's exclusivism, from a profound understanding of the Christian
faith.

According to Sivaraman, the present context calls for "a reappraisal
of one's own religious tradition and a reoriented approach to other
religious traditions."[104] Sheshagiri Rao, maintaining that there are and will
continue to be differences between religions and that these must be
respected and preserved, had this to say about the task ahead:

> Traditional theology, developed in religious isolation has now become
> inadequate, if not obsolete. It does not permit the different religious
> traditions to live side by side. . . . As far as we can see human community
> will continue to be religiously pluralistic. Each religion should come to
> terms with this fact, and attempt to do justice to the religious experience
> of mankind as a whole. By a deep and a thorough investigation of its
> respective heritage, each tradition should open up a new spiritual horizon
> hospitable to the faiths of other people.[105]

The Hindus are not looking for further adjustments to Hindu–Christian
relationships in order to accommodate their spiritual experience. Nor are
they, at least in the thinking of these two representatives, looking for any
kind of theology of religions, or any extensions of Christian doctrine that
would assure them and the Christians that they would also be 'saved.'
What they are seeking is a dynamic restatement of Christian belief that
takes account of the reality of religious pluralism in terms of its own
faith. Without this, no amount of dialogue could cure the justified suspicion that has crept into Hindu–Christian relations, which otherwise might
be sublimely enriching.

What have been the barriers to such a dynamic theology of religious
pluralism? To answer this question we must turn to the second issue at
the centre of the ecumenical debate, namely, Christology.

---

103 *Ibid.,* p. 165.
104 *Towards World Community* (Colombo Papers), p. 30.
105 *Dialogue in Community,* p. 162.

Issue II:

Are 'Uniqueness' and 'Finality' Appropriate Theological Categories to Understand the Significance of Christ?

The Unresolved Issue

The second unresolved issue in the ecumenical discussion of Christian relationships with other faiths has to do with the 'uniqueness' and 'finality' of Christ. Even though we have chosen these words as the focus of the discussion, the issue of the centrality of Christ to the faith has taken different forms of expression in the underlying debate.

In Jerusalem (1928) the delegates from continental Europe rejected what they saw as a disquieting relativism in some of the preparatory materials and called on Christians to "stand decidedly and even stubbornly with both feet" on the "unique way of salvation proclaimed with one voice in the Bible."[106] The Jerusalem message itself stressed the person of Christ and the revelation made through him. "He is the revelation of what God is and of what man through him may become."[107]

Tambaram (1938) dealt with the issue primarily in terms of religion and revelation: the 'gospel message' interpreted as an act of God demanded a response from sinful people. Rather than 'uniqueness' and 'finality,' Tambaram underlined the 'decisiveness' of the Christ-event.[108] The same emphasis has found other forms of expression. Thus Whitby spoke of the urgency of bringing the world to "acknowledge and serve the Kingship under which we stand,"[109], and Willingen referred to the "unique Lordship of Christ."[110] The report of the Mexico City meeting warned against loss of conviction as to the "finality" of Christ.[111]

All these expressions point to some of the familiar Protestant themes which have constituted the fundamental theological formation on Christology that has played such a crucial role in shaping Christian attitudes to other faiths. To put the matter crudely in order to facilitate our discussion, there is at the heart of this theological formation a belief that God has revealed his saving will in the birth, life, death, and resurrection of Jesus Christ, and it is only by responding to this unique/decisive/full/final/once-and-for-all initiative of God that humankind can hope to achieve

---

106 Report on the speech by Julius Richter, *JMR*, I, p. 153 ff.

107 The Statement of the Council, *JMR*, I, p. 480.

108 O. V. Jathanna in a detailed analysis of the theological dialogue among Kraemer, Hogg, Hocking, and Chenchiah, interprets it as a dialogue on the 'decisiveness of the Christ-event,' *op. cit.*

109 See discussion in Chapter V, p. 93.

110 See discussion in Chapter V, p. 95.

111 See discussion in Chapter V, p. 124.

salvation. From this absolute vision derives the urgency of mission to a world that would perish if it did not embrace this salvation.

This is surely an oversimplication of the issue, for such a belief was considerably modified and qualified when it was considered in relation to the attending beliefs about creation, God's providence, and the various ways in which God's will has partially been revealed to humanity. Certainly, there is no single Protestant theology, and one should remember that within the wcc discussions Orthodox insights are also articulated, although never with the frequency and intensity that they deserve.

It is our contention, however, that the position articulated by Kraemer at Tambaram, which made the Christ-event ultimately decisive and set Christ as the only way to salvation, has never really been tested in ecumenical discussion. Kenneth Cragg, as we have seen, sought to open up the debate with the support of the Roman Catholic theologians present at the Kandy meeting, but this attempt proved to be a non-starter.[112]

As the Dialogue programme developed within the wcc, several assumptions were made about the theological 'status' of other faiths and the validity of the religious experience of the people who lived by them, and many of these were by implication contradictory to the other main theological formation that the Council had inherited from the IMC. In spite of sustained interaction and communication between the CWME and the subunit on Dialogue, and despite the fact that both emphases have their origin in the discussions within the IMC it was evident that these two foci within the wcc were building on two distinct theological emphases and sets of theological assumptions about the significance of other faiths. No effort was made to reconcile these assumptions; nor were they easily reconcilable. This tension is manifest in *Mission and Evangelism: An Ecumenical Affirmation,* prepared by the CWME and adopted by the Central Committee in 1982 and received by the Vancouver Assembly. We have referred to this document earlier but should take a closer look at it here in terms of the present discussion.[113]

The text certainly tried very hard to incorporate the fruit of the work on dialogue, and affirmed the need for a dialogical relationship with people of other faiths. This has been enabled by the overall Trinitarian framework in which the statement is set, its emphases on the Kingdom of God and on God's love as basis of the apostolic calling of the church.

The section dealing with "Witness Among People of Living Faiths" (Section 7, para. 41-45) depended heavily on the *Guidelines on Dialogue,* and an important section of the *Guidelines* was incorporated into the appendix. The Affirmation dealt with the difficult question of salvation in

---

112 See discussion in Chapter V, pp. 123-124.
113 *Mission and Evangelism: An Ecumenical Affirmation* (Geneva: WCC).

two ways. First, there was the confession: "In him is *our* salvation" [emphasis ours]. But there was also a disagreement: "Among Christians there are still differences of understanding as to how *this* salvation in Christ is available to people of diverse religious persuasions" [emphasis ours]. The phrase "how *this* salvation *in Christ* is available," affirmed salvation as something that God offered to all in Christ, leaving open the question how this offer of salvation related to the experience of salvation to which people of other faiths testified.

The authors made a studied attempt to avoid triumphalistic language and they issued an unmistakable call for "mission in Christ's way," which was interpreted also in terms of solidarity with the oppressed and marginalized in society. The *Affirmation* dealt with the sensitive issue of the 'Lordship' of Christ in terms of the confession of the early church:

> The early Church confessed Jesus Christ as Lord, as the highest authority at whose name every knee shall bow, who in the cross and in the resurrection has liberated in this world the power of sacrificial love. (para. 2)

On the question of the person and work of Christ, it avoided such terms as 'finality,' 'uniqueness,' 'decisiveness,' etc., which had been very common in earlier documents relating to evangelism. It chose, instead, the word 'complete':

> Jesus Christ was in himself the complete revelation of God's love, manifested in justice and forgiveness through all aspects of his earthly life. (para. 5)

One should also note that the expression 'complete revelation' was further tempered by the addition of the phrase, 'of God's love' thus diverging from earlier statements that had spoken of Christ as the revelation *of God* or of God's will.

The sensitivity of the wcc document on Mission and Evangelism to the challenge of rethinking triumphalistic affirmations in the light of the new awareness of plurality stood out in marked contrast with the statement made on the same issue at about the same time in the Lausanne Covenant. The latter declaration, in our opinion, further fortified the Tambaram response to the awareness of plurality:

> We affirm that there is *only one* Saviour and *only one* Gospel although there is a wide diversity of evangelistic approaches. We recognize that all men have some knowledge of God through his general revelation in nature. But we deny that this can save, for men suppress the truth by their unrighteousness. We also reject as derogatory to Christ and the Gospel every kind of syncretism and dialogue which implies that Christ speaks equally through all religions and ideologies. Jesus Christ being himself the *only Godman,* who gave himself as the *only ransom* for sinners, is the *only mediator* between God and man. There is *no other name* by which we must be saved. ... To proclaim Jesus as "the saviour

of the world" is not to affirm that all men are either automatically or ultimately saved, still less to affirm that all religions offer salvation in Christ. ... Jesus Christ has been exalted above every other name; we long for the day when *every knee shall bow* to him and every tongue shall confess him Lord.[114] [Emphasis ours]

The strength of the *Ecumenical Affirmation* lies in its assertion of the centrality of the person and the work of Christ to Christian faith and the Christian vocation to witness to this with a sensitive awareness of the way such assertions should be made in today's world. There are also cautious attempts to push the boundaries within which the work of Christ was understood in past statements. In many ways the *Ecumenical Affirmation* thus attempted to walk the theological tight-rope between the Tambaram heritage and the insights received through the churches' new awareness of pluralism. But did it help?

The same assembly that received and endorsed the *Ecumenical Affirmation* locked itself into controversy over the sentence about "God's creative work in the religious experience of people of other faiths," which appeared in the report that CWME and Dialogue had prepared together. Anticipating objection, the drafting committee had, in the first instance, prefaced this statement with the clause: "While affirming the *uniqueness* of the birth, life, death, and resurrection of Jesus, to which we bear witness, we recognize God's creative ... ," etc. But as we have already seen, this draft was rejected because of its theological 'confusion' as one of the interventions put it.

Hence the question with which we began this section: Are 'uniqueness' and 'finality' appropriate categories for understanding the significance of Christ? Behind the question lie the deeper theological issues articulated in the *Guidelines* as needing further attention:

> What is the relation between the universal creative/redemptive activity of God towards all humankind and the particular creative/redemptive activity of God in the history of Israel and in the person and work of Jesus Christ?[115]

The ecumenical community can ill afford to avoid the Christological question, for it can no longer function on the implicit assumption that Christian relationships to people of other faiths and the Christian understanding of mission and evangelism can be carried further without a more conscious reconsideration of the Christology in vogue since Tambaram. This rethinking is necessary not simply because of the deep divisions at the Assemblies which were themselves symptoms of the need to address

---

114 Quoted in S. Wesley Ariarajah, *The Bible and People of Other Faiths* (Geneva: WCC, 1985), p. 37
115 *Guidelines on Dialogue, op. cit.,* p. 13.

the issue. It is our conviction that neither the CWME nor the Dialogue sub-unit can make any further contribution to the overall debate on Christian relationships with other faiths, or indeed to a theology of pluralism, without considering fully the current attempts at reformulating the Christo-logical affirmations so that they may speak meaningfully in a pluralistic milieu. Here again one should take account of some of the contemporary discussions to see what lessons may be learnt.

Some Aspects of the Contemporary Discussions

Christopher Duraisingh makes a useful distinction between 'uniqueness' and 'finality,' indicating the different ways in which 'finality' has been under-stood. There are four senses in which Christ's work could be understood to be 'final.' First, that it is an exclusive act: the one act through which God intends to save humanity. All who should be saved should respond to this act in Christ. Second, finality could be interpreted as an inclusive act by which the one act alters the general and universal situation in a radical way. Third, it is also possible to interpret finality in a non-tem-poral way as that which transcends the normal historical process. And lastly, finality may still be maintained while understanding the act as temporal-processive, giving significance to the historical process. In whichever way it is interpreted, 'finality' endows the act with some form of 'decisiveness.' Duraisingh sees 'uniqueness' as a derivative concept. "It arises," he says, "out of the concern of individuals or the community of faith to advdance their claim for Christ in terms of change which they experience in their lives."[116]

When claims to the finality of Christ, however, are brought into the context of religious pluralism, one has enormous difficulties in relating them to the religious experience of the people of other faiths. This was the difficulty encountered by those who responded to the questionnaire of Commission IV of the Edinburgh meeting. The absolute claims of Christian theology did not match experience in the field. Kraemer's response was to deny any ultimate significance to the religious experience of the people of other faiths. He had thus to perceive even the deeply devotional religion of Ramanuja, which represented a total self-giving and surrender to the love and grace of God, as being within the "vitalistic, eudemonistic" variety of religious life.

Once Kraemer's option is rejected, the range of options dwindles. Here we shall take a few examples of how this issue is being addressed among contemporary theologians to see what might help in reassessing the

---

116 Christopher Duraisingh, "World Religions and the Christian Claim for the Unique-ness of Jesus Christ," *The Indian Journal of Theology* XXX 3-4 (July–December 1981): 176.

situation. We shall turn first to Karl Rahner and Raimundo Panikkar, two Roman Catholics who seek to resolve the issue by an 'inclusive' approach.

(a) 'Anonymous Christians'

Karl Rahner is generally considered to be 'the major architect' of the post-conciliar Roman Catholic contribution to this subject.[117] Rahner could too easily be misunderstood if one did not recognize that he looks at pluralism from the point of view of the dogmatic theologian. He himself is clear that his reflection on the non-Christian faiths arises from his own self-understanding as a Christian; indeed, most of his discussion about non-Christian faiths is to be found in his 20 volume work on dogmatic theology. The second important consideration in understanding Rahner is his own theological context of Vatican II. In a real sense, Rahner has fleshed out the declarations of Vatican II, which were themselves more affirmations than developed theological positions.

We have noted earlier that there are three lines of thinking in the Vatican II documents. First, God wills salvation to the whole created order; his salvific will is active in the world. Second, God fulfils his salvific will through the paschal mystery of Christ, of which the Church is the sacramental embodiment. Third, in the exact words of the document, "those also can attain to everlasting salvation who through no fault of their own do not know the gospel of Christ or His church, yet sincerely seek God and, moved by His grace, strive by their deeds to do His will as it is known to them"[118]

Rahner began with a strong affirmation of the universal salvific will of God:

> Christian faith is aware of a universal history of salvation, common to all mankind, existing from the very outset, always effective, universally present as the most radical element of the unity of mankind. . . . The universalism of the one salvific will of God in regard to all mankind, which establishes the final unity of mankind, is the sustaining ground of all particular history of salvation and religion.[119]

But at the same time Rahner was committed to the paschal mystery of salvation, of which the church was the sign and sacrament: God's salvation is mediated and fulfilled in every one's life through grace made available in Christ and mediated through the church. Rahner's theology of religions was thus an elaborate attempt to reconcile these two theological emphases

---

117 Cf. Alan Race, *Christians and Religious Pluralism,* p. 45.

118 "The Dogmatic Constitution of the Church," Chapter II, The People of God, para. 16, in *The Documents of the Vatican II,* p. 35.

119 "Unity of the Church — Unity of Mankind," *Theological Investigations,* Vol. 10 (London: Darton, Longman, and Todd, 1966), p. 160f.

within Roman Catholic thinking. This led him to the concept of the 'anonymous Christian' which has been much discussed and strongly criticized, not always with an adequate understanding of his basic concern. In his words,

> When we have to keep in mind both principles together, namely, the necessity of Christian faith and the universal salvific will of God's love and omnipotence, we can only reconcile them by saying that somehow all men must be capable of being members of the church; and this capability must not be understood merely in the sense of an abstract and purely logical possibility, but as a real and historically concrete one.[120]

In seeking this reconciliation, Rahner took sides on an issue which had been much debated at Tambaram, namely, the relationship between nature and grace. Kraemer, in keeping with the mainline Protestant tradition, had made a clear distinction between 'nature' and 'grace.' The natural man —the man in his religion— needed to be redeemed from his 'natural' state by the grace of God revealed in Christ as God's free gift. Devoid of this revelation, man's religion could not lead him to God. Such Asian theologians as D. G. Moses and T. C. Chao had expressed strong reservations on this position.[121]

Rahner adopted the Roman Catholic position — 'grace built into nature': The salvific will of God is already active in all religious life despite the fact that it is 'mixed up with human depravity.' The important emphasis here is that this grace, already active in non-Christian life, is not 'non-Christian' in the last analysis, for it is given 'on account of Christ.' In other words, God's grace in Christ is already available for salvation, whether one has consciously acknowledged the paschal mystery or not — hence the possibility of the 'anonymous Christian.'[122] This means that there are not two separate phases in human life of the individual and community, one 'natural' and the other 'grace-filled,' one 'outside the saving act of God' and the other 'in the community of the saved.' It also means that non-Christian religions could also be considered as 'vehicles of salvation' insofar as they, albeit unconsciously, are within the total salvific will of God which He would bring to fulfilment in the grace of Christ.

Knitter has given us a useful summary of Rahner's understanding of the relationship of Christ and of the Christ-event to the total salvific will of God:

---

120 *Theological Investigations,* Vol. 6, p. 391.
121 See discussions in the Tambaram volume, *The Authority of the Faith,* pp. 25-89.
122 *Theological Investigations,* Vol. 5, pp. 121-25.

First, Christ is the *constitutive cause* of salvation (this term is not Rahner's). Whatever saving grace is present in the world has to be constituted
and caused by the event of Jesus Christ. Rahner, however, does not
consider Christ as an *efficient* cause of grace, as if Jesus had to *do*
something to bring about God's universal love. Rather, Christ is the *final*
cause of God's universal salvific will: What God, from the beginning of
time, had in mind in calling and offering grace to all humankind. Jesus
of Nazareth is, then, the final goal, the end product of the entire process
of universal revelation and grace. For Rahner, the final goal is a necessary
cause of salvation. Without the goal, realized in one historical individual,
the entire process would not take place: God desires the salvation of
every one; and this salvation is the salvation won by Christ. ... *This*
relationship of God to man (the supernatural existential) ... rests on the
incarnation, death, and resurrection of the one Word of God become
flesh.[123] [Emphasis Knitter's]

Rahner's system thus seeks an inclusive understanding of salvation without
sacrificing the centrality of the Christ-event and the church, affirming at
the same time the salvific value of other religions.

The church in this understanding is not a community plucked out of
the perishing world with the mission to 'save' as many as possible before
it is too late. Rather it becomes the 'embodiment' of the salvific power of
Christ which has always (even before the incarnation) been active, historically manifested in the Christ-event, and through which alone all salvation
is finally accomplished. The mission of the church, therefore, is to bring
to explicit consciousness the grace of God in Christ which has been
accepted implicitly by the non-Christian.

Rahner's concept of the 'anonymous Christian' has been attacked from
many angles. In a biting criticism of the whole concept as "offensive to
the non-Christians, reflecting the chauvinism and paternalism that creates
barriers," Hick called the notion of anonymous Christians "an honorary
status granted unilaterally to people who have not expressed any desire for
it."[124] A similar criticism, expressed in a lighter vein, came from
C. J. Eichhorst, who suggested that "whereas it was once extremely hard to
be inside the church, in this interpretation it is extremely hard to be
outside" of it.[125] It is unfortunate that Rahner used the phrase 'anonymous
Christians' in his attempt to develop an inclusivist Christology, for the
phrase itself was open to attack as being insensitive towards people of
other faiths.

123 Paul Knitter, *No Other Name?* pp. 128-29. Knitter has taken his quotation from
Theological Investigations, pp. 118, 122.

124 John Hick, *God Has Many Names,* Westminster Press, Philadelphia, p. 68.

125 "From Outside the Church to the Inside," *Dialogue* 12 (Summer 1973): 195;
quoted by Christopher Duraisingh, *op. cit.,* p. 177.

More substantive criticisms related to the ecclesiology behind Rahner's Christology. Hans Küng's criticism, for example, centred on Rahner's implicit reaffirmation of the formula that 'outside the church there is no salvation.' Küng's charge was that, by vaporizing the church into a universal presence, Rahner had made the church everywhere and nowhere.[126] Van Straelen complained about the missiological implications of Rahner's ecclesiology for, in his view, Rahner's universalizing of the church had rendered conversion superfluous and removed the possibility of any religious demand that might legitimately be made of non-Christians.[127]

There have also been a number of sympathetic voices, hailing Rahner's position as the most viable way of holding on to a universalist understanding of salvation and also preserving the normative character of the person and work of Christ. Gavin D'Costa, for example, felt that, while it would be possible to abandon the concept of the 'anonymous Christian,' it was not possible to give up the "underlying conviction and reality it denotes — that when a person is saved, it is by God's grace that they are saved." It is D'Costa's conviction that Rahner's position "avoids the a priori Barthian exclusivism which characterizes the partner's life and religion as erroneous, and reductive forms of pluralism which neglect real differences between dialogue partners."[128] In a detailed comparison between the exclusivist position taken by Kraemer at Tambaram and what was at the heart of Rahner's proposal, D'Costa concludes that a more developed inclusivist position is the most viable option open as long as one seeks to do full justice to "the two most important Christian axioms: that salvation comes through God in Christ alone, and that God's salvific will is truly universal."[129]

D'Costa puts his finger on the unresolved Christological tension evidenced at every ecumenical meeting we have considered. But before we turn to the ways in which the question may be taken up in the future, it would be profitable to see how the exclusivist view had been applied specifically to the Hindu context by another well-known Roman Catholic theologian, Raimundo Panikkar.

(b)   The 'Unknown Christ'

Like Rahner, Panikkar emphasized the universal salvific will of God as present and active in all religions. At the same time he also contended that Christians could have no grounds for understanding salvation except

---

126 Hans Küng, *On Being a Christian* (New York: Doubleday, 1976), p. 98.

127 H. van Straelen, *The Catholic Encounter with World Religions*, 1966, p. 97; quoted by Eric J. Sharpe, *Faith Meets Faith*, p. 130.

128 Gavin D'Costa, *Theology and Religious Pluralism*, p. 90.

129 *Ibid.,* p. 136.

in Christ. He dealt with the issue by developing the cosmic-ontic aspect of Christ which had been one of the themes in Christology from the very beginning:

> We believe that the Logos himself is speaking in that religion (Hinduism) which for millenia has been leading and inspiring hundreds and millions of people. *Vac,* the Logos, is the First-born of truth and was with the absolute from the beginning.[130]

For Panikkar, therefore, the essential aspect of the Hindu–Christian relationship is for the Christian to recognize the 'unknown' dimensions of Christ in Hinduism.

In order to do this Panikkar gives greater emphasis to Christ as the second person of the Trinity, the ontological —temporal and eternal— link between God and the world. "This then," Panikkar says, "is Christ: that reality from whom everything has come, in whom everything subsists, to whome everything that suffers the wear and tear of time shall return. He is the embodiment of Divine Grace who leads every man to God; there is no other way but through him."[131]

Developing this idea further in *The Trinity and the Religious Experience of Man,* Panikkar uses his deep knowledge of Hinduism to build a strong case for Hindu–Christian dialogue based on the inclusivist position.[132] If Christ is the one mediator between the Father and humankind and the light "that illumines every human being coming into the world," then we cannot but discern Christ to be already present and active within Hinduism:

> The Spirit of Christ is already at work in Hindu prayer. Christ is already present in every form of worship, to the extent that it is adoration directed to God. The deep-thinking Christian declines to judge Hinduism. God alone judges through Christ. So long as men are pilgrims on earth, Christianity has not the right to separate the wheat from the chaff. Rather, in meeting and accepting Hinduism as it is, the Christian will find Christ already there.[133]

Panikkar's inclusiveness was open to much of the criticism levelled against Rahner for Panikkar, despite his caution, appeared to insist on interpreting the heart of Hinduism entirely in Christian terms. In his long introduction to the revised version of *The Unknown Christ of Hinduism,* Panikkar attempted to clear what he considered to be a misunderstanding of his

---

130 Raimundo Panikkar, *The Unknown Christ of Hinduism* (1964; revised and enlarged edition, Maryknoll, N. Y.: Orbis, 1981), pp. 1-2.

131 *Ibid.,* p. 49.

132 Raimundo Panikkar, *The Trinity and the Religious Experience of Man* (Maryknoll, N. Y.: Orbis, 1973).

133 *The Unknown Christ of Hinduism,* p. 49.

proposal among both Christians and Hindus. Explaining the intention of the book's title, Panikkar said:

> My main concern was not to speak of (a) the unknown Christ of Hindus 'known' by the Christians, nor (b) of an unknown Christ of Christians who is 'known' to Hindus, under whatever form or name. . . . But my primary intention was to speak (c) about the 'unknown' Christ of Hinduism, which can be either unknown, or known *qua* Christ, to Christian and Hindu alike. . . . The title does not say the *Hidden Christ* as though Christians knew the secret and Hindus did not. I wanted to lay stress on the presence of the one mystery (not necessarily the 'same' mystery) in both traditions.[134]

Panikkar's Christology thus portrayed Christ as the real source of all genuine spiritual life. While the Christian approach to the 'mystery' of Christ was rooted in the life, death, and resurrection of Jesus Christ, Christ was 'more' than all that Christians had conceived him to be. In this respect, Panikkar said that one could write also of "The known Christ of Christianity," for there was no attempt here to speak of Christian superiority over Hinduism:

> I speak neither of a principle unknown to Hinduism, or of a dimension of the divine unknown to Christianity, but of that unknown *reality*, which Christians call Christ, discovered in the heart of Hinduism, not as a stranger to it, but as its very *principle of life*, as the light that illumines every man who comes into the world.[135]

We have rather inadequately presented the overall positions of Rahner and Panikkar on the theology of religions. Our purpose, however, was not to expound their views but to use them to illustrate the fundamental Christological issue confronting the ecumenical discussion.

Tambaram's emphasis on the uniqueness and decisiveness of Christ led to an 'exclusivist' view that would come under increasing pressure in the context of religious pluralism. As we have seen in our discussion of Rahner and Panikkar, an 'inclusivist' position which still insists on the finality of Christ does not necessarily resolve the problem if we intend to understand the significance of Christ in the context of pluralism in ways that respect the authenticity of the other religious traditions.

(c) Other Explorations

Both Roman Catholics and Protestants who have tried to find a third way out have had considerable difficulty in reconciling the uniqueness and finality attributed to the incarnation with a pluralist view of the world. It

---

134 *Ibid.,* pp. 25-26.
135 *Ibid.,* pp. 19-20.

is beyond the scope of our discussions to examine these in detail, for they are many and varied. Hick and Robinson, for example, have interpreted belief in the incarnation as a 'myth,' thus attempting to dissociate the exclusivism of the language from the significance of the event. In so far as both the incarnation and the divinity of Jesus are mythic, these scholars hold that not only are beliefs about Jesus open to interpretation, but our Christian responsibility requires us to interpret them for our own times.[136]

The second option is to reject both the exclusive and the inclusive in its ontic sense, but to emphasize the 'normative' character of the Christ event. Hans Küng, for example, and W. C. Smith, by implication, seem to affirm this line of thinking. Here Christ is the decisive demonstration of God's love and therefore any uniqueness of Christ's lies in the 'normative' function of this experience in evaluating all other experience.[137]

Samartha and Knitter have attempted to deal with the issue in terms of 'relational uniqueness.' Samartha bases his argument for this concept on the principle that Christians should grow in awareness of the 'mystery' that they confront when they talk about ultimate reality. Therefore, any claims to uniqueness which may be a part of the Christian understanding of Christ must be put alongside other claims, for the Christian and the Hindu are both dealing with a mystery that is beyond their grasp.[138]

Having argued for a theo-centric model of relationships, Knitter also insists that uniqueness of Christ has to be defined in a way that would relate it to other claims to uniqueness. Nevertheless, Knitter reveals his own Christian bias by stating that one among all the limited historical expressions of divine life may well be more complete than the others. "Perhaps," he muses, "Jesus of Nazareth will stand forth (without being imposed) as the unifying symbol, the universally fulfilling and normative expression, of what God intends for all history."[139] Knitter is quick to add that if such an eventuality should occur it would have to be a 'side-effect' and not the central purpose of inter-faith dialogue. "Nevertheless," comments Allan Brockway in his review of Knitter's book, "the question to Knitter must be: But what if Moses or Mohammad or Krishna emerges as the culmination point of all religions? What then for Christians?"[140] Knitter's hope and Brockway's comment illustrate both the dynamic

---

136 J. A. T. Robinson, *op. cit.* See Robinson's discussion on "Defining without Confining," p. 120 ff.

137 Cf. Hans Küng, *On Being a Christian* (New York: Doubleday, 1979), pp. 110-24.

138 See especially Samartha's article on "The Lordship of Jesus Christ and Religious Pluralism" (pp. 102-4), and "Ganga and Galilee: Two Responses to Truth" (pp. 150-54), both in *Courage for Dialogue.*

139 Paul Knitter, *No Other Name?, op. cit.,* p. 231.

140 Allan R. Brockway, Review of *No Other Name?,* by Paul Knitter, *The Ecumenical Review* XXXVII (Oct. 1985): 515.

possibilities and the inherent fears involved in the search for a pluralist Christology.

We should consider two other currents within the contemporary discussions before we link this whole question to Hindu–Christian relations. The first has to do with the concern most insistently held within the Indian context by M. M. Thomas, Niles, and Devanandan, who interpret Christology primarily in terms of the "spiritual dynamic of the new humanity."[141] Without necessarily working out a systematic theological frame of reference for dealing with the 'ontic' Christ, nor even appealing specifically to logos Christology, they have argued that the risen Christ in the power of the Holy Spirit is the forerunner and guarantor of the new humanity tht God offers in Christ to all of humankind. Here we have an attempt to cross the barrier between the religious and the secular, for Thomas speaks of a "Christ-centred secular ecumenism" or a "secular fellowship in Christ," placing the emphasis on the new humanity and the renewal of all human life; Christians should draw their confidence and hope in such humanity from what God has done in Jesus Christ.[142]

The second current has to do with the way in which the awareness of life and theology in one religious community impinges on that in another. We have already noted the call of Hick and Cantwell Smith for a 'global' or 'world' theology which would attribute the whole of the religious life to the whole of humanity. In his new volume, *The Christ and the Faiths,* Kenneth Cragg develops the idea of "Theology in Cross-Reference."[143] Already at Kandy in 1967, Cragg was challenging the idea of 'discontinuity' and arguing that the credence of the gospel depended on its ability to be heard by the persons of another religious tradition. He therefore rejected the "trade-mark mentality" in doing theology which would allow "only brand names and no open truths in common."[144] After examining the whole issue of the frontiers of theology, Cragg has concluded that the need to be 'attentive' to each other's faith and the increasing pressures to make common responses to common issues would mean that "the theology of cross-reference is the only theology there is."[145] Conceding that each religion tends to be overly conscious "of its version of what is final," Cragg holds that "when such versions (claims to finality) meet, when they effectively discover that they are not alone in interpreting the mystery and

---

141 See especially M. M. Thomas' chapter on "Modern Man and the New Humanity in Jesus Christ" in his *Man and the Universe of Faith* (Bangalore: Christian Institute for the Study of Religion and Society, 1975), pp. 129-57.

142 *Ibid.,* p. 141.

143 Kenneth Cragg, *The Christ and the Faiths: Theology in Cross-Reference* (London: SPCK, 1986).

144 *Ibid.,* p. 344.

145 *Ibid.*

the world, they must converse and articulate their finality where it can no longer be assumed, it is then that they face, or it may well be evade, the double obligation to waive their finality and re-learn how to commend it."[146]

It is this conviction about the need to do theology in cross-reference that Cragg himself seeks to exercise in his *Muhammad and the Christian: A Question of Response*. In this work, he invites Christians to examine their own relationships with Muslims, and Stuart E. Brown has observed that Cragg "provides an articulate and sufficient rejoinder to those of his critics for whom Muslim–Christian relations can never reach beyond an austere if respectful aloofness."[147]

Cragg is in the company of an increasing number of theologians like Harold Coward, Ulrich Schoen, and Aloysius Pieris, who would render Christian theology more 'attentive' to other faiths.[148] Pieris, for example, sees the religious heritage of Semitic thought and the religious insights and values of the Hindu–Buddhist–Taoist traditions as two distinct 'impluses' or, to use his own terms, "the *agapeic* and *gnostic* idioms." In his view these two impulses, far from being contradictory, "are in fact complementary and *mutually corrective*.... They are two instincts emerging dialectically from within the deepest zone of each individual, be he Christian or not. Our religious encounter with God and man would be incomplete without this interaction."[149] Pieris develops his thesis further in advocating a *participatory approach* to theology. It is only through total participation through baptism in Asian religiosity and poverty, the two distinct realities of Asia, and out of such theo-praxis, that an authentic theology can develop.[150]

Implications for the Ecumenical Debate

Our rather selective and all too sketchy sampling of contemporary theological debates reveals a widening gap between current general thinking on the question of Christology and official discussions within the WCC. Almost all the major meetings up to the Vancouver Assembly have tried to preserve and protect the 'uniqueness,' 'finality' or 'decisiveness' of Christ

146 *Ibid.,* p. 310.

147 Stuart E. Brown, Review of *The Muhammad and the Christian: A Question of Response,* by Kenneth Cragg, *The Ecumenical Review* XXXVII 4 (Oct. 1985): 516.

148 Harold Coward, *Pluralism: Challenge to World Religions,* pp. 105-9; Ulrich Schoen, "The Event and the Answers: In Quest of a Theology of Religions for Today," in German, *Das Ereignis und die Antworten: Auf der Suche nach einer Theologie der Religionen heute* (Göttingen/Zürich: Vandenhoeck and Ruprecht, 1984), 166 pp.

149 Aloysius Pieris, "Western Christianity and Asian Buddhism: A Theological Reading of Historical Encounters," *Dialogue,* p. 64.

150 *Ibid.,* pp. 83-85.

in the sense used at Tambaram in 1938. Despite the new emphasis on dialogue and the reduction of triumphalistic language and despite all intentions to work with the rest of humanity in the search for a "just, participatory, and sustainable society," the WCC constituency has made no major attempt to re-examine its Christological assumptions, many of which have come under the close scrutiny which we have just reviewed. There are signs that the entirely exclusivist alternative is being subjected increasingly to serious questioning. But, as we have already seen, the tentative exploration of this issue from the side of Dialogue led at both Nairobi and Vancouver to sharp controversies and the consequent reaffirmation of the exclusivist stand. The importance of the issue also bears on the Council's concern for mission and evangelism. As long as its Christological assumptions have not been tested against the challenge of religious plurality and the emerging consensus about the need for a theology of religious pluralism, the Council cannot hope to have a dynamic understanding of mission and evangelism that will carry any conviction in the hearts and minds of the churches which live and witness in religiously pluralistic societies.

On Hindu–Christian Relations

What are some of the implications of all this for Hindu–Christian relations? We have noted that a Christology which begins with finality, uniqueness, or any such term inevitably arrives either at the inclusivist position represented in our discussion by Rahner and Panikkar, or at the exclusivist position that has lingered unchallenged in the Council's statements ever since it was reaffirmed at Tambaram.

Commenting on both Panikkar and Rahner, Eric Sharpe has expressed dismay at the way Christians would still want "to impose *a priori* theories on the religions of the world in the interest of comparative religion." Noting that we have learned, painfully, to speak and think of non-Christian religions as totalities or units each one subject to its own judgments, with its own theological, sociological, and psychological presuppositions, he contended that Panikkar and Rahner are "either unaware of this intellectual development, or bent on ignoring it."[151] As for the Hindu attitude, he commented:

> Christian apologetics are of course always cooly received by non-Christians; the more the apologist has strained himself to produce a version of Christianity which he has felt might be acceptable to the non-Christian, or (in this case) a version of the non-Christian religions which might be acceptable to the guilt-ridden Christian, the less actual communication has taken place. The Hindu is not going to thank you for even suspecting that

151 Eric Sharpe, *Faith Meets Faith,* p. 129.

he might be a Christian without knowing it. The attempt may be as well-meaning as you please; but in dialogical terms, it is fatal. What the Hindu undoubtedly does respect, on the other hand, is open and total Christian commitment. He may not agree with it, but he does not as a rule despise it.[152]

On the exclusivist view we need not comment. Outstanding interpreters of Hinduism like Vivekananda, Radhakrishnan, and Gandhi have interpreted Christian exclusivism as arrogance born out of a defective conception of Truth. More recently, Anantanand Rambachan has said that the Christian preoccupation with finality and uniqueness has clouded the deeply spiritual dimension of the personality of Jesus and the challenge it presents for an authentic spiritual life. "I think," said Rambachan, "that this primary aspect of the personality of Christ is not always sufficiently emphasized in presenting him. I imagine that it will always be difficult to represent one who cared so little for the comforts and possessions which are usually the focus of our energies and aspirations. ... But perhaps in its concern to stress the uniqueness and originality of Jesus, Christianity has ignored some of the identities in the definition of the spiritual life which Jesus shares with the tradition of Hinduism."[153]

Rambachan's comments shed some light on the possibility of a more sympathetic evaluation of the attempts of Panikkar and Rahner, which Sharpe had so severely criticized. Our question is: Are both the exclusivist and the inclusivist views so overly preoccupied with defending the finality and uniqueness of Christ that they pass by the true significance of Christ for a pluralist milieu?

Reviewing the pluralist situation in India and Hindu–Christian relations within it, Arvind Nirmal has said that the only way forward lies in asking some painful theological questions. In his review of the Chiang Mai papers of the Dialogue sub-unit he complained that even the dialogue concern had not really attempted to face the hard theological issues raised by pluralism in India:

> Very often our theological approaches to dialogue try to put the cart before the horse. We ask for an 'adequate' theological basis for dialogue rather than re-examining our theological traditions and formulations in the light of specific dialogical experiences. We are preoccupied with our concern to safeguard the uniqueness of Jesus Christ or the finality of Jesus Christ or total commitment to Jesus Christ before entering into a dialogical situation, rather than examining the adequacy of the doctrine

---

152 *Ibid.*

153 Reproduced in *My Neighbour's Faith and Mine: Theological Discoveries Through Interfaith Dialogue,* a Study Guide (Geneva: WCC, 1986), pp. 18-19.

of the uniqueness of Jesus or the nature of our committment to him in the light of actual dialogue experience.[154]

Our study of developments within the ecumenical movement has shown that every attempt to reflect theologically about other faiths that has begun with the finality of Jesus Christ, interpreted in its various forms, has ended in Christian chauvinism and paternalism. With regard to Hinduism, Panikkar had gone the furthest, interpreting 'Christ' in the broadest possible sense, so much so, despite Panikkar's protest to the contrary, the 'ontic' Christ loses almost all connection with the historical Jesus. It would appear that whatever connection there is has survived because the theological tradition has always expected this connection to be crucial for theological orthodoxy. And yet, for the Hindu, Panikkar would appear to be as imperialistic as Rahner, for both of them, in the last analysis, insist on the finality of Christ in one sense or another.[155] Whatever useful purpose the terms finality and uniqueness may once have served in interpreting the salvific purpose of God, their usefulness is past. We should abandon these two concepts, along with the theological constructs associated with them.

Let us immediately attempt here to remove a possible misunderstanding. We do not mean that we should give up the centrality of Christ for the Christian faith, in both its historical and transcendental dimensions. This the Hindu understands. Nor do we mean that we should not witness to the experience of salvation in Christ as an offer open to the whole of humanity. This too the Hindu would understand. We advocate neither an easy relativism nor a compromise of the central and challenging elements of the Christian faith. But we do contend that these elements need not necessarily depend on the concepts of finality and uniqueness. In other words, we should re-examine the assumption commonly heard in WCC discussions, that it is the uniqueness and finality of Christ which governs, defines, and limits our understanding of and approach to the Hindu or to any other person of faith. For it is not the positive affirmation of the centrality of Christ to the Christian understanding of the world and human life that makes these words obsolete in a religiously plural world, but the negative implications inherent in a concept of uniqueness or finality.

---

154 Arvind P. Nirmal, "Redefining the Economy of Salvation," *The Indian Journal of Theology* XXX 3-4 (July–December 1981): 214.

155 In his Introduction to the revised version of *The Unknown Christ of Hinduism*, Panikkar contends that what he has done does not deserve this interpretation: "If Christians, believing in the truth of their own religion, recognize truth outside it, they will be inclined to say that a 'Christian' truth has been discovered there. ... Similarly, when a Hindu discovers a positive value outside his own religion, he will either try to incorporate it without any 'copyright' qualms or recognize that it was also present, although perhaps dormant, in his own religion," p. 7.

In fact, a detailed examination of the way they have been used at Nairobi and Vancouver would show that, far from articulating an ecumenical theological consensus among Christians on the question of salvation, they have become emotive words that satisfy a stream within the movement that would protect its particular understanding of mission and evangelism, at a time when it has long since come under serious questioning in the light of the new awareness of pluralism.

Within the long history of relationships between Hindus and Christians, these words give the wrong signals and can no longer be reinterpreted for new content. Nor are we arguing for new words that would convey the same meaning. What we seek is a new theological orientation to bring together the two issues which we have raised. If religious plurality is within God's providence, then a Christology that rejects it is at cross-purposes with God.

Towards a Theology in Relationship

In a recent study, José Miguez-Bonino has cautioned that, even though the WCC endorses the Trinitarian faith, its Christological affirmations have a tendency towards Christo-monism. "To be sure," says Miguez-Bonino, "the early Christological emphasis was not anti-trinitarian. But it tended to interpret the first and the third articles in relation to the second." Thus creation, providence, pneumatology, and eschatology were "all seen in a Christo-centric —and sometimes even in a Christo-monistic— way."

Unfortunately, and despite the particaption of the Orthodox churches in the ecumenical discussions there has been no serious attempt to see Christology itself within a dynamic understanding of the Trinitarian faith — or as Miguez-Bonino puts it, "to interpret the second article in relation to the first and third, both creationally and pneumatologically."[156] Such an understanding would certainly help to counter the sterile pronouncements on finality that turn a blind eye on the new awareness of pluralism which we have noted in our opening chapter.

It is beyond the scope of our present interest to examine whether the trinitarian or any other avenue we have considered would prove to be the way forward. But we are convinced that the contemporary efforts towards a third position, which we have reviewed in bare outline, offer a number

---

156 The WCC has a membership of over 310 churches from more than 100 countries. All the major branches of the Protestant and Orthodox traditions are represented in the Council. The Roman Catholic Church is not an official member, but works in close collaboration with the WCC through a Joint Working Group. Official representatives of the Roman Catholic Church, however, are full and voting members of the Commission on Faith and Order.

of the elements necessary for an overall reassessment of Christian theology in the context of pluralism:

–A profound awareness of the mystery which attends any exploration of Truth or of the meaning of Christ (Samartha, Race);

–A broadening appreciation of the nature of doctrine, its cultural-linguistic idiom, and its regulative function within given faith communities (Lindbeck);

–An acknowledgment of the inevitable limitations imposed by human thought and language on the explication of an event (Hick, Robinson);

–A willingness to understand claims to uniqueness, finality etc., in their relationship to other such claims (Knitter, Cragg);

–An openness to enrichment and transformation through contact with other faiths (Cobb);

–A searching for realistic, moral, and community-building ways of explicating one's faith in a pluralist world (Hick);

–A growing respect for the Divine — human relationship that lies beyond all human attempts to grasp or limit it, and a readiness to do theology that takes account of the spiritual history of all of humankind (Cantwell Smith);

–The challenge to Christology, and indeed to all Christian theology which has been developed in one cultural tradition and perception, to be 'baptised' into Asian spirituality and weaned from theo-praxis (Pieris); and

–The need to explicate one's faith in terms of dynamic for the renewal and humanization of all of life (Thomas).

These are some of the considerations that should govern the explication of the centrality of Jesus Christ to the Christian understanding of life supported by exclusivist (Kraemer) and inclusivist (Rahner, Panikkar) alike. This explication, furthermore, must affirm the totality of the Christian faith (including creation and the Holy Spirit).

Such a Christology can only emerge from a thorough realization in practice of the two kinds of ecumenism we mentioned in opening this discussion: a greater integration of the various confessional and cultural streams of theological thought that comprise the Christian ecumenical movement, and the practice, in living dialogue, of the 'wider' ecumenism which informs, corrects, and enriches Christian life and thought. Therein also lies the context for future Christian–Hindu relations.

The Ecumenical Task: A Concluding Comment

In this study we have argued the need for a theology of religious plurality as an essential part of the explication of the fundamentals of our faith, and for an authentic Christology that moves away from an entirely missiological explanation of the significance of Christ. This twofold request appears at first sight to be a most daunting agenda, but we are convinced that such a theological reconstruction is not too much to ask of the ecumenical community.

For the ecumenical movement, with the World Council of Churches as one of its primary instruments, gathers churches of a variety of cultures and traditions into a fellowship of mutual enrichment and correction. Represented within it is almost every stream of Protestant, Orthodox, and Roman Catholic theological thinking, expresssing among them a wide variety of theological responses to religious plurality and a broad range of approaches to the Christological question.[157] The Council, therefore, seems better placed than any other body to provide the venue for an exploration of the elements necessary for a considered theological understanding of religious plurality. We insist that religious plurality is now more than a missiological issue and of much wider import than the theology of religions in the restricted sense of the term. Religious plurality has to do with the explication of the Christian faith, and the task it demands must therefore be the *common* responsibility of the Faith and Order, Mission, and Dialogue aspects of the work of the Council.[158]

At its Louvain meeting in 1971, the Faith and Order Commission thus recognized the importance of this question for Christian theology and for its own work:

> ... There was also a strong feeling that dialogue contributes to our understanding of the gospel and of Christian unity. It breaks down our 'tribalism' and enlarges the horizons within which we think of the church's catholicity. It makes us more aware, and in new ways, of the 'concentrality' of Jesus Christ. It helps us think more clearly about the relation between unity and diversity.[159]

The report went on to acknowledge that the concern had to do with the "readiness to let new ground be broken for Faith and Order thinking."[160]

---

157 José Miguez-Bonino, "Report on the Concern for a Vital and Coherent Theology" (WCC Archives, 1986), pp. 7-8 –draft.

158 The Commission on Faith and Order, The Commission on World Mission and Evangelism and the Programme on Dialogue with People of Living Faiths are subunits which together with Church and Society from the Unit on Faith and Witness.

159 *Faith and Order, Louvain, 1971: Study Reports and Documents,* Faith and Order Paper no. 59 (Geneva: WCC, 1971), p. 191.

160 *Ibid.*

In her report to the sixth meeting of the WCC Dialogue Working Group, its moderator Diana Eck recalled the theological challenge facing the ecumenical movement and urged the Commission on Faith and Order to respond to the challenge of religious pluralism: "How do we account theologically for the fact of human religious diversity? ... Theology has come to grips with Aristotle, just as theology has had to come to grips with science and with the fact that the sun does not circle the earth. Coming to grips with the world's religious pluralism is equally challenging to Christian theology today." She continued with this thought-provoking quotation:

> As Wilfred Cantwell Smith has put it: "Not only are Christian answers not the only answers, but Christian questions are not the only questions." Smith, writing nearly twenty years ago, predicted: "The time will soon be with us when a theologian who attempts to work out his position unaware that he does so as a member of a world community in which other theologians, equally intelligent, equally devout, equally moral, are Hindus, Buddhists, Muslims, and unaware that his readers are likely perhaps to be Buddhists, or to have Muslim husbands, or Hindu colleagues — such a theologian is as hopelessly out of date as one who attempts to construct an intellectual position unaware that Aristotle has thought, or unaware that the earth is a minor planet in a galaxy that is vast only by terrestrial standards." That time has come, and in the next period of our WCC work, we look forward to closer collaboration with the Faith and Order Commission on the theological task of one world.[161]

In his illuminating study on "God and the Nations" and his probing exegesis of the apparently exclusive verses in the Bible, Kenneth Cracknell draws on his own Methodist tradition for his contribution to this theological task. His and other attempts, in different parts of the world, to understand the Bible in relation to other faiths, and the sub-unit on Dialogue's longterm study project on *My Neighbour's Faith — And Mine: Theological Discoveries Through Inter-faith Dialogue* are all meant to facilitate this theological reconstruction.[162]

Our mind, however, goes back to the work of Commission IV at the Edinburgh meeting of 1910. This report, more than any other we have considered, was able to assess the true dimensions of the challenge which

---

161 *Dialogue with People of Living Faiths,* Minutes of the Sixth Meeting of the Working Group, Swanwick, U. K., March 1985 (Geneva: WCC, 1985), p. 27.

162 We refer here to chapters in Kenneth Cracknell, *Towards a New Relationship,* and S. Wesley Ariarajah, *The Bible and People of Other Faiths* (Geneva: WCC/WSCF, 1985), as well as Krister Stendahl, "Notes for Three Bible Studies," *Christ's Lordship and Religious Pluralism,* Gerald H. Anderson and Thomas F. Stransky, eds. (Maryknoll, N. Y.: Orbis, 1981). *My Neighbour's Faith and Mine* is the Study Guide for a four-year programme to raise awareness of religious pluralism in the churches (Geneva: WCC, 1986).

Christian theology was facing in its encounter with the spiritual tradition of Hinduism. Comparing this encounter to the one between the Christian faith and the Graeco-Roman world, the authors observed that "the mind of the church is deeply stirred" by its meeting with Hinduism. This was a 'new emergency' that was 'pregnant with new possibilities,' for it would drive the church to search for ever more profound dimensions of the gospel. "New faith," the Commission believed, "is born out of new emergency," and the church was called to a radical reappraisal of its own theology.[163]

And so we say: Never mind Vancouver 1983! Let us pick up the discussion from where we left it in 1910. If it has the will, the ecumenical movement has both the resources and the stamina it needs.

---

163 From the Report of the Edinburgh 1910 meeting. Here the text closely follows the concluding part of our Chapter IV.

Bibliography

(A) Consultations and Reports
(in chronological order)

World Missionary Conference 1910: Reports. Edinburgh/London: Oliphant, Anderson, and Ferrier, 1910

VOL. I   *Carrying the Gospel to All the Non-Christian World: Report of Commission I,* with supplement: Presentation and Discussion of the Report in the Conference on 15th June 1910.

VOL. II   *The Church in the Mission Field: Report of Commission II,* with supplement: Presentation and Discussion of the Report in the Conference on 16th June 1910.

VOL. IV   *The Missionary Message in Relation to Non-Christian Religions: Report of Commission IV,* with supplement: Presentation and Discussion of the Report in the Conference on 18th June 1910

VOL. IX   *The History and Records of the Conference together with Addresses Delivered at the Evening Meetings.*

Commission on the Missionary Message. (Bound volumes containing typescripts of the answers received to the questionnaire distributed by Commission IV).

Hinduism, VOL. I
Andrews, C. F., pp. 24-46.
Campbell, W. H., pp. 99-116.
Eddy, G. S., pp. 163-67.
Farquhar, J. N., pp. 169-211.
Hogg, A. G., pp. 400-65.
Hume, R. A., pp. 495-510.

Hinduism, VOL. II
Kingsbury, F., pp. 24-32.
Lahore, Bishop of, pp. 34-56.
Lucas, B., pp. 92-107.
Macnicol, N., pp. 108-34.
Mukerjee, N. C., pp. 207-14.
Slater, T. E., pp. 315-404.

Steinthal, F. W., pp. 414-57.

Report of the Jerusalem Meeting of the International Missionary Council,
March 24th–April 8th 1928. London/New York: IMC, 1928.

VOL. I   *The Christian Life and Message in Relation to Non-Christian*
          Systems.

VOL. II   *The Relations Between the Younger and Older Churches.*

VOL. VIII *Addresses and Other Records.*

The World Mission of the Church: Findings and Recommendations of the
Meeting of the International Missionary Council, Tambaram, Madras,
December 12-29, 1938. London/New York: IMC, 1939.

VOL. I   *The Authority of the Faith.*

VOL. II   *The Growing Church.*

VOL. III *Evangelism.*

VOL. VII *Address and Other Records.*

Preparatory Volume:

Hendrik Kraemer. *The Christian Message in a Non-Christian World.* London: Edinburgh House Press (for the IMC), 1938.

The Witness of a Revolutionary Church: Statements Issued by the Committee
of the IMC, Whitby, Ontario, Canada, July 5-24, 1947. London/New
York: IMC, 1947.

C. W. Ranson, ed. *Renewal and Advance: Christian Witness in a Revolution-*
ary World. London: Edinburgh House Press, 1948.

W. A. Visser 't Hooft. *The First Assembly of the World Council of Churches*
held at Amsterdam, August 22nd to September 4th 1948. London: SCM
Press Ltd., 1949.

Man's Disorder and God's Design: The Amsterdam Assembly series. New
York: Harper and Brothers Publishers, 1948.
VOL. 1. *The Universal Church in God's Design.*
VOL. 2. *The Church's Witness to God's Design.*

The Christian Prospect in Eastern Asia: Papers and Minutes of the EACC,
Bangkok, December 3-11, 1949. New York, 1950.

N. Goodall, ed. *Missions Under the Cross: Addresses Delivered at the*
Enlarged Meeting of the Committee of the IMC at Willingen, Germany,
1952, with Statements issued by the Meeting. London: IMC, 1953.

Assembly Work Book: Prepared for the Second Assembly of the WCC at
Evanston, 1954. Geneva, 1954.

W. A. Visser 't Hooft, ed. *The Evanston Report: The Second Assembly of the WCC.* London/New York: SCM Press, 1955.

Consultation on "Christianity and Non-Christian Religions," Davos, Switzerland, July 21-25, 1955.

Report in the *Bulletin of the World Council of Churches Division of Studies,* I 2 (1955): 22-25.

Papers and Record of Discussions in mimeo in the WCC Archives.

Committee of the Department of Missionary Studies, July 19-22, 1956.

Papers by D. T. Niles and by A. Th. van Leeuwen on "How Should We Continue the Post-Tambaram Discussions" in mimeo in the WCC Archives.

R. K. Orchard. *The Ghana Assembly of the IMC,* 28th December 1957 to 8th January 1958. London: Edinburgh House Press, 1958.

Bossey Consultation March 14-18, 1958: First Meeting of the Committee for the Study on "Living Faiths."

Papers, study document and decisions — mimeo in the WCC Archives.

Report of the Consultation published in *Bulletin of the WCC Division of Studies* IV 1 (1958): 22-30.

U Kyaw Than, ed. *Witness Together: Being the Official Report of the Inaugural Assembly of the EACC,* held at Kuala Lumpur, Malaya, May 14-24, 1959. Rangoon, Burma, 1959.

Nagpur Colloquium on "Hindu and Christian Views of Man," October 10-13, 1960, Reports and papers in the WCC Archives, Report on the meeting by J. B. Carman in *Occasional Bulletin.* WCC: Research Department, no date.

Nagpur Meeting, March 11-15, 1961.

Interim statement (Findings) of the study on *The Word of God and the Living Faiths of Men* published in the *Bulletin of the WCC Division of Studies* VII 1 (1961): 3-10.

Evanston to New Delhi, 1954–1961: Report of the Central Committee to the Third Assembly of the WCC. Geneva: WCC, 1961.

W. A. Visser 't Hooft, ed. *The New Delhi Report: Report of the Third Assembly of the WCC.* London: SCM Press, 1962.

R. K. Orchard, ed. *Witness in Six Continents: Records of the Meeting of the Commission on World Mission and Evangelism of the WCC* held in Mexico City, December 8-19, 1963. London: Edinburgh House Press, 1964.

Second Assembly of the EACC, Bangkok, Thailand, February 25–March 4, 1964, Statement on "Christian Encounter with Men of Other Beliefs" published in *The Ecumenical Review* XVI 3 (July 1964): 451-55.

Kandy Consultation on "Christian Dialogue with Men of Other Faiths," February 27–March 6, 1967, the statement "Christians in Dialogue with Men of Other Faiths" published in *Study Encounter* III 2 (1967): 52-72. Other papers are in the WCC Archives.

New Delhi to Uppsala, 1961–1968: Report of the Central Committee to the Fourth Assembly of the WCC, Uppsala, 1968. Geneva: WCC, 1968.

N. Goodall, ed. *The Uppsala '68 Report: Official Report of the Fourth Asssembly of the WCC,* Uppsala, July 4-20, 1968. Geneva: WCC, 1968.

Albert H. van den Heuvel, ed. *Unity of Mankind: Speeches from the Fourth Assembly of the World Council of Churches,* Uppsala, 1968. Geneva: WCC, 1969.

S. J. Samartha, ed. *Dialogue Between Men of Living Faiths: Papers Presented at a Multi-Faith Consultation,* held at Ajaltoun, Lebanon, March 16-25, 1970. Geneva: WCC, 1971. (Contains the *Ajaltoun Memorandum.*)

"Christians in Dialogue with Men of Other Faiths," the Zürich Consultation which produced the *Zürich Aide-Mémoire.* Text in *International Review of Missions* LIX 236 (Oct. 1970).

Central Committee of the WCC — Addis Ababa Meeting, January 10-21, 1971. "An Interim Policy Statement and Guidelines" published in *Living Faiths and the Ecumenical Movement.* S. J. Samartha, ed. Geneva: WCC, 1971.

Faith and Order — Louvain 1971, Study Reports and Documents, Faith and Order Paper, no. 59. Geneva: WCC, 1971.

Bangkok Assembly, 1973: Minutes and Reports of the Assembly of the Commission on World Mission and Evangelism of the WCC, December 31, 1972 and January 9-12, 1973. Geneva: WCC, 1973. (mimeo)

S. J. Samartha, ed. *Towards World Community: The Colombo Papers, Report of the Multi-lateral Dialogue* held in Colombo, April 1974. Geneva: WCC, 1975.

David Johnson, ed. *Uppsala to Nairobi, 1968–1975: The Report of the Central Committee to the Fifth Assembly of the WCC,* Nairobi 1975. Geneva: WCC, 1975.

David M. Paton, ed. *Breaking Barriers, Nairobi 1975: The Official Report of the Fifth Assembly of the WCC,* Nairobi, 23 November–10 December 1975. SPCK; Grand Rapids: Wm. B. Eerdmans; Geneva: WCC, 1976. (Other related papers are in WCC Archives.)

Castro, Emilio, ed. *Your Kingdom Come, Mission Perspectives: Report of the World Conference of CWME,* Melbourne. Geneva: WCC, 1980.

Nairobi — Vancouver, 1975–1983: Report of the Central Committee to the Sixth Assembly of the WCC. Geneva: WCC, 1983.

David Gill, ed. *Gathered for Life: Official Report, VI Assembly, World Council of Churches,* Vancouver, Canada, 24 July–10 August 1983. Grand Rapids: Wm. B. Eerdmans; Geneva: WCC, 1983.

(B) Minutes of Meetings

World Missionary Conference

Minutes of the Continuation Committee (WCC Archives)
Edinburgh – 1910
Bishop Auckland – 1911
Lake Mohonk – 1912
The Hague – 1913

Meeting of the Ad Hoc Committee of the International Missionary Council

Crans – 1920

Minutes of the Committee of the International Missionary Council

Canterbury – 1922
Atlantic City – 1925
Rättirk – 1926
Herrnhut – 1932
Northfield – 1935

Minutes of the Ad Interim Committee of the International Missionary Council

Salisbury – 1934
Old Jordans – 1936
London – 1937

Minutes of the International Missionary Council

Lake Mohonk – 1921
Oxford – 1923
Jerusalem – 1928
Tambaram – 1938
Whitby – 1947
Willingen – 1952
Ghana – 1957
New Delhi – 1961

Also Considered:

(a) Minutes of the meetings of the Executive and Central Committee meetings of the wcc 1948–1983.

(b) Minutes of the meetings of the Commission on World Mission and Evangelism — New Delhi (1961), Mexico City (1963), Bangkok (1972), Melbourne (1980).

(c) Minutes of the sub-unit on Dialogue with People of Living Faiths (and Ideologies): 1st Athens (March 1973); 2nd New Delhi (Sept. 1974); 3rd Trinidad (May 1978); 4th Matrafüred (April 1980); 5th Bali (Dec.–Jan. 1981/82); 6th Swanwick (March 1985); 7th Potsdam (July 1986).

Significant Documents

WCC

Guidelines on Dialogue with People of Living Faiths and Ideologies. Geneva: wcc, 1979.

Mission and Evangelism: An Ecumenical Affirmation. Geneva: wcc, 1982.

Vatican Secretariat for Non-Christians

The Attitude of the Church Towards the Followers of Other Religions. (Reflections and Orientations on Dialogue and Mission). Vatican City, Pentecost 1984.

Dialogue Commission of the Catholic Bishops' Conference of India

Guidelines for Inter-Religious Dialogue. Varanasi: cbci, 1977.

(C) Books

Abbot, Walter M. *The Documents of Vatican II: All Sixteen Official Texts Promulgated by the Ecumenical Council, 1963–1965.* New York: Guild Press, 1966.

Abhedananda, Sw. *Why a Hindu Accepts Christ and Rejects Christianity?* Calcutta: Ramakrishna Vedanta Math, 1965.

Abhishitkananda, Sw. *Hindu–Christian Meeting Point Within the Cave of the Heart.* Bombay: Institute of Indian Culture, 1969.

——. *Saccidananda: A Christian Approach to Advaitic Experience.* Delhi: ispck, 1974.

——. *The Future Shore, Two Essays: Sannyasa and the Upanishads, An Introduction.* Delhi: ispck, 1975.

Abrecht, Audrey, ed. *History's Lessons for Tomorrow's Mission.* Geneva: WSCF, no date (1960?).

Akhilananda, Sw. *Hindu View of Christ.* New York: Philosophical Library, 1949.

Amalorpavadass, D. S., ed. *Research Seminar on Non-Biblical Scriptures.* Bangalore: National Biblical, Catachetical and Liturgical Centre, 1974.

Ambalavanar, D. J., ed. *The Gospel in the World: Essays in Honour of Bishop Kulandran.* Madras: CLS, 1985.

Anderson, Gerald H., ed. *Christ and Crisis in Southeast Asia.* London: Friendship Press, 1968.

——, ed. *Asian Voices in Christian Theology.* Maryknoll, N. Y.: Orbis, 1976.

—— and Thomas F. Stransky, eds. *Christ's Lordship and Religious Pluralism.* Maryknoll, N. Y.: Orbis, 1981.

——, ed. *Mission Trends no. 5: Faith Meets Faith.* New York, London/ Toronto: Paulist Press; Grand Rapids: Wm. B. Eerdmans, 1981.

Appasamy, A. J. *The Gospel and India's Heritage.* London/Madras: SPCK, 1942.

——. *The Christian Task in Independent India.* London: SPCK, 1951.

——. *The Theology of Hindu Bhakti.* Madras: CLS, 1970.

Appleton, G. *Glad Encounter: Jesus Christ and the Living Faiths of Men.* London: Edinburgh House Press, 1959.

Archbishop of Canterbury, ed. *Lambeth Essays on Faith.* London: SPCK, 1969.

Ariarajah, S. Wesley. *Dialogue.* Singapore: Christian Conference of Asia, 1980.

——. *The Bible and People of Other Faiths.* Geneva: WCC/WSCF, 1985.

Asirvatham, E. *Christianity in the Indian Crucible.* Calcutta: YMCA, 1955.

Ayrookuzhiel, Abraham, A. M. *The Sacred in Popular Hinduism.* Madras: CLS, 1983.

Baago, Kaj. *Pioneers of Indigenous Christianity.* Madras: CLS, 1969.

Bent, Ans van der, Compiler. *Major Studies and Themes in the Ecumenical Movement.* Geneva: WCC, 1981.

——. *Six Hundred Ecumenical Consultations 1948–1982.* Geneva: WCC, 1983.

——. *A Guide to Essential Ecumenical Reading.* Geneva: WCC, 1984.

Beyerhaus, Peter and Carl F. Hallencreutz. *The Church Crossing Frontiers: Essays on the Nature of Mission in Honour of Bengt Sundkler.* Uppsala: Gleerup, 1969.

Bouquet, A. C. *Christian Faith and Non-Christian Religions.* London/ New York: Harper and Brothers, 1958.

——. *Is Christianity the Final Religion?.* London: Macmillan, 1921.

Boyd, R. H. S. *An Introduction to Indian Christian Theology.* Madras: CLS, 1969.

——. *Indian and the Latin Captivity of the Church: The Cultural Context of the Gospel.* Cambridge: Cambridge University Press, 1974.

Braybrooke, Marcus. *Together to the Truth: A Comparative Study of Some Developments in Hindu and Christian Thought since 1800.* Delhi: ISPCK; Madras: CLS, 1971.

Bria, Ion, ed. *Martyria/Mission: Witness of the Orthodox Churches Today.* Geneva: WCC, 1980.

BCC. *Can We Pray Together: Guidelines on Worship in a Multifaith Society.* London: BCC, 1983.

Brown, David. *All Their Splendour: World Faiths, The Way to Community.* London: Collins/Fount, 1982.

Camps, A. *Partners in Dialogue: Christianity and Other World Religions.* Maryknoll, N. Y.: Orbis, 1983.

Castro, Emilio. *Freedom in Mission: The Perspective of the Kingdom of God, An Ecumenical Inquiry.* Geneva: WCC, 1985.

Caves, S. *Hinduism or Christianity: A Study in the Distinctiveness of the Christian Message.* London: Hodder & Stoughton, 1939.

Chakkarai, V. *The Cross and Indian Thought.* Madras: CLS, 1932.

Chirgwin, A. M. *These I Have Known* (William Temple, William Paton, W. A. Visser 't Hooft, Martin Niemöller). London: London Missionary Society, 1964.

Cobb Jr., John B. *Beyond Dialogue: Toward a Mutual Transformation of Christianity and Buddhism.* Philadelphia: Fortress Press, 1982.

Coward, Harold. *Pluralism: Challenge to World religions.* Maryknoll, N. Y.: Orbis, 1985.

Cracknell, Kenneth. *Why Dialogue? A First British Comment on the WCC Guidelines.* London: BCC, 1980.

——. *Towards a New Relationship: Christians and People of Other Faith.* London: Epworth Press, 1986.

——— and Christopher Lamb. *Theology on Full Alert*. Revised and enlarged edition; London: BCC, 1986.

Cragg, Kenneth. *The Christ and the Faiths: Theology in Cross Reference*. London: SPCK, 1986.

———. *The Christian and Other Religion: The Measure of Christ*. London: Mowbrays, 1977.

———. *The Call of the Minaret*. 1956; rpt. New York: Oxford University Press, 1964.

———. *The Muhammad and the Christian: A Question of Response*. London: Darton, Longman and Todd; Maryknoll, N. Y.: Orbis, 1984.

Cupitt, D. *Christ and the Hiddenness of God*. London: Lutterworth Press, 1971.

Davis, C. *Christ and the World Religion*. London: Hodder and Stoughton, 1970.

Dave, Donald G. and John B. Carman, eds. *Christian Faith in a Religiously Plural World*. Maryknoll, N. Y.: Orbis, 1978.

D'Costa, Gavin. *Theology of Religious Pluralism: The Challenge of Other Religions*. London/New York: Basil Blackwell, 1986.

Devanandan, P. D. *Living Hinduism: A Descriptive Survey*. Bangalore: CISRS, 1958.

———. *The Gospel and the Hindu Intellectual: A Christian Approach*. Bangalore: CISRS, 1958.

———. *Resurgent Hinduism: Review of Modern Movements*. Bangalore: CISRS, 1958.

———. *Christian Concern in Hinduism*. Bangalore: CISRS, 1961.

———. *The Gospel and Renascent Hinduism*. Geneva: WCC, 1959.

Devasahayam, D. M. and A. N. Sudarisanam, eds. *Rethinking Christianity in India*. Madras: CLS, 1939.

Devasahayam, D. M. *The Presentation of Christianity to Non-Christians: Being the Report of the Bangalore Conference Continuation Commission on the Presentation of Christianity to Non-Christians*. Madras: Albinion Press, 1918.

Devadas, Nalini. *Svami Vivekananda*. Bangalore: CISRS, 1968.

Dewart, L. *The Future of Belief: Theism in a World Come of Age*. New York: Herder and Herder, 1966.

Doraisawmy, Solomon. *Christianity in India: Unique and Universal Mission*. Madras: CLS, 1986.

Dunn, J. G. *Christology in the Making.* London: SCM, 1980.

Dusen, Henry Pitney van. *One Great Ground of Hope: Christian Missions and Christian Unity.* London: Lutterworth Press, 1961.

Eliaden, M. and J. M. Kitagawa, eds. *The History of Religions: Essays on the Problem of Understanding.* Chicago: Chicago University Press, 1967.

——. *Images and Symbols: Studies in Religious Symbolism.* New York: Harvill Press, 1961.

——. *The Quest: History and Meaning in Religion.* Chicago: University of Chicago Press, 1969.

Elwood, Douglas J., ed. *What Asian Christians are Thinking: A Theological Source Book.* Quezon City: New Day Publishers, 1976.

Evans-Pritchard, E. E. *Theories of Primitive Religion.* Oxford: Clarendon Press, 1965.

Fabella, Virginia and Sergio Torres, eds. *Irruption of the Third World: Challenge to Theology.* Maryknoll, N. Y.: Orbis, 1983.

Farmer, Herbert H. *Revelation and Religion: Studies in the Theological Interpretation of Religious Types.* London: Nisbet & Co. Ltd., 1954.

Farquhar, J. N. *The Crown of Hinduism.* 1913; rpt. Oxford: Oxford University Press, 1930.

Ferre, N. F. S. *The Finality of Faith and Christianity Among the World Religions.* New York: Harper and Row, 1963.

Fleming, D. J. *Attitudes Towards Other Faiths.* New York: Association Press, 1928.

Forrester, Duncan B. *Caste and Christianity: Attitude and Policies on Caste of Anglo-Saxon Protestant Missions in India.* London/Dublin: Curzon Press, 1980.

Francis, Dayanandan. *New Approaches to Inter-Faith Dialogue.* Sweden: Church of Sweden Mission, 1980.

Freytag, Walter. *The Gospel and the Religions.* London: SCM Press, 1957.

Furtado, Christopher L. *The Contribution of Dr. D. T. Niles to the Church Universal and Local.* Madras: CLS, 1978.

Gairdner, W. H. T. *Edinburgh 1910: An Account and Interpretation of the World Missionary Conference.* Edinburgh/London: Oliphant, Anderson & Ferrier, 1910.

Galloway, A. D. *The Cosmic Christ.* New York: Harper, 1951.

Gispert-Sauch, George. *God's Word Among Men: Papers in Honour of Fr. Joseph Putz, s. j.* Delhi: Vidyajyoti, 1973.

Goodall, N. *The Ecumenical Movement: What It Is and What It Does.* London/New York: Oxford University Press, 1961.

——. *Ecumenical Progress: A Decade of Change in the Ecumenical Movement, 1961–1971.* London: Oxford University Press, 1972.

Green, Michael, ed. *The Truth of God Incaranate.* London: Hodder and Stoughton, 1977.

Gurukul Theological Research Group of the Tamilnad Christian Council. *The Christian Theological Approach to Hinduism.* Madras: CLS, 1956.

Hallencreutz, Carl F. *Kraemer Towards Tambaram: A Study in Hendrik Kraemer's Missionary Approach.* Uppsala: Gleerup, 1966.

——. *New Approaches to Men of Other Faiths, 1938–1968: A Theological Discussion.* Geneva: WCC, 1970.

Hargreaves, Cecil. *Asian Christian Thinking: Studies in Metaphor and its Message.* Delhi: ISPCK; Madras: CLS, 1972.

Harr, W. C., ed. *Frontiers of the Christian World Mission since 1938: Essays in Honour of K. S. Latourette.* New York/London: Harper and Brothers, 1962.

Herklots, H. G. G. *Looking at Evanston: A Study of the Second Assembly of the World Council of Churches.* London: SCM Press, 1954.

Hick, John. *The Second Christianity.* 1968; rpt. London: SCM, 1983.

——. *God and the Universe of Faiths.* London: Collins/Fount, 1977.

——. *Faith and Knowledge.* 2nd ed., London: Collins/Fount, 1978.

——. *God Has Many Names.* London: Macmillan, 1980.

——, ed. *The Myth of God Incarnate.* London: SCM, 1977.

——, ed. *Truth and Dialogue: The Relationship Between World Religions.* London: Sheldon Press, 1974. Also published as *Truth and Dialogue in World Religions: Conflicting Truth Claims.* Philadelphia: Westminster Press, 1974.

—— and B. Hebblethwaite, eds. *Christianity and Other Religions.* London: Collins/Fount, 1980.

Hillman, E. *The Wider Ecumenism: Anonymous Christianity and the Church.* London: Burns and Oates, 1968.

Hocking, W. E. *Living Religions and a World Faith.* New York: The Macmillian Company, 1940.

——. *The Coming World Civilization.* New York: Harper and Brothers Publishers, 1956.

——— and others. *Rethinking Missions: A Layman's Inquiry After One Hundred Years.* New York/London: Harper and Brothers Publishers, 1932.

Hogg, A. G. *Karma and Redemption: An Essay Toward the Interpretation of Hinduism and the Re-statement of Christianity.* 1909 by CLS of India; rpt. with an Introduction by Eric J. Sharpe, Madras: CLS, 1970.

———. *Redemption of this World or the Supernatural in Christianity.* London: T. & T. Clark, 1922.

———. *The Christian Message to the Hindu: Being the Duff Missionary Lectures for 1945 on the Challenge of the Gospel in India.* London: SCM Press, 1947.

———. *Towards Clarifying My Reactions to Doctor Kraemer's Book.* Madras: Diocesan Press, 1938.

Hogg, W. R. *Ecumenical Foundations: A History of the International Missionary Council and its Nineteenth-Century Background.* New York: Harper and Row, 1952.

Hopkins, Howard C. *John R. Mott, 1865–1955: A Biography.* Geneva: WCC; Grand Rapids: Wm. B. Eerdmans, 1979.

Howell, Leon. *Acting in Faith: The World Council of Churches since 1975.* 3rd ed., Geneva: WCC, 1983.

Hughes, Edward J. *Wilfred Caantwell Smith: A Theology for the World.* London: SCM, 1986.

Hutchinson, John A. *Paths of Faith.* 2nd ed., New York: McGraw Hill, 1975.

Jathanna, C. D. *Dialogue in Community: Essays in Honour of S. J. Samartha.* Mangalore, India: The Karnataka Theological Research Institute, 1982.

Jathanna, O. V. *The Decisiveness of the Christ-Event and the Universality of Christianity in a World of Religious Plurality.* Berne, Frankfort/M., Las Vagas: Peter Lang, 1981.

Job, G. V., V. Chakkarai, and others. *Rethinking Christianity in India.* Madras: Hogarth Press, 1950.

Jones, Stanley. *The Christ of the Indian Road.* 1925; rpt. Lucknow: Lucknow Publishing House, 1964.

Kirkpatrick, D., ed. *The Finality of Christ.* Nashville: Abingdon Press, 1966.

Klostermaier, K. *Hindu and Christian in Vrindaban.* London: SCM Press Ltd., 1969.

——. *Kristvidya*. Bangalore: CLS, 1967.

Knitter, Paul F. *No Other Name? A Critical Survey of Christian Attitudes Towards the World Religions*. Maryknoll, N. Y.: Orbis, 1985.

Kraemer, Hendrik. *The Christian Message in a Non-Christian World*. London: Edinburgh House Press (for the IMC), 1938.

——. *Religion and the Christian Faith*. London: Lutterworth Press, 1956.

——. *The Communication of the Christian Faith*. London: Lutterworth Press, 1957.

——. *World Cultures and World Religions: The Coming Dialogue*. London: Lutterworth Press, 1960.

——. *Why Christianity of all Religions?*. London: Lutterworth Press, 1962.

Kulandran, Bishop S. *Resurgent Religions*. Geneva: WCC, London: Lutterworth Press, 1957.

——. *Facing a Renaissance*. Culcutta: YMCA Publishing House, 1957.

——. *Grace: A Comparative Study of the Doctrine in Christianity and Hinduism*. London: Lutterworth Press, 1964.

——. *Concept of Transcendence: A Study of it in Various World Religions*. Madras: CLS, 1981.

Küng, Hans. *On Being a Christian*. London: Collins, 1974.

Lamb, Christopher A. *Belief in a Mixed Society*. London: Lion, 1985.

Latourette, K. S. and W. R. Hogg. *Tomorrow is Here: A Survey of the World Wide Mission and Work of the Christian Church*. London: Edinburgh House, 1948.

——, eds. *The Gospel, the Church, and the World*. New York: Harper, 1946.

Leeuwen, Arend Th. van. *Christianity in World History: The Meeting of the Faiths of East and West*. London: Edinburgh House Press, 1964.

Lewis, H. D. *Jesus in the Faith of Christians*. London: Macmillan, 1981.

Lindbeck, George A. *The Nature of Doctrine: Religion and Theology in a Postliberal Age*. Philadelphia: Westminster Press, 1984.

Löffler, Paul. *Conversion to God and Service to Man: A Study Document on the Biblical Concept of Conversion*. Geneva: WCC, 1967.

Lombardi, R. *The Salvation of the Unbeliever*. London: Burns and Oates, 1956.

Macnicol, N. *Indian Theism*. Oxford: Oxford University Press, 1915.

——. *Is Christianity Unique? A Comparative Study of the Religions*. London: SCM, 1936.

Manikam, R. B., ed. *Christianity and the Asian Revolution.* Madras: CLS, 1954.

Mattam, J. *Land of Trinity: A Study of Modern Christian Approaches to Hinduism.* Bangalore: Theological Publications of India, 1975.

McKain, D. W., ed. *Christianity — Some Non-Christian Appraisals.* New York: McGraw Hill, 1964.

Moses, David G. *Religious Truth and the Relations Between Religions.* Madras: CLS, 1950.

Mott, John R. *The Decisive Hour of Christian Missions.* New York: Student Volunteer Movement for Foreign Missions, 1915.

Moule, C. F. D. *The Origin of Christology.* Cambridge: Cambridge University Press, 1977.

Neill, Stephen. *Colonialism and Christian Missions.* London: Lutterworth Press, 1966.

——. *Bhakti: Hindu and Christian.* Madras: CLS, 1974.

——. *Salvation Tomorrow: The Originality of Jesus Christ and the World Religions.* London: Lutterworth Press, 1976.

——. *Christian Faith and Other Faiths: The Christian Dialogue with Other Religions.* Oxford: Oxford University Press, 1970.

Nelson, Robert J., ed. *No Man is Alien: Essays on Unity of Mankind.* Leiden: E. J. Brill, 1971.

Neuner, J., ed. *Christian Relation to World Religions.* London: Burns and Oates, 1967.

Newbigin, Lesslie. *A Faith For This One World.* London: SCM Press, 1961.

——. *The Finality of Christ.* London: SCM Press, 1969.

——. *Christian Witness in a Plural Society.* London: BCC, 1977.

——. *The Relevance of Trinitarian Doctrine for Today's Mission.* London: Edinburgh House Press, 1963.

——. *Unfinished Agenda.* Geneva: WCC, 1986.

Nichols, James Hastings. *Evanston: An Interpretation.* New York: Harper Brothers Publishers, 1954.

Niles, D. T. *The Message and Its Messengers.* Nashville and New York: Abingdon Press, 1966.

——. *Eternal Life Now: A Presentation of the Christian Faith to the Buddhist.* Jaffna: St. Joseph's Catholic Press, 1946.

——. *The Preacher's Calling to be Servant: The Warwick Lectures for 1957–1958.* London: Lutterworth Press, 1960.

——. *The Preacher's Task and the Stone of Stumbling.* London: Lutterworth Press, 1958.

——. *Upon the Earth: The Mission of God and the Missionary Enterprise of the Churches.* London: Lutterworth Press, 1962.

Northcott, Cecil. *Answer from Amsterdam: Congregationalism and the World Church.* London: Independent Press, No date (1948?).

Otto, R. *India's Religion of Grace and Christianity Compared and Contrasted.* New York: Macmillan, 1930.

Oxtoby, Willard. *The Meaning of Other Faiths.* Philadelphia: Westminster Press, 1983.

——, ed. *Religious Diversity: Essays by Wilfred Cantwell Smith.* New York: Harper and Row, 1976.

Panikkar, Raimundo. *The Interreligious Dialogue.* New York: Paulist Press, 1978.

——. *The Unknown Christ of Hinduism: Towards an Ecumenical Christophany.* 1964; Revised and enlarged edition, Maryknoll, N. Y.: Orbis, 1981.

——. *The Trinity and the Religious Experience of Man: Icon, Person, Mystery.* London: Darton, Longman, and Todd, 1973.

Pannenberg, W. *Basic Questions in Theology,* VOL. 2. London: SCM, 1971.

Parrinder, G. *Comparative Religion.* London: George, Allen, 1962.

——. *Avatar and Incarnation.* London: Faber and Faber, 1970.

——. *The Christian Debate: Light from the East.* New York: Doubleday, 1966.

Pathrapankal, J., ed. *Service and Salvation: Nagpur Theological Conference on Evangelization.* Bangalore: Theological Publications of India, 1973.

Paton, William. *The Faiths of Mankind.* London: SCM, 1932.

——. *A Faith for the World: Jerusalem 1928.* London: Edinburgh House Press, 1929.

——. *Jesus Christ and the World Religions.* London: CMS, 1916.

Perry, E. *The Gospel in Dispute: The Relationship of Christian Faith to Other Missionary Religions.* New York: Doubleday, 1958.

Potter, Philip A. *Life in All Its Fullness: Reflections on the Central Issues of Today's Ecumenical Agenda.* Geneva: WCC, 1983.

Prabhavananda, Sw. *The Sermon on the Mount According to Vedanta.* London: Allen and Unwin, 1964.

Rahner, Karl. *Theological Investigations*. London: Darton, Longman, and Todd, v, vi, x, 1966.

——. *Foundations of Christian Faith: An Introduction to the Idea of Christianity*. London: Darton, Longman, and Todd, 1978.

—— and Wilhelm Thüsing. *A New Christology*. London: Burns and Oates, 1980.

Race, Alan. *Christians and Religious Pluralism: Patterns in the Christian Theology of Religions*. London: SCM Press, 1983.

Radhakrishnan, S. *The Hindu View of Life*. 1927; rpt. London: George, Allen, and Unwin, 1971.

——. *East and West in Religion*. London: George, Allen, and Unwin, 1954.

——. *The Present Crisis of Faith*. Delhi: Hind Pocket Books, 1970.

Richardson, A. *Religion in Contemporary Debate*. London: SCM Press, 1966.

Robinson, Gnana, ed. *Influence of Hinduism on Christianity*. Madurai: Tamil Nadu Theological Seminary, 1980.

Robinson, John A. T. *Truth is Two-Eyed*. London: SCM Press, 1979.

Rouner, C. S. *Philosophy, Religion, and the Coming World Civilization: Essays in Honour of William Ernest Hocking*. The Hague: Martinus Nijhoff, 1966.

Rousseau, Richard W. *Interreligious Dialogue: Facing the Next Frontier*. Scranton, USA: Ridge Row Press, 1981.

Rupp, G. *Christologies and Cultures: Toward a Typology of Religious World-View*. The Hague: Mouton, 1974.

Samartha, S. J. *Courage for Dialogue: Ecumenical Issues in Inter-religious Relationships*. Geneva: WCC, 1981.

——. *The Hindu View of History*. Bangalore: CISRS, 1959.

——. *Introduction to Radhakrishnan*. New York: Association Press; New Delhi: YMCA Publishing House, 1964.

——. *The Hindu Response to the Unbound Christ: Towards a Christology in India*. Bangalore: ÇISRS, 1974.

Samartha, S. J., ed. *Dialogue Between Men of Living Faiths*. Geneva: WCC, 1971.

——. *Living Faiths and the Ecumenical Movement*. Geneva: WCC, 1973.

——. *Living Faiths and Ultimate Goals*. Geneva: WCC, 1973.

——. *Faith in the Midst of Faiths.* Geneva: WCC, 1978.

——. *Towards World Community.* Geneva: WCC, 1975.

Samuel, V. C. *The Ramakrishna Movement: The World Mission of Hinduism.* Bangalore: CISRS, 1959.

Sharpe, Eric J. *The Theology of A. G. Hogg.* Madras: CISRS/CLS, 1971.

——. *Faith Meets Faith: Some Christian Attitudes to Hinduism in the Nineteenth and Twentieth Centuries.* London: SCM Press, 1977.

——. *Not to Destroy But to Fulfil: The Contribution of J. N. Farquhar to Protestant Missionary Thought in India before 1914.* Lund: CWK, Gleerup, 1965.

Singh, H. J., ed. *Inter-Religious Dialogue.* Bangalore: CISRS, 1967.

Slack, Kenneth. *The Nairobi Narrative: The Story of the Fifth Assembly of the World Council of Churches.* London: SCM Press, 1976.

——. *Uppsala Report: The Story of the World Council of Churches Fourth Assembly,* Uppsala, Sweden, 4-19 July 1968. London: SCM Press, 1968.

Slater, R. L. *Can Christians Learn from Other Religions?* New York: Seabury Press, 1963.

——. *World Religions and World Community.* New York: Seabury Press, 1963.

Smart, N. *A Dialogue of Religions.* London: SCM Press, 1960.

——. *The Phenomenon of Religion.* London: Mowbrays, 1978.

——. *The Religious Experience of Mankind.* London: Collins, 1977.

Smith, Wilfred Cantwell. *The Faith of Other Men.* New York: New American Library Mentor Books, 1965.

——. *The Meaning and End of Religion: A New Approach to the Religious Traditions of Mankind.* New York: Mentor, 1964.

——. *Questions of Religious Faith.* New York: Charles Scribner's Sons, 1967.

——. *Belief and History.* Charlottesville: University Press of Virginia, 1977.

——. *Faith and Belief.* Princeton: Princeton University Press, 1979.

——. *Towards a World Theology: Faith and the Comparative History of Religion.* Philadelphia: Westminster Press; London: Macmillan, 1981.

Song, Choan-Seng. *Christian Mission in Reconstruction.* Madras: CLS, 1975.

Speer, R. E. *The Light of the World: A Brief Comparative Study of Christianity and Non-Christian Religions.* West Melford: United Study of Missions, 1911.

Stowe, D. M. *When Faith Meets Faith.* New York: Friendship Press, 1966.

Straelen, H. van. *The Catholic Encounter with World Religions.* London: Burns and Oates; New York: Newman Press, 1966.

Swearer, Donald K. *Dialogue: The Key to Understanding Other Religions.* Philadelphia: Westminster Press, 1977.

Taylor, Richard W. *Society and Religion: Essays in Honour of M. M. Thomas.* Bangalore: CISRS, 1976.

——. *The Contribution of E. Stanley Jones.* Madras: CISRS/CLS, 1973.

Thangasamy, D. A. *The Theology of Chenchiah, with Selections from his Writings.* Bangalore: CISRS/YMCA, 1966.

Thomas, M. M. *Salvation and Humanization: Some Critical Issues of the Theology of Missions in Contemporary India.* Bangalore: CISRS/CLS, 1971.

——. *The Acknowledged Christ of the Indian Renaissance.* Madras: CISRS/CLS, 1970.

——. *The Secular Ideologies of India and the Secular Meaning of Christ.* Madras: CLS, 1976.

——. *Man and the Universe of Faiths.* Madras: CISRS/CLS, 1975.

——. *The Christian Response to the Asian Revolution.* London: SCM Press, 1966.

——. *Some Theological Dialogues.* Madras: CISRS/CLS, 1977.

Thomas, P. T. *The Theology of Chakkarai with Selections from his Writings.* Bangalore: CISRS, 1968.

Thundy, Zacharias P. and others, eds. *Religions in Dialogue: East and West Meet.* Lanham: University Press of America, 1985.

Tillich, Paul. *Christianity and the Encounter of the World Religions.* New York/London: Columbia University Press, 1963.

——. *What is Religion?* New York: Harper and Row, 1969.

Todd, J. M. *Catholicism and the Ecumenical Movement.* London: Longmans, 1956.

Toynbee, Arnold J. *Christianity Among Religions of the World.* London: Oxford University Press, 1958.

Troeltsch, Ernst. *The Absoluteness of Christianity and the History of Religions.* 1902 (German); rpt. London: SCM Press, 1972.

Vicedom, G. F. *The Challenge of the World Religions.* Philadelphia: Fortress Press, 1963.

Visser 't Hooft, W. A. *The Genesis and Formation of the World Council of Churches.* Geneva: WCC, 1982.

——. *Has the Ecumenical Movement a Future?* Belfast: Christian Journals Ltd., 1974.

——. *No Other Name: The Choice Between Syncretism and Christian Universalism.* London: SCM Press, 1963.

Wach, J. *Types of Religious Experience, Christian and Non-Christian.* Chicago: University of Chicago Press, 1951.

Warren, M. A. C. *The Relationship between Christianity and Other World Religions.* London: Prism, 1966.

——. *Social History and Christian Mission.* London: SCM, 1967.

WCC. *Religious Resources for a Just Society: A Hindu–Christian Dialogue.* Geneva, 1981.

Webb, Pauline. *Salvation Today.* London: SCM, 1974.

——. *Faith and Faithfulness: Essays on Contemporary Ecumenical Themes: A Tribute to Philip A. Potter.* Geneva: WCC, 1984.

Weber, Hans-Ruedi. *Asia and the Ecumenical Movement.* London: SCM, 1964.

Weger, H. *Karl Rahner: An Introduction to his Theology.* London: Burns and Oates, 1980.

Yannoulatos, Archim. Anastasios. *The Purpose and Motive of Mission from an Orthodox Theological Point of View.* Athens: 1968.

Young, Robert D. *Encounter with World Religions.* Philadelphia: The Westminster Press, no date.

Zaehner, R. C. *Christianity and Other Religions.* New York: Hawthorn Books, 1964.

——. *At Sundry Times.* London: Faber and Faber, 1958.

——. *The Concordant Discord.* Oxford: Oxford University Press, 1970.

——. *The Catholic Church and World Religions.* London: Burns and Oates, 1964.

(D) Articles

(There is a list of abbreviations at the end of this section)

Abhishiktananda, Swami. "The Church in India — A Self-Examination." *Religion and Society* XV 3 (Sept. 1968): 5-19.

Addison, J. T. "The Changing Attitude toward Non-Christian Religions." *International Review of Mission* 27 (1938): 110-21.

Amaladoss, M. "Dialogue and Mission: Conflict or Convergence?" *Vidya-jyoti* L 2 (Feb. 1986): 62-86.

Anastasios, Bishop of Androussa (Yannoulatos). "Mexico City 1963: Old Wine into Fresh Wineskins." *IRM* LXVII 267 (July 1978): 354-64.

Andrews, C. F. "A Quest for Truth." *YMI* 40 (1928): 443-45.

Appasamy, A. J. "An Approach to Hindus." *IRM* 17 (1928): 472-82.

———. "The Christian Approach to Hinduism." *NCCR* 57 (1937): 239-49.

———. "Our Relations with Those of Other Faiths: A Study Outline." *YMI* 48 (1936): 35-42.

Ariarajah, S. Wesley. "Towards a Theology of Dialogue." *Ecumenical Review* XXIX 1 (Jan. 1977): 3-11.

———. "Ecumenical Issues in Dialogue." *Current Dialogue* 9 (Dec. 1985): 9-12, 17.

Azariah, V. S. "The Christian Message in Relation to Non-Christian Religions, IV, India and Christ." *IRM* 17 (1928): 145-59.

Bassham, Rodger C. "Seeking a Deeper Theological Basis for Mission." (On the Willingen Meeting of the IMC). *IRM* LXVII 267 (July 1978): 329-37.

———. "Mission Theology, 1948–1975." *OBMR* IV 2 (April 1980): 52-58.

Berthrong, John. "Interfaith Dialogue in Canada." *The Ecumenical Review* XXXVII 4 (Oct. 1985): 462-70.

Bitton, W. W. "Report of the Proceedings of the World Missionary Conference in Edinburgh, From June 13 to 23." *CR* 41 (1910): 530-49.

Bose, N. J. "Difficulties in Presenting the Gospel to Non-Christians." *The Guardian* (Oct. 29, 1925): 508-9; (Nov. 5, 1925): 521-22; (Nov. 12, 1925): 533-34; (Nov. 19, 1925): 543-45.

Brockman, F. S. "Impressions of the World Missionary Conference." *CR* 41 (1910): 608-10.

Brockway, Allan R. Review of *No Other Name?*, by Paul Knitter. *The Ecumenical Review* XXXVII 4 (Oct. 1985): 513-15.

———. "Vancouver and the Future of Interfaith Dialogue." *Current Dialogue* 6 (Spring 1984): 4-7.

———. "Notes on Interreligious Dialogue." *Current Dialogue* 7 (Autumn 1984): 13-15.

Brown, Stuart E. Review of *The Muhammad and the Christian: A Question of Response,* by Kenneth Cragg. *The Ecumenical Review* XXXVII 4 (Oct. 1985): 515-17.

Buck, P. S. "The Laymen's Mission Report." *The Christian Century* (March 23, 1932): 1434-35.

Butsellaar, Jan van. "Dialogue and Witness." *The Ecumenical Review* XXXVII 4 (Oct. 1985): 398-405.

Cairns, D. S. "A Comparison of Thought in 1910 and in 1928." *IRM* 18 (1929): 321-31.

Carino, Feliciano V. "Partnership in Obedience (Whitby)." *IRM* LXVII 267 (July 1978): 316-28.

Chakkarai, V. "Christianity as Bhakti Marga." *NMI* 20 (1926): 163-64.

——. "The Kingdom of God vs. The Church at Tambaram Conference." *The Guardian* (April 6, 1939): 197-98.

——. "Rethinking Mission." *The Guardian* (March 30, 1933): 148-49; (April 4, 1933): 161-62; (April 13, 1933): 173-74; (April 20, 1933): 186-87.

Chandran, J. R. "Christianity and World Religions — The Ecumenical Discussion." *IJT* XXX 3-4 (Jul.–Dec. 1981): 186-203.

——. "Emerging Issues in the Discussion of Third World Theologians." *Religion and Society* XXV 3, 64f.

de Chardin, Teilhard. "The Confluence of Religion." *Theology Today* XXVII 1 (April 1970): 63-70.

Chenchiah, P. "The Christian Message in a Non-Christian World: As an Indian Christian Views Dr. Kraemer's Book." *The Guardian* (Oct. 6, 1938): 628-30; (Oct. 13, 1938): 644-45; (Oct. 27, 1938): 676-77; (Nov. 3, 1938): 692-93; (Nov. 10, 1938): 708-10; and (Nov. 17, 1938): 724-27.

——. "Wherein Lies the Uniqueness of Christ? An Indian Christian View." *SW* 22 (1929): 398-412.

Chetsingh, R. M. "Impressions of Tambaram." *NCCR* 59 (1939): 131-32.

Conway, Martin. Review of *Questions of Religious Truth* by Wilfred Cantwell Smith. *Student World* 61 (1967): 357-59.

Cox, James L. "Faith and Faiths: The Significance of A. G. Hogg's Missionary Thought for a Theology of Dialogue." *SJT* (1979), 241-56.

Cracknell, Kenneth. "Within God's Gracious Purposes: Interfaith Dialogue in Britain." *The Ecumenical Review* XXXVII 4 (Oct. 1985): 452-61.

Craig, A. C. "Impressions of the Tambaram Meeting." *IRM* 28 (1939): 185-90.

Crosthwaite, A. "Hindu Hopes and Their Christian Fulfilment." *EW* 12 (1914): 83-95.

Devanandan, P. D. "After Tambaram — What? An Indian Christian Layman's Point of View." *The Guardian* (Jan. 26, 1939): 42-43.

Deweick, E. C. "Christ, the Lord of All Religions." *YMI* 37 (1925): 144-55.

Dupuis, J. "The Presence of Christ in Hinduism." *Religion and Society* XVIII 1 (March 1971): 33-45.

Duraisingh, Christopher. "World Religions and the Christian Claim for the Uniqueness of Jesus Christ." *IJT* XXX 3-4 (Jul.–Dec. 1981): 168-85.

Eck, Diana L. "Inter-religious Dialogue as a Christian Ecumenical Concern." *The Ecumenical Review* XXXVII 4 (Oct. 1985): 406-19.

——. "What do we Mean by 'Dialogue'?" *Current Dialogue* 11 (Dec. 1986): 5-15.

Farmer, H. H. "The Faith by Which the Church Lives." *IRM* 28 (1939): 174-84.

Farquhar, J. N. "Are All Religions True?" *YMI* 32 (1920): 417-27.

——. "The Greatness of Hinduism." *CR* 48 (1910): 647-58.

——. "The Relation of Christianity to Hinduism." *IRM* 3 (1914): 417-32.

Frick, H. "Is a Conviction of the Superiority of his Message Essential to the Missionary?" *IRM* 15 (1926): 625-46.

——. "The Sense of Superiority in the Missionary Movement." *IRM* 16 (1927): 126.

Gavie, A. E. "The Christian Challenge to the Other Faiths." *IRM* 1 (1912): 659-73.

——. "The Evangelical Faith and Other Religions." *IRM* 22 (1933): 353-61.

Gibson, P. S. P. "The Presentation of Christianity in Ceylon." *IRM* 8 (1919): 341-57.

Gilkey, Langdon. "A Theological Voyage with Wilfred Cantwell Smith." Review of 'The Meaning and End of Religion,' 'Belief and History,' 'Faith and Belief,' 'Towards a World Theology,' by Wilfred Cantwell Smith. *RSR,* no. 7 (Oct. 1981): 293-306.

Gort, Jerald D. "Jerusalem 1928: Mission, Kingdom and Church." *IRM* LXVII 267 (July 1978): 273-98.

Gregorios, Paul. "Dialogue with World Religions — Basic Approaches and Pratical Experience." *IJT* XXIX 1 (Jan.–March 1980): 1-11.

Hartenstein, K. "The Theology of the World and Missions." *IRM* 20 (1931): 210-27.

Hayward, V. E. "Three Kandy Meetings." *Study Encounter* 3 (1967): 51-52.

Heim, K. "The Message of the New Testament to the Non-Christian World." *IRM* 17 (1928): 133-44.

Hick, John. "On Conflicting Truth Claims." *Religious Studies* 19 (1983): 485-91.

———. "The Theology of Religious Pluralism." *Theology* 86 (1983): 335-40.

———. "Pluralism and the Reality of the Transcendent." *Christian Century* 98 (1981): 45-48.

Hoedemaker, Libertus A. "The Legacy of Hendrik Kraemer." *OBMR* IV 2 (April 1980): 60-64.

Hollenbach, David. "Human Rights and Interreligious Dialogue: The Challenge to Mission in a Pluralist World." *IBMR* VI 3 (July 1982): 98-101.

Hume, R. E. "What is the Christian Attitude toward Non-Christian Religions?" *YMI* 41 (1929): 665-69.

Job, G. V. "The Christian Approach to Popular Hinduism." *NCCR* 57 (1937): 120-27.

Jones, Stanley. "Madras Missed its Way." *The Christian Century* (March 15, 1939): 351-52.

———. "What I missed at Madras." *The Christian Century* (May 31, 1939): 704-8.

Jones Jr., Tracy K. "History's Lessons for Tomorrow's Mission." *IBMR* X 2 (April 1986): 50-53.

Knak, S. "Some Theological Problems Arising from the Tambaram Conference." *The Gospel Witness* (1939): 282-86.

Kraemer, H. "Impressions of Tambaram." *NCCR* 59 (1939): 76-77.

Latourette, K. S. "The Laymen's Foreign Mission Inquiry: The Report of its Commission of Appraisal." *IRM* 22 (1933): 153-73.

Leung, S. C. "The Meaning and Message of the Madras Conference." *CR* 70 (1939): 215-19.

Lonning, Per. "Dialogue: A Question about 'Religiology'." *The Ecumenical Review* XXXVII 4 (Oct. 1985): 420-29.

Lyon, W. "Some Impressions of the Jerusalem Meeting." *CR* 59 (1928): 409-13.

Macnicol, N. "Beyond Syncretism and Europeanism." *SW* 27 (1934): 298-307.

——. "The Christian Message and the Missionary Presentation of It." *NCCR* 48 (1928): 70-79.

——. "Hindu Devotional Mysticism." *IRM* 5 (1916): 210-23.

——. "Interreligionism in India." *HF* 53 (1933): 508-17.

Michael, S. M. "Sociological Perspectives of Conversion in India." *IMR* v 1 (Jan. 1983): 40-52.

Mott, John R. "At Edinburgh, Jerusalem, and Madras." *IRM* 27 (1938): 297-320.

——. "The Continuation Committee of the World Missionary Conference, Edinburgh, 1910." *HF* 30 (1910): 347-50.

——. "The Possibilities of the Tambaram Meeting." *NCCR* 59 (1939): 3-12.

Mulder, D. C. " 'None Other Gods' — 'No Other Name'." *The Ecumenical Review* XXXVIII 2 (April 1986): 209-15.

Nambiaparambil, Albert. "Identity and Openness after the Vatican Council — Tension of Dialogue." *IJT* XXX 3-4 (July–Dec. 1981): 204-10.

Niles, D. T. "The Uniqueness of Christ and the Presentation of His Message." *SW* 27 (1934): 315-25.

Niles, D. Preman. "Christian Mission and the Peoples of Asia." *CTC Bulletin* III 1 (April 1982): 34-48.

Nirmal, Arvind P. "Redefining the Economy of Salvation." *IJT* XXX 3-4 (July–Dec. 1981): 211-17.

Oldham, J. H. "After Twenty-Five Years." *IRM* 24 (1935): 297-314.

O'Neill, F. W. S. "What We May Hope from the Jerusalem Meeting." *CR* 59 (1928): 222-28.

Paton, W. "The International Missionary Council and the Future." *IRM* 25 (1936): 106-15.

——. "The Jerusalem Meeting of the International Missionary Council." *IRM* 17 (1928): 3-10.

——. "The Jerusalem Meeting and After." *IRM* 17 (1928): 435-44.

——. "The Meeting of the International Missionary Council at Tambaram, Madras." *IRM* 28 (1939): 161-73.

——. "An Open Letter from William Paton on the Madras Conference." *SW* 31 (1938): 291-99.

——. "The Syncretistic Mood in East and West." *SW* 27 (1934): 308-14.

Pannikar, R. "The Internal Dialogue: The Insufficiency of the so-called Phenomenological 'Epoche' in the Religious Encounter." *Religion and Society* XV 3 (Sept. 1968): 55-72.

Pieris, Aloysius. "Western Christianity and Asian Buddhism: A Theological Reading of Historical Encounters." *Dialogue,* New Series, VII 2 (May–Aug. 1980): 49-85.

——. "The Place of Non-Christian Religions and Cultures in the Evolution of a Third World Theology." *CTC Bulletin* III 2 (Aug. 1982): 43-61.

Philip, T. V. "Issues in Evangelism Among the Educated Secularized Indians." *Religion and Society* XV 4 (Dec. 1968): 35-41.

——. "Pluralism and the Early Church." *Religion and Society* XVII 1 (March 1970): 7-21.

Phillips, P. O. "The Jerusalem Meeting." *NCCR* 48 (1928): 283-311.

Pickard Jr., William M. "Truth in Religious Discourse." *The Ecumenical Review* XXXVII 4 (Oct. 1985): 437-51.

Quick, O. C. "The Jerusalem Meeting and the Christian Message." *IRM* 17 (1928): 445-54.

Ratnayake, Shantha. "A Buddhist–Christian Monastic Dialogue." *Dialogue,* New Series VI 3 (Sept.–Dec. 1979): 85-90.

Reetz, Dankfried. "Raymond Panikkar's Theology of Religions." *Religion and Society* XV 3 (Sept. 1968): 32-54.

Richter, J. "Missionary Apologetic: Its Problems and its Methods." *IRM* 2 (1913): 520-42.

Samartha, S. J. "Dialogue as a Continuing Christian Concern." *Religion and Society* XVIII 1 (March 1971): 11-23.

——. "Partners in Community: Some Reflections on Hindu–Christian Relations Today." *OBMR* IV 2 (April 1980): 78-82.

——. "Christian Concern for Dialogue in India." *Current Dialogue* 9 (Dec. 1985): 3-9.

——. "Interreligious Relationships in a Secular State." *Current Dialogue* 11 (Dec. 1986): 22-28.

Sawyerr, Harry. "The First World Missionary Conference: Edinburgh 1910." *IRM* LXVII 267 (July 1978): 256-72.

Schoonhoven, Evert Jansen. "Tambaram 1938." *IRM* LXVII 267 (July 1978): 299-315.

Scott, David C. "Hindu and Christian *Bhakti*: A Common Human Response to the Sacred." *IJT* XXIX 1 (Jan.–March 1980): 12-45.

Sharpe, Eric J. "The Legacy of A. G. Hogg." *IBMR* VI 2 (April 1982): 65-69.

Smith, W. C. "Participation: The Changing Christian Role in Other Cultures." *Religion and Society* XVII 1 (March 1970): 56-74.

Speer, R. E. "The Edinburgh Missionary Conference." *EW* 8 (1910): 369-80.

——. "Jerusalem and Edinburgh." *SW* 21 (1928): 365-70.

Stockwell, Eugene L. "What Word from Vancouver on Mission?" *IBMR* VII 2 (April 1983): 50-53.

Suh, David Kwang-Son. "The Christology of Karl Rahner." *NAJT* 4 (March 1970): 88-105.

Sundkler, B. "Dare in Order to Know: The International Missionary Council from Edinburgh to New Delhi." *IRM* 51 (1962): 4-11.

Taylor, John V. "Bangkok 1972–1973." *IRM* LXVII 267 (July 1978): 365-70.

Temple, William. "The Message of Jerusalem." *The Student World* 21 (1928): 361-64.

Thangasamy, D. A. "Theological Pioneering in India." *Religion and Society* XVII 1 (March 1970): 75-87.

Thomas, M. M. "The Absoluteness of Jesus Christ and Christ-Centred Syncretism." *The Ecumenical Review* XXXVII 4 (Oct. 1985): 387-97.

——. "Post-Colonial Crisis in Mission — A Comment." *Religion and Society* XVIII 1 (March 1971): 64-70.

——. "Christology and Pluralistic Consciousness." *IBMS* X 3 (July 1986): 106-8.

Thomas, T. K. "The Christian Task in Asia: An Introduction to the Thought of Bernard Lucas." *RS* 15 (1968): 20-31.

Underhill, M. M. "A German View of the Jerusalem Meeting." *IRM* 18 (1929): 266-72.

Vineeth, V. F. "The Concept of Dialogue and the Economy of Salvation." *IJT* XXX 3-4 (July–Dec. 1981): 152-57.

Visser 't Hooft, W. A. "Questions about the Future of the World Council of Churches." *The Ecumenical Review* XXXVIII 2 (April 1986): 133-39.

Wickremesinghe, Lakshman. "Togetherness and Uniqueness: Living Faiths in Interaction." *Dialogue,* New Series VII 1 (Jan.–April 1980): 4-22.

Wilfred, Felix. "Understanding Conversion in India Today." *IMR* v 1 (Jan. 1983): 61-73.

Winter, Ralph D. "Ghana: Preparation for Marriage." *IRM* LXVII 267 (July 1978): 338-53.

———. "Precarious Milestones to Edinburgh 1980." *OBMR* IV 2 (April 1980): 64-66.

Wood, H. G. "Theological Issues at Madras." *EWR* 5 (1939): 119-25.

Zago, Marcello. "Dialogue in the Mission of the Churches of Asia: Theological Bases and Pastoral Perspectives." *Kerygma* 17 (1983): 185-204.

Abbreviations

CBCI	Catholic Bishops' Conference of India
CISRS	Christian Institute for the Study of Religion and Society
CLS	Christian Literature Society
CMR	Church Missionary Review
CR	The Chinese Recorder
CWME	Commission on World Mission and Evangelism
EACC	East Asia Christian Conference
EW	The East and the West
EWR	East West Review
IBMR	International Bulletin of Missionary Research
IJT	Indian Journal of Theology
IMC	International Missionary Council
IMR	Indian Missiological Review
IRM	International Review of Mission(s)
ISPCK	Indian Society for the Propagation of Christian Knowledge
JMR	Jerusalem Meeting Report
NAJT	The Northeast Asia Journal of Theology
NCCR	National Christian Council Review
NMI	National Missionary Intelligencer
OBMR	Occasional Bulletin of Missionary Research
RS	Religious Studies
RSR	Religious Studies Review
SJT	The Scottish Journal of Theology
SPCK	Society for the Propagation of Christian Knowledge
SW	The Student World
YMI	Young Men of India

Edinburgh   1910

IMC

Life and Work

Faith and Order

Stockholm
1925

Lausanne
1927

Jerusalem
1928

Tambaram
1938

Oxford
1937

Edinburgh
1937

Whitby
1947

Willingen
1952

Amsterdam
1948

WCC

Evanston
1954

Ghana
1957–8

New Delhi
1961

CWME

Mexico City
1963

Uppsala 1968

Addis Ababa 1971

Bangkok
1972

Dialogue

Nairobi
1975

Chiang Mai
1977

Melbourne
1980

Vancouver
1983

*World Conference on
Mission and Evangelism*
San Antonio (Texas)
1989

7th Assembly
Canberra
1991

*4 year study on
my neighbour's
faith and mine*
1989

DATE DUE

12-30-93		
APR APR 20 2006		
JUN 02 2007		
NOV 21 2007		
GAYLORD		PRINTED IN U.S.A.